CASSELL
Illustrated
Dictionary of
Lacemaking

CASSELL
Illustrated
Dictionary of
Lacemaking

ALEXANDRA STILLWELL

CASSELL

CASSELL
First published in the UK 1996 by
Cassell Publishers Ltd
Wellington House, 125 Strand, London WC2R 0BB

Text and illustrations © Alexandra Stillwell 1996

Distributed in the United States by Sterling Publishing Co. Inc.
387 Park Avenue South, New York, NY 10016–8810

Distributed in Australia by Capricorn Link (Australia) Pty Ltd
2/13 Carrington Road, Castle Hill, NSW 2154

British Library Cataloguing in Publication Data
A catalogue record for this book is available from the
British Library

ISBN 0–304–34145–2

Designed by Gwyn Lewis
Typeset by Keystroke, Jacaranda Lodge, Wolverhampton
Printed and bound in Great Britain by Hillman Printers Ltd

Acknowledgements
The quotation from the *Concise Oxford
Dictionary* on page 7 is reproduced by permission of
Oxford University Press.

Contents

Introduction

When the City and Guilds Lacemaking Course was introduced, it became clear that lacemakers in different places were using different terms. The same word or phrase sometimes has more than one meaning, while conversely, several words or phrases may have the same meaning. This book has been compiled to systematize these various usages and to reflect the vocabulary of lacemaking as it is currently used. Where a technique or application has several names, the definition has been given under the name that has been found to be the most commonly used, and cross-references from alternative names have been included as appropriate. This does not mean that one name is more correct than another or is to be preferred; there has been no attempt to indicate which of several terms is the most 'correct'. However, it is sometimes the case that the different meanings that have accrued to a single term can lead to confusion, and there may be an alternative term that has only one meaning.

During the recent revival in interest in lacemaking many terms have been introduced by well-known teachers and authors. These terms are also included in this Dictionary, as are many Anglicized versions of French terms. It often happens that these phrases do not have exactly the same meaning as the original French and they may be grammatically incorrect – Belle point de Venise, for example. *Point* is a masculine noun in French, and the adjective qualifying it should also be masculine: *beau*. Moreover, the shapes in this filling are called bells, even though the French word belle actually means beautiful. However, as this phrase is most commonly used in its Anglicized version, it is entered here in this form.

The following statement appears in the H.W. Fowler's Acknowledgements in the *Concise Oxford Dictionary*:

> A Dictionary-maker, unless he is a monster of omniscience, must deal with a great many matters of which he has no first-hand knowledge. That he has been guilty of errors and omissions in some of these he will learn soon after publication.

This makes me realize that I am not alone in my concern about the accuracy of information I have collated. While every effort has been made to avoid errors and omissions there will probably be some, for these my apologies.

My thanks go to Margaret Susans, who painstakingly checked my manuscript, picked up many of my mistakes, made suggestions and gave me the incentive to continue. Thanks also to Grace Hartley for minding my Ps and Qs and for checking my grammatical, typing and spelling errors, and to my many friends and students for their support and suggestions.

A

à pièces rapportées *See* PART LACE.

accrochetage (bobbin) *See* SEWING (Fr.).

acetate film (bobbin) Used for REPEATING PATTERNS when designing and pricking patterns. Overhead projector film is suitable.

acid free tissue paper (general) This paper does not contain acid. Most paper and cardboard is acid, and lace stored in it may be damaged.

active chain (tatting) The CHAIN making the JOIN when one chain joins to the PICOT of another. *See also* PASSIVE CHAIN.

active pair (bobbin) *See* WORKER.

adding bobbins/pairs (bobbin) The process of introducing extra BOBBINS, usually in pairs. (1) Across the top of open areas within the lace for making a filling in that area. (2) Into the work as it is made, thus increasing the density of the lace. In Bedfordshire lace the new pair is slipped over the WORKERS at the end of a row, taken behind the pin and laid next to the PASSIVES, the worker returning through this pair first (figure a). Pairs are hung in similarly in Bucks point. In Honiton lace the new pair is placed inside the edge DOWNRIGHT when working WHOLE STITCH (figure b), and the resulting second pair of downrights

may be twisted when working HALF STITCH (figure c). Also called fil attaché and hanging-in bobbins/pairs. *See also* HANGING IN PAIRS FOR LATER USE.

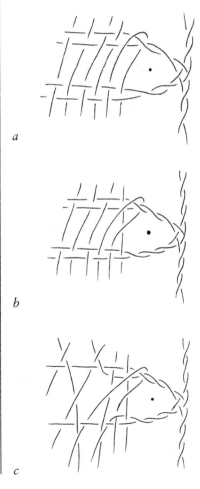

a

b

c

adding pairs horizontally (bobbin) The process of introducing extra pairs at the side of the work, as the work increases suddenly in width.

additionals (bobbin) Extra bobbins added into the work. *See also* ADDING BOBBINS.

afficot (needle) The tool used on needle lace to enhance the RAISED EDGE and for GLOSSING needle lace. Originally lobster claws were used, but they are now made from polished bone, horn, wood and so on (figure). *See also* COLD IRONING.

aficot (needle) *See* AFFICOT.

aglet lace (bobbin) *See* EYELET LACE.

Agnes Forty (bobbin) A corruption of AQUA FORTIS.

a'jours (general) A decorative FILLING.

à l'aguille (needle) French for 'by needle'.

Alençon beads (needle) Needle lace FILLING used within narrow spaces. BUTTONHOLE STITCHES, with their loops arranged opposite each other, are worked along both sides of the space. A working thread is fastened on at one end of the lower edge, and the first loop is whipped once. * The needle is taken down through the first stitch of the upper edge and up through the opposite one*, with the overcasting process from * to * repeated up to three times. The 'bead' is completed by whipping once

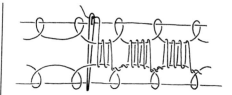

into the lower loop. The threads linking the loops must lie next to each other and not cross. When complete, the 'beads' can be pressed flat with the back of a thumb nail (figure). Also called bead stitch insertion.

Alençon ground/mesh (needle) The GROUND used for Alençon and Burano laces. Originally the ground was worked with the needle pointing away from the worker. If it is made with the needle pointing towards the worker, the twists

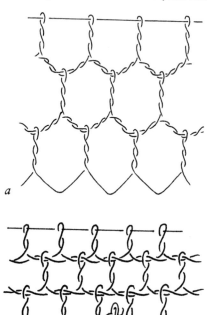

a

b

and whips will face the other way. (1) Rows of TWISTED BUTTONHOLE STITCHES each with the threads crossing three times and each whipped on the return row with the needle passing upwards twice through each loop of the previous row. Subsequent rows of buttonhole stitches are worked through the mesh (figure a). Also called point feston doublé and Greek stitch. (2) As (1) but with the threads crossing only once and whipping once only through each loop (figure b). Also called petit réseau and réseau ordinaire. Alençon lace was made with slack whipping, allowing the mesh to take on a hexagonal shape. Burano copies were made with a tighter whipping thread, resulting in a squarer mesh. *See also* BRIDES TORTILLÉE(S), BURANO GROUND, POINT D'ANVERS, TWISTED BUTTONHOLE STITCH.

allover lace (machine lace) Lace that is sufficiently wide to cut out pieces for making garments. It usually has the same design repeated widthwise and lengthwise.

alpine point (needle) *See* PUNTO AVORIO.

amulet bead (bobbin) A bead believed to ward off evil, used to weight bobbins – e.g., EVIL EYE BEAD.

angle to the footside (bobbin) The angle between the FOOTSIDE pins and a line of GROUND pins sloping downwards from it (figure a). For Bucks point lace, usually measured within the ground since the spacing between the footside, catch pins and the first vertical line of ground pins is wider than for the remainder of the ground (figure b).

annular ring (bobbin) A glass ring sometimes used as part of a SPANGLE.

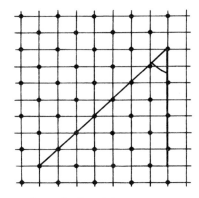

a angle to the footside

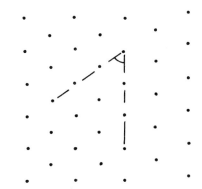

b angle to the footside

Antwerp edge (needle) Used to edge TAPE LACE. After working a BUTTONHOLE STITCH into a tape, another is made across it (figure). *See also* SORRENTO EDGING.

application/applied lace *See* APPLIQUÉ LACE.

applied piece (needle) Small pieces worked separately from the main piece to which it is later sewn. Usually sewn along part of its edge only, allowing the piece to stand up three-dimensionally. Also called detached leaf, flap and raised needle lace.

appliqué lace (general) Consisting of small decorative motifs, made by bobbin, needle, tatting and so on, and sewn to a continuous machine net or, rarely, bobbin-made net. Also called application lace and applied lace. Not to be confused with REGROUNDING.

aqua fortis (bobbin) Concentrated nitric acid used to decorate wooden bobbins by darkening them. This chemical is *very dangerous* and should not be used without training. Also known as AGNES FORTY. *See also* MOTTLED BOBBIN.

Arab lace (needle) *See* BEBILLA.

architects' linen (general) The pale blue translucent, glazed linen formerly used by architects. Matt-finished, coloured plastic film is often used as a substitute. Oil cloth was formerly used if the translucent quality was not required.

Ardenza (point) bar (needle) Work pairs of FACING BUTTONHOLE STITCHES along both sides of one, or more (usually three), threads stretched across a space or couched down (figures a and b). It is also occasionally used as an

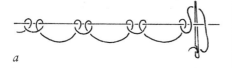

a

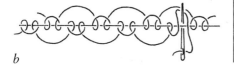

b

alternative to BUTTONHOLE STITCH when TOP STITCHING.

Ardenza point (needle) A FILLING stitch consisting of pairs of FACING BUTTONHOLE STITCHES (figure).

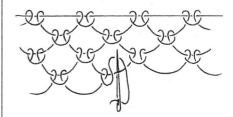

Argentan ground (needle) The GROUND for Argentan lace. *See also* BRIDE(S) BOUCLÉE(S), BRIDE(S) CLAIRE(S), BRIDE(S) PICOTÉE(S), BRIDE(S) TORTILLÉE(S).

armaletta (needle) *See* DARNING STITCH.

Armenian knot stitch (needle) (1) Working to the left, with the point away from you, pass the needle through the upper edge of the fabric or loop of previous stitch and behind the thread emerging from the fabric or previous stitch. Take the thread, from the eye-end, from left to right behind the needle (figure a, p.13) and pull through (figure b, p.13). (2) Working to the left, with the point away from you, pass the needle through the upper edge of the fabric or loop of previous stitch and behind the thread emerging from the fabric or previous stitch. Take the thread, from the eye-end, from right to left behind the needle (figure c, p.13) and pull through (figure d, p.13). Also called DOUBLE KNOT. For subsequent rows, the work can be turned around, so that all stitches are worked in the same direction, or the stitch can be reversed and the rows worked in the other direction. *See also* BEBILLA, RODI STITCH.

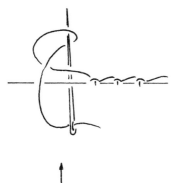

a

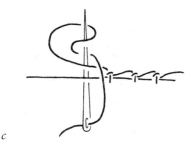

b

c

Armenian lace (needle) *See* BEBILLA. *See also* ARMENIAN KNOT STITCH.

armure (bobbin) A Continental term for the complicated, patterned GROUNDS characteristic of Binche and early Valenciennes lace.

aux fuseaux (bobbin) (Fr.) Made with bobbins.

auxiliary pin (bobbin) A pin that is used only temporarily, sometimes being removed before the next row on that side is started, sometimes as the next row reaching that side is pinned. Also called temporary pin. *See also* GIMP STITCH.

auxiliary thread (tatting) When a CHAIN is made, the thread held across the hand over which the shuttle makes the stitches. *See also* BALL THREAD, SHUTTLE THREAD.

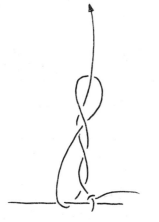

d   *Armenian knot stitch*

B

baby bobbin (bobbin) A BOBBIN with a hollow SHANK containing a loose miniature bobbin, the baby. *See also* CHURCH WINDOW, COW-AND(IN)-CALF, GRANDMOTHER BOBBIN, MOTHER AND/ IN/'N BABE, TWISTED CHAMBER BOBBIN.

baby Irish crochet (crochet) A term often used for a lighter style of Irish crochet, containing small motifs that are often amalgamated into medallions, worked in fine, white thread and trimmed with ribbons.

baby lace (bobbin) A narrow bobbin lace, usually Bucks point, with a simple, usually geometric, design, which was used to decorate babies' clothes, especially caps.

back (bobbin) Working WHOLE, HALF STITCH or a FILLING over raised work (RIB, ROLL, VEIN and so on) in Honiton lace.

back cloth (bobbin) Folded COVER CLOTH pinned across the pillow, just behind the lace as it is freed from the pins (figure a). Frequently a white cloth is used because its function is to keep the lace clean. It is sometimes folded and the lace placed between the folds (figure b); sometimes the rear edge of the cloth is turned over the lace. If it is sufficiently large it will protect all the lace, and the thread on the bobbins, from dust (figure

c). Also called hind cloth. *See also* DRAWTER.

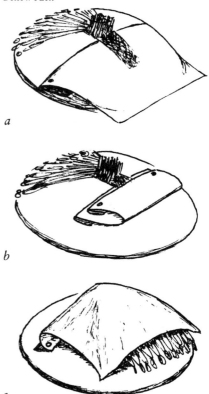

a

b

c

back stitch (bobbin) The technique by which the WORKERS are kept at right angles to the line of work when they show a tendency to slope, achieved by using a pinhole twice. (1) In Beds and Bucks point the last pin, of the side that slopes down, is removed and the loop of

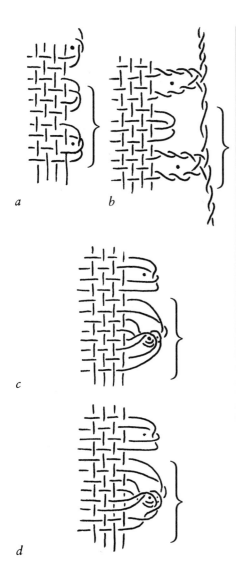

a

b

c

d

(figure b). (3) In some types of lace, particularly the coarser ones, the pin is not removed from the hole, the workers being wrapped around it, on top of the previous pair(s) (figure c). The last pair of passives is not always worked immediately before using the pin a second time, typically in Bruges flower lace. Instead, it is twisted three times, passed around the pin and worked back through the passives in the normal way (figure d).

back stitched centre (needle) When used in Tenerife lace the web threads at the centre are divided into groups and the needle taken under, back over and under each group in turn (figure). *See also* CENTRE.

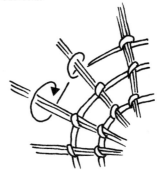

backing (needle) A double layer of fabric, sufficiently tough for hard use, onto which the FOUNDATION THREAD is couched when making needlepoint lace. Also called foundation (fabric). *See also* EMERALD FOUNDATION.

balance marks (bobbin) The marks drawn across the join where two parts of a PRICKING meet. When they are matched, they ensure the pieces line up accurately. *See* Appendix.

ball and shuttle (tatting) The shuttle thread is tied to the end of the ball

thread ignored when the hole is reused (figure a). Also called gaining on a pin. (2) When used in Honiton lace the process is similar but before the edge stitch is worked, on the low side, the runners are twisted once, the pin set and the runners returned across the work, the edge pair remaining unworked. On returning to that side the pin is removed and the edge stitch worked as usual

thread, which may be of a different colour, or left continuous with the ball thread. When the ball thread is held across the fingers, as the AUXILIARY THREAD, although the shuttle makes the stitches they are transferred to the ball thread when the stitch is CAPSIZED. Thus the chain takes the colour of the ball thread.

ball thread (tatting) The thread coming from the ball of thread that passes over the fingers of the left hand when making a CHAIN and over which the stitches are made. *See* AUXILIARY THREAD.

ballpoint scissors (needle) Scissors with one pointed blade and the other with a rounded projection that prevents it from passing through net. They are used for trimming fabric away from the motifs of Carrickmacross and for similar purposes where net might be cut if pointed blades were used. These scissors are generally used with the pointed blade uppermost (figure).

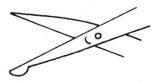

baluster-turned bobbin (bobbin) An ORNAMENTALLY TURNED bobbin the shape of which imitates the baluster stems of eighteenth-century English wine glasses (figure).

bandage stitch (bobbin) *See* CLOTH STITCH.

banding (crochet) The term for the chain and space foundation row of an edging, which is carefully worked around a filling to smooth the outline.

bar (bobbin) (1) *See* BAR (general). (2) The twisted pair before, and after, the STITCH ABOUT A/THE PIN is made at the footside (figure). Used by Honiton workers and others.

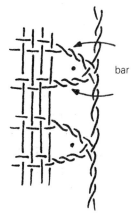

bar (general) Narrow connections in the lace that link its different motifs and sections together. There are many techniques for making these connections. Also called bride, bridge, coxcomb, leg, plait, straps and tie. *See also* BAR (BOBBIN), BUTTONHOLE(D) BAR, CORDED BAR, BAR IN DOUBLE BUTTONHOLE STITCH, PLAIT, TWISTED BAR, WOVEN BAR.

bar cluster (needle) A decorative stitch used to fill narrow spaces by throwing a thread across a space and whipping across it back to the original side (as many times as required to give a close twisted appearance). This is repeated a little way further on, then another

baluster-turned bobbin

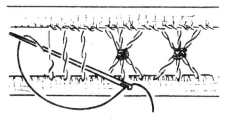

started the same distance from the second and whipped back to the centre, where all three bars are joined by five buttonhole stitches worked around all bars, then the whipping of the last bar is completed (figure). *See also* WHEATSHEAF.

bar in buttonhole stitch (needle) *See* BUTTONHOLE(D) BAR.

bar in cording (needle) *See* CORDED BAR.

bar in darning stitch (needle) *See* WOVEN BAR.

bar in double buttonhole stitch (needle) Three threads are thrown across a space and a row of slightly spaced BUTTONHOLE STITCHES worked back to the original side. The work is turned up the other way and a similar row worked with the stitches of the

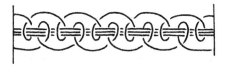

second row being worked between those of the first row (figure). Also called doublesided buttonhole bar.

bar in overcasting (needle) *See* TWISTED BAR.

bar pattern filling (needle) A NEEDLERUN filling (figure).

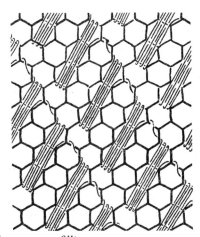

bar pattern filling

bar rosette (needle) (1) A SQUARE FOUNDATION is laid across a space, sometimes with knots where the threads cross. The working thread is fastened on and whipped along one of the threads until it reaches a cross thread. A small rosette is worked with the working thread passing over and under the same threads each time. The rosettes may touch or there may be spaces between them, in which case the working thread is whipped along the thread connecting the two rosettes (figure a). Also called circles in darning stitch, darned circles

a

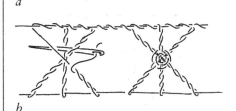

b

and darned rosette. *See also* POINT D'ANGLETERRE, POINT D'ANGLETERRE BAR. (2) Throw a thread diagonally across a space and whip back across it to the original side (as many times as required to give a close, twisted appearance). A little way further on another twisted bar is worked across the centre of the first, then another is started the same distance from the second and angled so that it crosses the other two. This thread is whipped back to the centre only when all three bars are joined by a rosette. Finally the remaining thread is whipped out to the edge (figure b).

bar stitch (needle) Found in the needle-knotted lace PUNTO AVORIO. The bar is produced by working two or more stitches horizontally above a single knotted stitch (figures a–f). Also called column. *See also* ARMENIAN KNOT STITCH

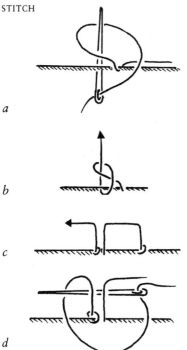

a

b

c

d

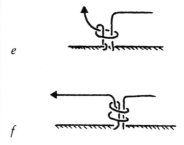

e

f

barred ground (general) A GROUND consisting of bars connecting the motifs. See *also* MESH GROUND.

barley straw (bobbin) Generally considered the best for pillow filling because it is soft and relatively free from nodes (i.e., lumps in the stem) that can impede the insertion of pins.

barleycorn (bobbin) Bedfordshire term for a long SQUARE-ENDED TALLY (figure). *See also* WHEATEAR.

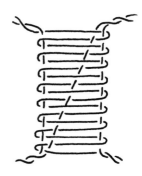

barleysugar twist (bobbin) A BOBBIN with a decoration of spiral grooves running down the shank (figure, p.19).

barrel (crochet) The straight part of a crochet hook that determines the size of the loop made around it and hence the part that determines the size of the crochet hook.

basket edge (bobbin) See GRAFTING OFF.

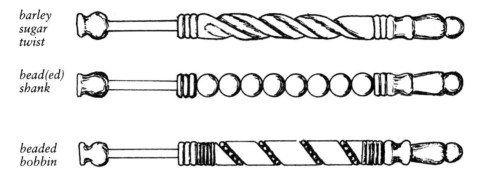

barley sugar twist

bead(ed) shank

beaded bobbin

basket stitch (needle) (1) *See* DARNING STITCH. (2) *See* WOVEN BAR.

basketwork bar (needle) *See* WOVEN BAR.

bâti (needle) *See* FOUNDATION THREAD.

bead edge (general) (1) An edge decorated with PICOTS. (2) *See* BEADING.

bead inlay (bobbin) *See* BEADED BOBBIN.

bead(ed) shank (bobbin) A BOBBIN with a SHANK of beads threaded on thick wire and fixed into the COLLAR at one end, and the TAIL at the other (figure).

bead stitch insertion (needle) *See* ALENÇON BEADS.

beaded bobbin (bobbin) A BOBBIN with a spiral groove, or narrowed section, in which is wound a fine wire threaded with beads (figure). Also called bead inlay and wire beaded.

beading (general) A narrow insertion with a simple design of bobbin or tape lace, to which lace, particularly fine or expensive lace, was attached. This was then attached to the garment. The insertion took the strain and remained attached to the lace when it was removed from the garment for washing or to be reused on another garment, so preventing the lace from being damaged during the unpicking. Also called bead edge, engrêlure and heading. *See also* DECORATED LINES.

beads (bobbin) Because these are used to weight bobbins, they should be made of a suitably heavy substance, such as glass or china. The different shapes and colours have no significance, but are merely decorative. *See also* SPANGLE.

bebilla (needle) Lace typically made using ARMENIAN KNOT STITCH and its variations. Also called Arab lace, Armenian lace, bibilla and Smyrna lace. *See also* RODI STITCH.

Bedford-fly (bobbin) *See* BUTTERFLY BOBBIN/INLAY.

Bedfordshire circle (bobbin) In Bedfordshire lace a CLOTH STITCHED circle with a hole in the centre connected to adjacent parts of the lace by PLAITS and/or LEAVES. The actual working and the number of pairs entering and leaving the work varies according to the number of pinholes in the pattern. Sometimes pairs need to be added at the start. At the end of the motif these pairs may be thrown out or incorporated into plaits (figure). Also called cloth stitch circle and Polo Mint circle/ring. *See also* DOUBLE PLAIT.

Bedfordshire foot(side) (bobbin) The WORKERS make CLOTH STITCHES with two or three pairs of PASSIVES, TWIST one to three times before working with the EDGE PAIR. The pairs change functions:

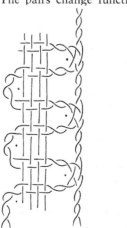

the workers become the edge pair and the former edge pair, now the workers, are twisted the same number of times and cloth stitched back across the passives. They are twisted two or three times as they pass around the pin at the inner edge. The edge pair is twisted two or three times (figure). Also called cloth stitch footside and whole stitch footside. *See also* TWISTED FOOTSIDE.

Bedfordshire spider (bobbin) A motif in Bedfordshire lace consisting of a circle of HALF STITCH surrounded by LEAVES and/or PLAITS, some of which bring

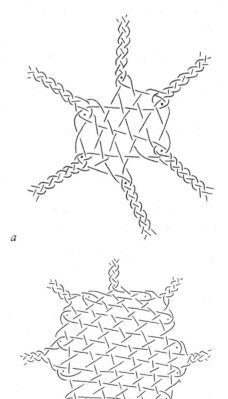

a

b

pairs into the circle while the others take them away (figure a). Sometimes the half stitch is connected to one or both sides by KISSES. There may be more pin-holes around the half stitch centre than plaits or leaves entering and leaving (figure b). *See* Appendix.

Bedfordshire trailer (bobbin) A Hunt-ingdon name for a thick bobbin, usually made of wood, although occasionally of bone, and sometimes made with a SINGLE NECK. Not all have SPANGLES. Some have wooden or pewter GINGLES; bone bobbins usually having bone gingles. Also called trolly bobbins.

Beds (bobbin) The abbreviation of Bedfordshire.

bee (needle) A small block of four stitches worked into an OPEN BRUSSELS STITCH. Made by oversewing four times into a mesh two or more rows above the one being worked (figure). Also called MOUCHE.

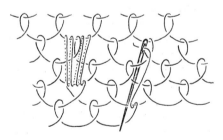

beehive tally (bobbin) A TALLY starting from a point and finishing with a square end (figure) or vice versa.

beeswax (bobbin) Regularly stabbing a PRICKER into beeswax, while making a pricking, makes it easier. The wax is a lubricant, easing the passage of the needle through the card. Candle wax is a suitable substitute.

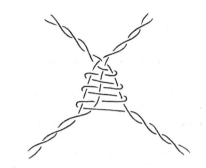

beehive tally

beggar's lace (bobbin) An early name for torchon lace.

Belgian bobbin (bobbin) A BOBBIN having a single head and a bulbous end to provide weight (figure). Slimmer versions are made for use with fine threads.

Belgian colour code (bobbin) Used for coding SCHEMATIC DIAGRAMS
   green: half stitch
   purple: cloth stitch
   red: cloth and twist
   yellow: individual thread, gimp or tally
   orange: half stitch, pin, half stitch twist
   brown: half stitch, twist, pin, half stitch, twist
   blue: two or four pair plait
SLASH MARKS lines indicate additional twists.

bell (needle) Special cluster of stitches made in BELLE POINT DE VENISE. Also called shell.

belle point de Venise (needle) A needle lace FILLING.

row 1: single BUTTONHOLE stitches leaving spaces for four buttonhole stitches between them

row 2: work four buttonhole stitches into the spaces

row 3: work buttonhole stitches into the spaces between the stitches of the groups of four of the previous row and miss the space between them, resulting in groups of three stitches

row 4: ** work buttonhole stitches into the spaces between the stitches of the groups of three of the previous row – i.e., two stitches; throw a thread back and make a stitch around the long thread leading to this pair; work from four to eight stitches over the thrown thread; this cluster of stitches constitutes the bell or shell

row 5: work single buttonhole stitches in the spaces between the groups

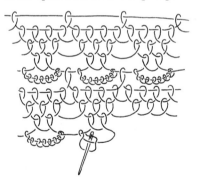

Repeat from ** for each group of three stitches. Repeat rows 2 to 5 as required (figure). Also called shell stitch.

berry pin (bobbin) A pin, usually steel, with a spherical glass head (figure).

bias ground (bobbin) A torchon FILLING of diagonal TRAILS, the pairs being twisted one or more times when they pass from one trail to the next (figure). Also called slanting.

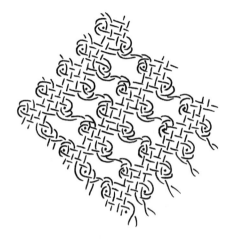

bibilla (needle) See BEBILLA.

big stitch (bobbin) See WINDMILL.

birdcage bobbin (bobbin) A hollow EAST MIDLAND'S BOBBIN with long openings, or windows, in the sides through which the beads can be seen. Sometimes with spiral wire binding to retain the beads (figure, p.23).

bird cage bead (bobbin) A bead used to weight bobbins, surrounded by tiny beads, threaded on fine wire. The wire covered with beads passes around the larger bead and through the hole. This is repeated as required, resulting in the beads forming lines from one end of the hole to the other (figure, p.23). See also BIRD CAGE SPANGLE.

bird cage spangle (bobbin) A SPANGLE with a BIRD CAGE BEAD as the bottom bead. This is usually suspended with its hole vertical (figure, p.23).

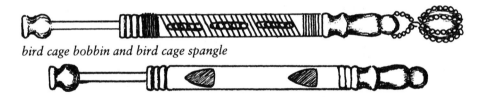

bird cage bobbin and bird cage spangle

bitted bobbin

bird's eye filling (tambour) A Coggeshall FILLING (figure a) and one of its variations (figure b).

bitted bobbin (bobbin) An INLAID BOBBIN with slanting cuts made in the shank and the projecting pieces removed

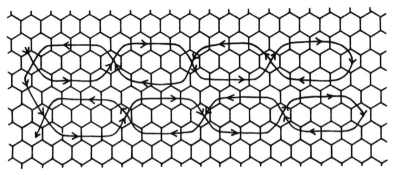

a bird's eye filling

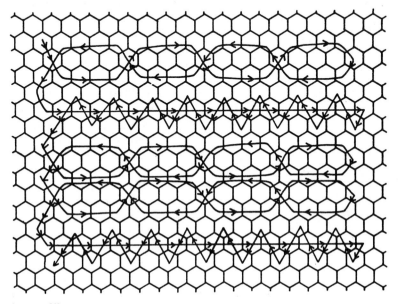

b bird's eye filling

and replaced with similar pieces of bone or wood of another colour (figure).

black beads (bobbin) *See* MOURNING BOBBIN.

blade (bobbin) *See* YARNINGLE.

blind pin (bobbin) A pin that is removed and reused when making a BACK STITCH.

blind spot (bobbin) A Bucks point technique used for a PICOT where there is no pair available from the GROUND, or required by the ground, to make that picot. Sometimes adjacent to HONEY-COMB when the available pair is required to complete the honeycomb. In these cases, one of the HEADSIDE PASSIVES, usually the second or third, is worked out to make the picot and returned (preferably not to the same position or a hole may form) (figure).

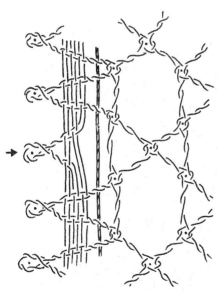

block pillow (bobbin) A rectangular, FLAT PILLOW with a shallow channel, some 7.5–12cm (3–5in) wide, down the centre in which are held square blocks, usually three, of a material that will support pins (figure). Also called Flemish pillow. Curved versions are available for making fans, collars and so on. *See also* U-SHAPED PILLOW.

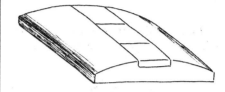

blocking (bobbin) In Bedfordshire lace working CLOTH STITCH areas – i.e., between the veins of leaves and flowers.

blocking out (general) The process of stretching and pinning lace back into shape after it has been washed and before it has dried. Also called pinning out. *See also* LILL(S) PINS.

blonde (bobbin) In the mid-eighteenth century the name for natural coloured silk imported from France. The name was later used for the CONTINUOUS LACE, made in that silk and first made around Caen at that time.

blossom filling (bobbin) (1) The PRICK-ING for the Honiton FILLING consists of blocks of four pins arranged in regular lines, with the spaces between the blocks wider than the spaces between the pins of the block (figure a).

    using pairs from PLAITS A and B
    pair 2 make RIGHT HAND PURL no. 1
    pair 1 as RUNNERS, WHOLE STITCH
    through pairs 2 & 3
    twist pairs 2 & 3
    whole stitch pairs 1 & 2 and 3 & 4*
    pair 1 make LEFT HAND PURL no. 2
    pair 4 make right hand purl no. 3
    whole stitch pairs 1 & 2 and 3 & 4

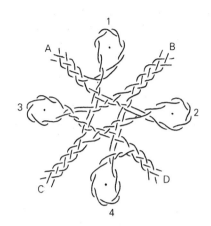

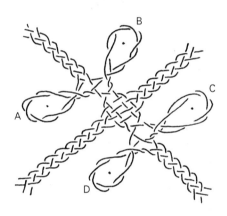

reaching the group of pins and another pair of picots, nos. 3 and 4, made as the plait leaves (figure b).

board (netting) *See* MESH BOARD/ GAUGE/STICK.

bobbin (bobbin) The implement, usually made of wood or bone, that holds the thread when making bobbin lace. Some have SPANGLES of beads to weight them, others rely on the weight of the wood only (figure). *See* DOUBLE HEAD, EAST MIDLANDS BOBBIN, HONITON BOBBIN, HOODED BOBBIN, LONG NECK, RIM, SHANK, SHORT NECK, SINGLE HEAD, SPANGLE, TAIL. *See also* CLEANING BOBBINS.

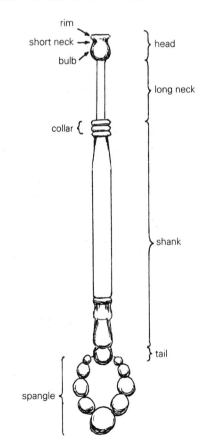

twist pairs 2 & 3
whole stitch pair 2 through 3 & 4
pair 3 make left hand purl no. 4
Make plaits with pairs 1 & 2 and 3 & 4 sufficiently long to reach the next group of four pinholes. (This filling can be made with pairs 2 & 3 twisted at *.)
(2) The Bedfordshire filling has an extra hole in the centre of each group of four. Plait, A reaches the group of four pins. A PICOT, no. 1, is made on one side of the plait, a HALF STITCH is worked with the two pairs and another picot, no. 2, is made on the other side. The pairs work a WINDMILL with the other plait, B,

bobbin bag (bobbin) A small bag, sometimes with two compartments, used to hold bobbins that are ready for use or temporarily out of use. When there are two compartments one is used for full bobbins, the other for recently emptied ones (figure).

bobbin box (bobbin) Box, usually made of wood, used for storing bobbins.

bobbin case (bobbin) (1) A container for bobbins made by folding part of a piece of fabric over and stitching it at intervals to form pockets that hold one or two bobbins, thus keeping them untangled and ready for use. A flap covers and protects them, and two strings are added to secure the case when rolled (figure a). (2) The more

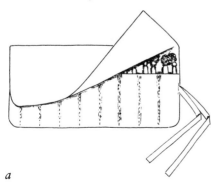

a

modern type has pockets made along both sides and a zip to secure it after the case has been folded (figure b).

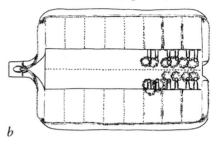

b

bobbin filet (bobbin) A form of torchon lace with a SQUARE GROUND. The solid areas, typical of filet lace, are SQUARE TALLIES. LEAVES may also be included. The edges may be finished with a footside or braid (figure). Also called filet ground.

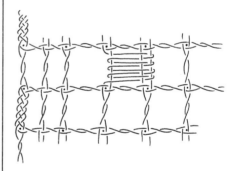

bobbin guipure (bobbin) A bobbin lace made without a ground – i.e., PART LACE, such as Honiton – or one that has trails and motifs connected by plaits, such as Bedfordshire.

bobbin lace (bobbin) Lace made using bobbins. Also called bone lace/point/work, caul lace/work, off-loom weaving, nuns' work and pin work.

bobbin net (bobbin) (1) Originally applied to nets and meshes made using bobbins. (2) Then, after machines were developed that could imitate bobbin-made meshes, the term became more generally applied to the machine-made variety, which was also called bobbinet. *See also* THREE-TWIST BOBBINET, TWO-TWIST BOBBINET.

bobbin tape lace (bobbin) TAPE LACE made using a hand-made bobbin braid. Also called MEZZO PUNTO.

bobbin winder (bobbin) A gadget designed to wind bobbins, usually worked by hand (figure) but sometimes electrically driven. Also called a turn and yarn winder. *See also* NOZZLE.

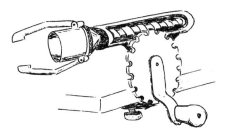

bobbinet (machine) *See* BOBBIN NET (2).

bobble (bobbin) *See* RAISED TALLY.

bobtailed bobbin (bobbin) *See* SOUTH BUCKS BOBBIN.

bold smuggler (tambour) Coggeshall FILLING consisting of small, filled circles (figure).

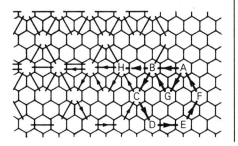

bolster (bobbin) Midland's pillow consisting of a tube of strong material, gathered at both ends and stuffed very firmly with straw. An average size is 43cm (17in) long with a circumference of 80cm (32in) (figure). *See also* ROUND PILLOW.

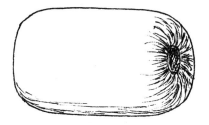

bone inlaid (bobbin) A bobbin with pieces of bone inlaid into the SHANK.

bone lace/point/work (bobbin) This name is said to have originated from the traditional beliefs that early lacemakers used animal bones for bobbins and/or fish bones for pins. *See* BOBBIN LACE.

booklice (bobbin) *See* PSOCID.

border (1) *See* EDGING. (2) A decorative edge along a straight headside with a repeating pattern that does not necessarily connect with the rest of the design but may complement it. (3) A gimp that encircles a motif.

boss (crochet) A padded ring, usually made by winding thread many times around a finger, knitting needle or other similar implement, closely covered with

bound bobbin

DOUBLE or TREBLE STITCHES and sometimes decorated with picots. These rings may be used singly as motifs, or they may be used as parts of flowers or sprays (figure). *See also* MESH.

bottom bead (bobbin) The central bead of a SPANGLE, usually larger and more ornate than the others. Also called centre bead.

bottom sewing (bobbin) TOP SEWING made around the lower BAR of the PIN-HOLE to which the sewing is to be made.

bottoming out (bobbin) *See* GRAFTING OFF.

bound bar (needle) *See* CORDED BAR.

bound bobbin (bobbin) A decorated bobbin having wire bound around its SHANK covering it completely, in band or spiralling. The wire is recessed into the wood or bone, so that it is not uncomfortable to use. Brass and silver wire are most used, with copper occasionally used (figure). Also called wire bound and wired bobbin.

bowed horse (bobbin) A stand for supporting a PILLOW for use. The name is derived from the curved piece of wood that supports the FRONT of the pillow (figure).

bow in (bobbin) Joining pairs from a PLAIT or FILLING to a braid by using a crochet hook or NEEDLEPIN to TAKE SEWINGS. The pairs may continue to make the filling or plait. A Honiton term.

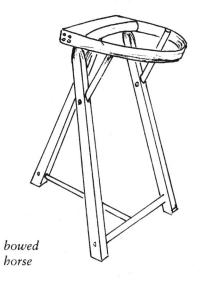

bowed horse

bow off (bobbin) Cutting off pairs in such a way that they remain knotted

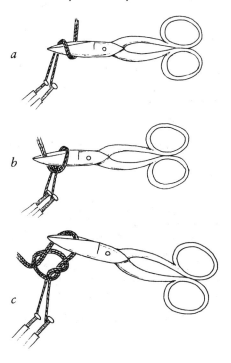

a

b

c

together. Lay the blades of the scissors flat on the pair of threads, wind the scissors around the threads (figure a), open the blades and close them, without cutting, over the threads on the far side (figure b) and draw the gripped threads through the loop around the blades, tighten the knot and cut the threads (figure c). A Honiton term. Also called cut off in couples.

bow out (bobbin) Fastening off pairs from a BRAID, PLAIT, FILLING and so on by using a crochet hook or NEEDLEPIN to TAKE SEWINGS. A Honiton term.

bow-tie (needle) *See* GAMOURCH.

box stand (bobbin) An open-topped box shaped to support a BOLSTER (figure). Early twentieth century.

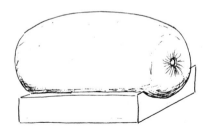

boxed pinhole (bobbin) In Bedfordshire lace, while working an area of CLOTH STITCH, the WORKERS are TWISTED twice during one row and a pin placed below the twists, the PASSIVES either side of the pin being twisted twice. The workers are twisted twice below the pin when working the return row. May be made singly or as a series, and may be worked

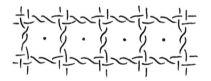

diagonally, horizontally (figure) or vertically. Also called windows.

boxed vein (bobbin) A vein consisting of a line of BOXED PINHOLES.

Brabançon stitch (needle) *See* POINT DE BRABANÇON.

Brabant ground (bobbin) The pricking for this torchon GROUND has alternate holes removed from alternate rows and is usually worked in one of the simpler torchon grounds – i.e., HALF STITCH, pin, half stitch (figure). Variations include adding one or two TWISTS after either or both stitches and substituting CLOTH STITCH AND TWIST for half stitch. Also called honeycomb filling/ground, mirror ground and torchon honeycomb. *See* Appendix for indicator.

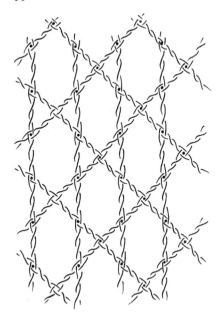

braid (general) A narrow strip of simple design often with both sides the same, made by bobbin or machine. Also called ribbon and tape. Not to be confused with machine-made tape. *See also* PLAIT.

braid dividing (bobbin) A braid dividing into two. (1) For most laces the WORKERS work through one pair further than the point at which it divides, a pin is set under the workers and a CLOTH

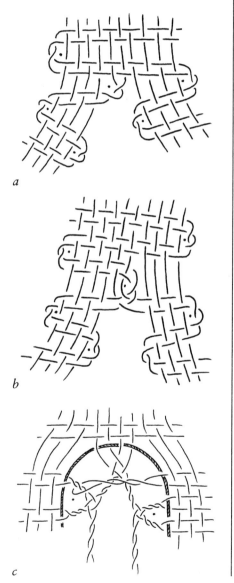

a

b

c

STITCH made, sometimes TWISTS are made. Both pairs are used as workers for their respective braids (figure a). A stitch may be worked with the two pairs of workers immediately following the pin (figure b). (2) In Honiton lace four threads are selected at the point of division, consisting of one pair with a half pair each side. A COARSE THREAD is threaded through these threads, keeping the 'weave' going, the four threads make a WHOLE STITCH, become 'pairs' and are twisted three times. The RUNNERS, approaching from one side, work through the COARSE PAIR, twist three times and a pin is set beneath them. A new pair is slipped up the runners and laid back. The edge of this braid is completed and the runners return. The new pair, twisted three times, become the runners for the other side, passing over the laid back pair, they work across this braid and back. When they return to the centre the remaining pair, from the original four threads, is twisted three times and becomes the edge pair for this braid (figure c).

braid lace (bobbin) A BRAID is made following a design on a pricking. The braid is joined, by SEWINGS, when it meets a previous section. Spaces between different sections of the braid are connected and decorated with bobbin-made BARS and FILLINGS. Also called trail lace. *See also* CHAIN LACE.

braids/trails combining (bobbin) Merging two BRAIDS/TRAILS into one by leaving one pair of WORKERS at the point where they join and continuing by using the remaining pair of workers across the PASSIVES of both trails. The workers should approach the pinhole, where they meet, at the same angle (figure a). The two pairs of workers may work a stitch immediately following the pin (figure b). Also called combining braids/ trails, merging braids/ trails.

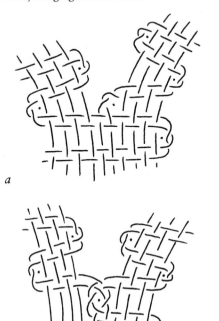

a

b

brake (bobbin) A fabric strip, having its ends pinned to a ROLLER and the back of a pillow, that prevents the roller from turning.

bran (bobbin) A traditional pillow filling. Because it is rather heavy its use is usually restricted to small pillows and rollers. It tends to 'pack down' in use, so the pillows require frequent refilling.

branched vein (bobbin) In Honiton lace a vein worked in RIB with side veins of rib branching off in turn as the central vein progresses. When veins branch to both sides from a single pinhole the one on the PIN SIDE is worked before the one on the PLAIN SIDE (figure). When the veining is complete the leaf is BACKED, the vein being retained in position by SELFSEWINGS.

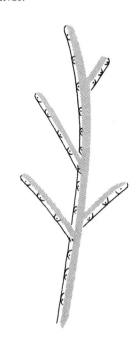

branching side vein (bobbin) BRANCHED VEIN with branches.

brass pinned bobbin (bobbin) *See* PINNED BOBBIN.

brass pins (bobbin) Traditionally brass pins have always been used by lacemakers because they do not rust; sometimes they are plated to resist corrosion. Stainless steel pins are also suitable.

brass wire (bobbin) Traditionally used to thread the SPANGLES and attach them to bobbins, also as decorative binding around the SHANK. *See* BOUND BOBBIN.

breaking thread (yarn) If a thread is broken the fibres on either side of the break are weakened, perhaps for as far as 10cm (4in) from the break. It is, therefore, better to cut threads than to break them.

breaking threads (bobbin) If bobbin threads keep breaking check that: (a) the thread is sufficiently strong (old thread can deteriorate and become brittle); (b) the bobbins are correctly wound without 'undoing' the twist on the thread (*see* WINDING BOBBINS); (c) the threads are not rubbing on the COVER CLOTH as the stitches are made. Polyester content in the fabric creates more friction and frays threads quicker than pure cotton does.

brick filling (bobbin) A Honiton filling (figure).

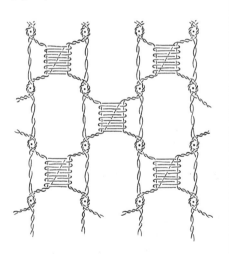

bride (general) *See* BAR (general).

bride(s) à picot(s) (needle) *See* BRIDE(S) PICOTÉE(S).

bride(s) bouclée(s) (needle) (1) Closely worked BUTTONHOLED BARS forming the hexagonal mesh used in the early GRAND BRIDE GROUND of Argentan lace. Also called Medici ground. *See also* BRIDE(S)

CLAIRE(S). (2) Occasionally used for a mesh as in (1), decorated with LOOP(ED) PICOTS. *See also* BRIDE(S) PICOTÉE(S). (3) Sometimes used to describe the later Alençon ground.

bride(s) claire(s) (needle) Closely

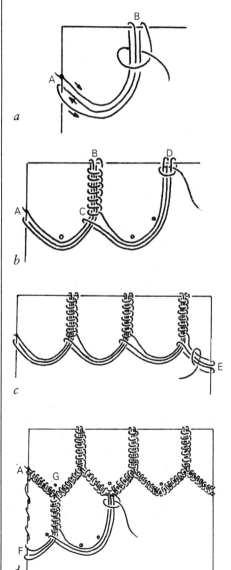

worked BUTTONHOLED BARS forming the hexagonal mesh used in the early GRAND BRIDE GROUND of Argentan lace. The working thread is attached to A and looped through the edge at B, leaving the thread slightly loose. This thread forms part of the foundation of the V at the base of a hexagon and one of its vertical sides. The size of the loop may be controlled by support pins at o. The thread returns to A and back to B; all three threads are the same length and form the foundation over which BUTTONHOLE STITCHES are worked (figure a). * Buttonhole stitches, traditionally between six and ten, are worked over the foundation from B to C, then the next section of foundation is laid between C and D (figure b). Repeat from * to the end of the row when the last small section of foundation is laid between C and the edge at E (figure c). Buttonhole stitches are worked across the lower Vs of the hexagons back to the start A. The working thread is whipped down the side of the work to the lowest position of the next hexagon F, and the foundation threads laid between here and the lowest point of the hexagon above G, where the needle may be taken through the bar (figure d) and continue. Also called Medici stitch.

bride(s) d'épingl(e)(s) (needle) The French word *épingle* means pin. Sometimes it is interpreted as referring to those used to control the size of the mesh when making the ground of regularly spaced bars on a pricked pattern. Otherwise it can refer to the pins used to support picots of the picotéed ground of point de France. *See also* BRIDE(S) CLAIRE(S), BRIDE(S) PICOTÉE(S).

bride de Venise (bobbin) *See* VENETIAN BAR.

bride ground (needle) A general term for the buttonholed needle lace grounds. *See also* BRIDE(S) BOUCLÉE(S), BRIDE(S) CLAIRE(S), BRIDE(S) D'ÉPINGL(E)(S), BRIDE(S) ORNÉE(S), BRIDE(S) PICOTÉE(S), GRAND BRIDE GROUND.

bride(s) ornée(s) (needle) A closely BUTTONHOLED BAR with elaborate decorations as used in Venetian gros point, point de neige and so on (figure).

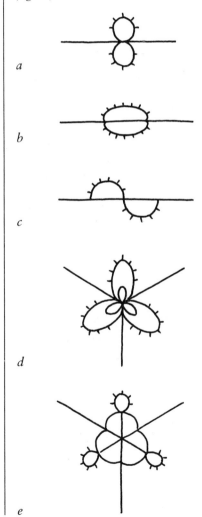

a

b

c

d

e

bride(s) picotée(s) (needle) Closely BUTTONHOLED BARS decorated with picots as used for the ground of point de France, where there may be three or four picots per bar, and coraline point. Also called bride(s) à picot.

bride(s) tortillée(s) (needle) Whipped bars worked over a foundation mesh having two threads per side forming the ground used for Alençon and the later Argentan lace (figure). *See also* ARGENTAN GROUND.

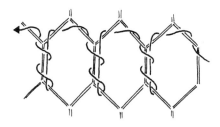

bridge (bobbin) (1) Tapering pad placed under a PRICKING to facilitate MOVING UP. Also called wedge (figure a). (2) When pins are pushed down when there is insufficient room for them to sit side-by-side and the head of one rests on the two adjacent pinheads (figure b). *See also* PIN DOWN. (3) *See* BAR (general).

a

b

bridge (general) *See* BAR (general).

bridge (needle) *See* GAMOURCH.

British Standard (yarn) *See* COTTON COUNT SYSTEM (Ne).

brodé, le (needle) (1) The term used in the Alençon Lace School for the FOUNDATION THREADS. (2) The raised outlining of needle lace produced by the TOP STITCHING.

broiders (needle) *See* TOP STITCHING.

broken thread (general) *See* BREAKING THREAD.

Bruges cord (bobbin) A thick gimp thread used in Bruges flower lace.

Bruges pull braid (needle) A machine-made BRAID specially produced for TAPE LACE, with an imitation FOOTSIDE and having one or more cords running through the centre, or a single one along one or both sides. The cord could be pulled up to gather the braid as required rather than whipping the edges to provide the means for gathering.

Brussels bobbin mesh/ground (bobbin) *See* DROSCHEL GROUND.

Brussels lace stitch (needle) *See* BRUSSELS STITCH.

Brussels net (machine) *See* THREE-TWIST BOBBINET.

Brussels stitch (needle) The simplest NEEDLE LACE GROUND, consisting of rows of SPACED BUTTONHOLE STITCHES each worked into the space between adjacent stitches of the previous row (figure). Sometimes qualified by the addition of a preceding word 'single' as the ground can be worked with two or more stitches worked together in each space. Also called Brussels lace stitch, buttonhole stitch, detached buttonhole stitch, net stitch, point de Brussels/ Bruxelles, point de Tulle, single Brussels/buttonhole stitch, single loop stitch and Tulle stitch. *See also* BUTTONHOLE STITCH, CLOSE STITCH, GREEK NET STITCH, POINT DE SORRENTO.

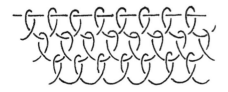

Buckinghamshire round (bobbin) A circular piece of Bucks point lace used for the back of a baby's bonnet. Also called crown.

buckle stitch (bobbin) *See* MITTENS.

Bucks (bobbin) Abbreviation of Buckinghamshire.

Bucks bobbin (bobbin) *See* EAST MIDLAND'S BOBBIN, SOUTH BUCKS BOBBIN.

Bucks point foot(side) (bobbin) The FOOTSIDE characteristic of Bucks point lace, worked by taking the last of the

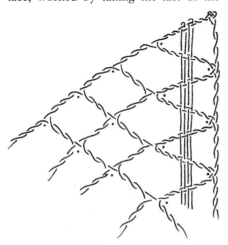

GROUNDWORK PAIRS, in CLOTH STITCH, through two FOOTSIDE PASSIVE pairs. The WORKERS TWIST * two, three or four times, according to taste and the thickness of thread relative to the pricking and a pin is SET UP under them. The workers make a cloth stitch with the EDGE PAIR, the returning workers being twisted the same number of times as * and the edge pair two, three or four times. The returning workers cloth stitch through the passives, are twisted three times and a pin, the CATCH PIN, set up under them (figure). *See also* OFF-SET FOOTSIDE.

Bucks point ground (bobbin) *See* POINT GROUND.

Bucks (point) stitch (bobbin) *See* POINT GROUND STITCH.

bud (bobbin) (1) A single component in CONTINUOUS (THREAD) LACE. (2) A small decorative motif within a piece of lace. (3) In Honiton lace a small hole in WHOLE STITCH. *See also* FOUR-PIN BUD, FIVE-PIN BUD.

bud (needle) A decorative hole in a densely worked stitch, made by missing one or more stitches when working one row and making up that number when making the next row of stitches. If there is a thread laid across, as in CORDED BUTTONHOLE STITCH, this may

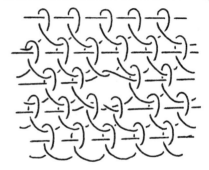

35

be whipped through the loop (figure). Also called opening, pinhole and porte.

bud filling/stitch (needle) Embroidered net FILLING of flower-shaped motifs made by working six small satin stitch blocks around a single hole in the net. The thread passes behind the net to the next position (figure).

bud grouping (crochet) A method of collecting loops along a strip of hairpin

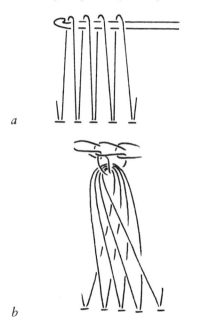

a

b

crochet. Holding the strip with the loops uppermost, insert a crochet hook through a series of loops with the hook passing through from back to front and secure together by finishing as a double crochet, each loop will be twisted (figures a and b). *See also* FAN GROUPING.

bugle (bobbin) South Bucks term for a decorated pin. Until 1824 pin heads were separate rings of wire fixed around the end of a pointed wire and, as these could be removed, beads could be pushed onto one pin and held in place by the head removed from another pin. Now glue is used to fix the beads in place (figure). *See also* LIMMICK, KINGPIN, STRIVER.

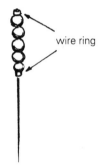

wire ring

bulb (bobbin) The rounded part of a bobbin between the short and long necks. *See also* BOBBIN.

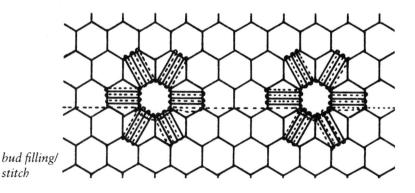

bud filling/ stitch

bullet hole lace (machine) Lace made on the pusher machine modified by John Snyer of Nottingham, patented 1825. This enabled the machine to produce a net patterned with larger holes, hence the name.

bullion bar (needle) A BUTTONHOLE(D) BAR decorated with BULLION PICOTS. *See also* RALEIGH BAR (GROUND).

bullion knot (tatting) A decorative knot made on CHAINS, worked by passing the AUXILIARY around the hand, as for making a RING, and winding the SHUTTLE THREAD around it a number of times (figure a), before pulling it up in the usual manner (figure b).

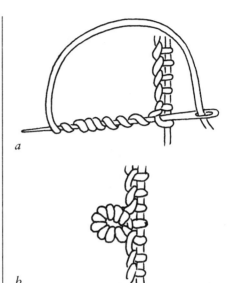

a

b

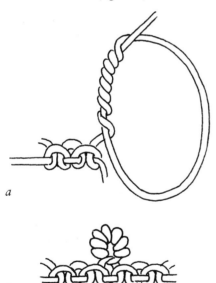

a

b

bullion lace (bobbin) Lace made from gold and/or silver thread, in the past usually used applied to fabric. *See also* DRIZZLING.

bullion (stitch) picots (needle) Usually used to decorate BUTTONHOLE BARS,

these picots are made by passing the needle back into the last BUTTONHOLE STITCH, winding the thread six or more times around the needle (figure a) and pulling the thread through. The picot is held in place by the next buttonhole stitch (figure b). Also called French eyelet, simple picot and picot in vapour stitch. *See also* BULLION BAR, FRENCH KNOT PICOT, POINT D'ESPAGNE EDGING.

bullion stitch (crochet) *See* ROLL STITCH.

bunch and tie (bobbin) Honiton technique for grouping threads and securing them together. Two pairs, or occasionally single bobbins, are crossed beneath the group (figure a). One thread from each of these pairs is used to make a REEF KNOT AND A HALF over the bunch of threads, then the other threads from each pair make a similar knot. The tie pairs may originate from the sides of the group, as at the end of a leaf, or from the centre, as where one section is sewn out into another, since this helps to control the loose ends.

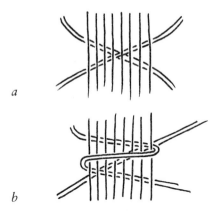

a

b

If the knot shows a tendency to loosen while it is being tied, one of the pairs may be wrapped tightly around the group of threads before knotting (figure b). Also called BUNCHING, SEWING OUT and tie out. *See* TYING TAIL TO TAIL.

bunching (bobbin) *See* BUNCH AND TIE.

Burano ground (needle) The characteristic ground of Burano lace, made as rows of TWISTED BUTTONHOLE STITCHES, which are whipped along the returning row. The twisted buttonhole stitches are best made in the continental manner – i.e., with the needle pointing away, to produce the correct number of twists – and the whipped row is pulled quite taut

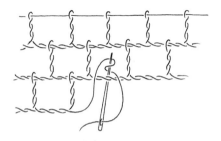

so that the mesh has square holes, rather than in ALENÇON GROUND where the whipped row is not pulled as tight, allowing the mesh to be more hexagonal (figure).

burat(t)o (needle) Lace produced by embroidering an openweave fabric that has a LENO WEAVE. Also called loome lace.

burnt-out lace (machine) *See* CHEMICAL LACE.

bur(r) head (bobbin) A pin decorated with a burr from cleavers or goose grass (Galium aparine). The green burr was skinned and pushed over the pinhead where it would shrink as it dried and so stay on (figure). Also called hard-head, hariffe pin and sweetheart. *See also* STRIVER.

butterfly bobbin/inlay (bobbin) An INLAID BOBBIN in which pewter band(s), inlaid around the SHANK, have been cut so that projections angle off. Sometimes the projections occur on only one side of the band, sometimes on both (figure). Also called Bedford-fly. *See also* COMPOUND INLAY BOBBIN, PEWTER INLAY.

butterfly stitch (needle) Needle lace FILLING, better suited to large areas,

butterfly bobbin

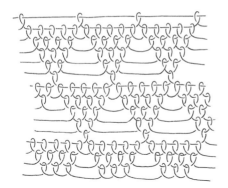

consisting of triangular blocks of BUT-
TONHOLE STITCHES formed by working
groups of five, into which are worked
four with a gap left to the next group,
then three with a gap left to the next
group, then two, and finally one stitch.
New triangles are started by working
five buttonhole stitches in the spaces
between the single stitches (figure). Also
called fan stitch, inverted pyramid
stitch, pyramid stitch, Tulle stitch, V-
ground/stitch and Venetian stitch.

buttonhole (bobbin) An opening in
Torchon lace (figure).

buttonhole(d) bar (needle) One to three
threads are laid across a space and
closely covered with buttonhole stitches
(figure). Also called bar in buttonhole
stitch and Venetian bar.

buttonhole(d) bar

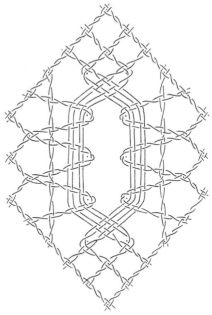

buttonhole

buttonhole(d) edging (netting) The
edge of FILET LACE may be neatened by
laying one or more threads along the
edge and buttonholing around the edge
and these threads.

buttonhole(d) edging (needle) After a
Tenerife medallion has been embroidered, the working thread is taken two
or more times around the circle of pins.
BUTTONHOLE STITCHES are worked over
these threads with one or two stitches
being worked into each loop of thread
supported by a pin as it is reached
(figure).

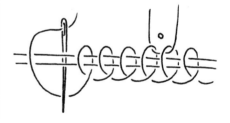

buttonholed loop (needle) From the appropriate place, lay three foundation threads and BUTTONHOLE STITCH closely around them (figure). Also called buttonholed ring picot, ring picot and rose point loop. *See also* COURONNE, LOOPED CORDONNETTE.

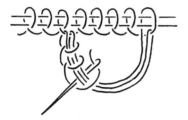

buttonhole(d) ring (needle) A decorative ring. (1) Made separately and attached to needle and other laces. Wind a thread as many times as required around the appropriately sized section of a RING STICK, and BUTTONHOLE STITCH closely around the windings. Sliding the windings down to the next, narrower, section of the stick makes the ring looser and easier to work (figure a). Finish by sliding the ring off the stick and passing the needle through the back part of the ring (figure b). Leave the working thread for stitching the ring in place. Also called buttonhole stitched ring. *See also* COURONNE. (2) A tiny ring made around one of the meshes of a GROUND. After making the ground, insert a pin in the selected mesh, secure the end of a thread at any convenient place and lay across to the pin, darn the thread through the surrounding meshes at least three times, passing the needle over and under the same threads. Remove the pin and buttonhole around the three rings of darning and the mesh they surround. Work three to six stitches in each space (figure c), fasten off the thread and pass to the next ring. Trim the thread leading to the first ring.

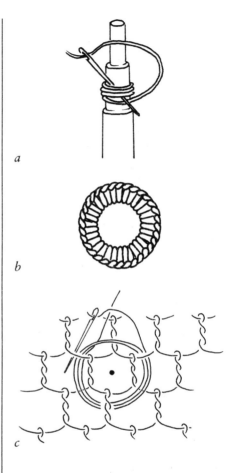

a

b

c

buttonhole(d) ring picot (needle) *See* BUTTONHOLED LOOP.

buttonhole stitch (needle) (1) The basic stitch of needle lace. It is made by taking a needle behind a thread and bringing it out through its own loop (figure). This is often called loop stitch, particularly by embroiderers who have a different stitch that they call buttonhole stitch. (2) The simplest needle lace ground consisting of rows of SPACED buttonhole stitches each worked into the space between adjacent stitches of the previous row. Also known as Brussels lace stitch, net stitch, point de Brussels/

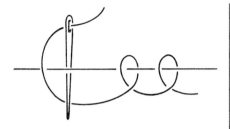

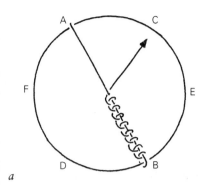

a

Bruxelles, point de tulle, single Brussels and tulle stitch. *See also* BRUSSELS STITCH, CLOSE STITCH, FACING BUTTONHOLE STITCHES, LOOP STITCH.

buttonhole stitched ring (needle) *See* BUTTONHOLE(D) RING.

buttonholed cobweb/spider (needle) From A a thread is stretched across a space, * fas.ened at B and BUTTONHOLE STITCHED back to the centre. The thread is laid to another point on the edge C (figure a), buttonholed back to the centre and a thread laid right across to D, to form the opposite 'spoke'. Repeat from * for points E, and F and buttonhole back to the centre. The remaining 'spoke' to A is buttonholed part way out. The thread is then taken, in a circle, around the centre, passing the needle through the bars. The circle is button-

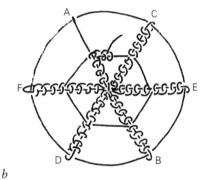

b

holed (figure b), then the remainder of the 'spoke' to A is worked. Also called Venetian cobweb.

C

cable gimp/in a braid (bobbin) RAISED GIMPS looking like a cord running through the lace. Two gimps are used as a pair, the right gimp is lifted and the workers are passed between them, then the gimps are twisted. By reversing the bobbin being lifted and crossing the gimps instead of twisting, the direction of 'twist' of the cord can be reversed (figure). When coloured gimps are used in this way there is an unbroken line of colour over the work, which is un-interrupted by the colour of the ordinary pairs as happens when gimps are used singly. Also called corded gimp, single cording. *See also* CHAIN CORDING/GIMP.

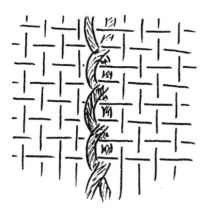

calyx-eyed needle (general) A needle that has a split, with a guiding slot, at the top of the eye and can be threaded by pressing the thread through the slot (figure). It is useful for TAKING SEWINGS.

camel beads (bobbin) Small, hand-wound, oval glass beads, flattened on two sides and with the hole through the shorter axis. They are usually opaque turquoise in colour, but opaque yellow ones are occasionally found. They were produced for trading with tribal people and are said to have been a popular ornament on camel harnesses, hence the name (figure).

candle block/stool (bobbin) A tall, three-legged stool with a socket in the centre to hold a candle, surrounded by several others that could support spherical flasks of water. This enabled several lacemakers to work using a single expensive candle (figure). Also called candle-block and flash stool. *See also* CUP, FLASH, FLASH CUSHION, HOLE BOARD, HUTCH, NOZZLE.

Candlemas day (tradition) 2 February, the feast of the Purification of the Virgin Mary and the presentation of Christ in the Temple, when candles are blessed. For lacemakers it was the day when candles were put away until the next winter.

candlewax (bobbin) *See* BEESWAX.

cane beads (bobbin) Beads cut from cane glass tubes with a shaped cross section, usually hexagonal, used to weight SPANGLES (FIGURE). *See also* FACETED BEAD.

cane bottom chair ground (bobbin) *See* POINT DE LA VIERGE.

cane ground (bobbin) *See* FLANDERS GROUND.

capsized knot (netting and tatting) When a knot is made with one thread over another, the supporting thread is relaxed while the thread making the knot is tightened, causing the thread making the knot to straighten and become a supporting thread, while the former supporting thread now forms the knot.

card (bobbin) *See* PRICKING.

Carrickmacross appliqué (needle) Lace made by COUCHING a thread around a design on fine fabric that is overlaying net, both mounted on a heavy fabric BACKING. The couching stitches pass through the fine fabric and net only. Portions of the fabric, between some of the couched threads, are cut away, leaving the net showing. Sometimes some of these areas are further decorated with needlerun fillings. The backing fabric is removed when the work is completed. *See also* POP, TWIRLING.

Carrickmacross guipure (needle) Lace made by COUCHING a thread around a design on fine fabric, mounted on a heavy fabric BACKING. The couching stitches pass through the fine fabric only. Portions of the fabric, between some of the couched threads, are cut away, leaving a lacy effect. The foundation fabric is removed when the work is completed. *See also* TWIRLING.

carrying pairs along a gimp (bobbin) Found especially in FLORAL BUCKS and similar laces. When pairs must be laid out of the clothwork to prevent it from becoming too thick, even though they are not required for the ground or for

43

filling, they may be taken across the GIMP, TWISTED twice and laid along the gimp. These pairs are treated as though they were part of the gimp when subsequent pairs cross (figure) and may be brought back into the work later on. Also called laying pairs along a gimp.

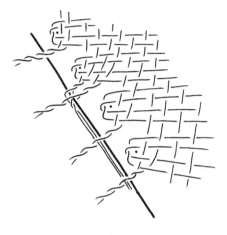

cartisan(e) (bobbin) A narrow strip of PARCHMENT closely bound with silk or metal thread and used as a GIMP. Also called parchment lace.

cartwheel (bobbin) A Honiton FILLING usually used in a circular or oval space. Three, four or five LEADWORKS may be worked above and below the centre with, respectively, three, four or five pins across the centre. Each leadwork entering the filling is supported by a pin, pairs being sewn in as required (figure).

With each two pairs work a whole stitch and three twists before the pin, close to the edge, is set.

Work a narrow leadwork, with each two pairs, to the corresponding pin of the upper row; twist each pair three times and leave the leadworks supported by the pins.

Discard a pair at each end, work a whole stitch and three twists with each set of two pairs across the centre. Include the pairs at each end, work a whole stitch and three twists with each set of two pairs across the centre. Set up pins across the lower row, between each two pairs.

Work a narrow leadwork with each two pairs; twist each pair three times and support with a pin close to the edge; work a whole stitch and sew out (figure).

Also called Devon cartwheel.

carved pillow (bobbin) A pillow carved from a block of POLYSTYRENE or STYROFOAM. *See also* MOULDED PILLOW.

casing (bobbin) A fabric envelope that, when stuffed with STRAW, BRAN or SAWDUST, becomes a lace PILLOW.

casket (needle) An area of GROUND bounded on all sides by more elaborate areas of design.

casting on (netting) Tie the STANDING END to a FOUNDATION LOOP. Hold the MESH STICK below the foundation loop and take the thread down the front of the stick, up behind it and through between the stick and the foundation loop. * Make a HALF HITCH by taking the thread up over the front of the foundation loop, down behind it and through between the stick and the foundation

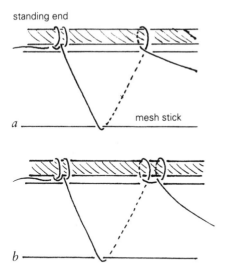

standing end

a _____ mesh stick

b _____

loop* (figure a). Firm up until the stick sits snugly below the foundation loop. Make another half hitch, working from * to *, to lock the stitch in place (figure b). Repeat for the number of meshes required.

catch pin (bobbin) Used in Bucks point and some similar laces, the pin that supports the POINT GROUND STITCH adjacent to the FOOT(SIDE) and occasionally

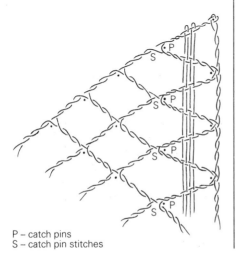

P – catch pins
S – catch pin stitches

found adjacent to a VERTICAL GIMP or HEADSIDE PASSIVES. Because the pairs entering and leaving the ground at this position are FIRMED UP more strongly, and the strain on individual threads has a different balance from the balance of strain caused by firming up ground, this pin is placed to the side of the stitch rather than in its usual place below it, thus counteracting the tendency for the stitch to be distorted (figure). *See also* CATCH PIN STITCH, REVERSE CATCH PIN STITCH.

catch pin stitch (bobbin) The stitch in Bucks point that has its pin, the CATCH PIN, placed to its side rather than between the two pairs (figure).

Catherine stitch (bobbin) In BRAID LACE a PLAIT decorated with a PICOT, which is SEWN to another braid or to another part of the same braid, and returns, decorated with a picot, to its point of origin (figure). *See* Appendix for guideline.

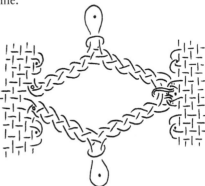

°single pinhole used twice

Cattern cake/day (tradition) Cattern is a corruption of Saint Catherine, the patron saint of lacemakers, whose day, 25 November (Cattern Day or Catterns), was celebrated by lacemakers. Special home-brewed drink and cakes were prepared, the Cattern cakes made of sweetened dough spiced with caraway seeds.

caught picot (bobbin) A SINGLE THREAD PICOT, often used to decorate PLAITS, made by taking a pin under the thread on the required side of the plait. (The illustration shows a picot being made to the left side.) The pin then passes over the other thread of the pair, which it pulls back under, and to the side of, the top thread (figure a). The point of the pin is taken over the top thread and down between them at A and, pointing away from you, between the threads at B. The resulting loop is lifted up through B (figure b), and the point of the pin is inserted in the required pinhole (figure c). Another method is to pull the pin to the right and to set up the pin on whichever side the picot is situated. Also called continental picot, Italian picot and knotted picot.

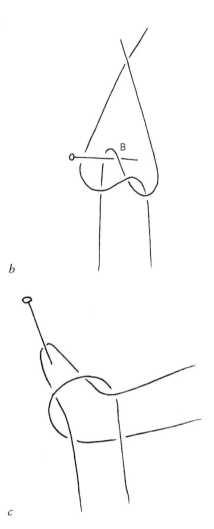

b

c

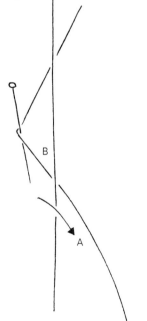

a

caul lace/work (bobbin) *See* BOBBIN LACE.

central ring (tatting) A method of starting a radially symmetrical piece in which a RING, bearing equally spaced PICOTS, is worked and usually tied off. This ring forms the centre of the piece, and subsequent work is made around it and joined to its picots as required (figure, p.47).

centre bead (bobbin) *See* BOTTOM BEAD.

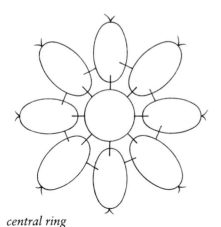

central ring

centre picot (tatting) A method of starting in the centre of a radially symmetrical piece where three or more RINGS or CHAINS meet. The first ring bears the central picot, to which all the subsequent rings or chains join. When finished, the central picot does not show: it is completely covered by the joins of the other rings or chains (figure).

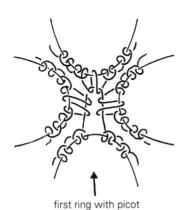

first ring with picot

centre (needle) The centre of a Tenerife lace medallion, where stitching holds the crossed threads of the web in place. *See also* BACK STITCHED CENTRE, DOUBLE DARNED CENTRE, GROUP DARNED CENTRE,

PROGRESSIVE DARNED CENTRE, SINGLE DARNED CENTRE, STEM STITCHED CENTRE.

chad pot (bobbin) *See* FIRE POT.

chain (crochet) With the crochet hook facing downwards, take up the thread and draw it through the loop on the hook (figure).

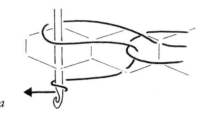

chain (tambour) Hold the thread below the net with the left hand and the hook

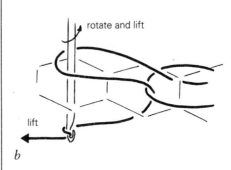

a

b

rotate and lift

lift

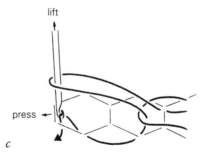

lift

press

c

between the right thumb and first finger. Insert the hook through one of the meshes, *wind the thread one and a half times round the hook, ending with the thread in line with the direction of work (figure a), rotate the hook through 180 degrees in the same direction, and start lifting (figure b). Press the back of the hook against the net and lift a loop through the net (figure c) and the previous stitch around the hook, rotate hook, in the opposite direction, back to its original position. Repeat from *. This stitch can be worked in any direction, horizontally, vertically or diagonally.

chain (tatting) With the last part of the previous work held between the left index finger and thumb, the ball thread is taken across the backs of the fingers of the left hand, and wound around the little, or third, finger to control the tension. DOUBLE STITCHES are worked with the shuttle over the section of ball thread between the first and second fingers (figure). *See also* AUXILIARY THREAD, TWISTED CHAIN.

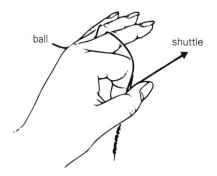

ball

shuttle

chain cording/gimp/stitch (bobbin) RAISED GIMPS creating a chain. Four gimps are used in two pairs. After starting by TWISTING the gimps of one pair, * the right gimp is lifted, the workers are passed between them and the gimps twisted*. The gimps of the other pair are

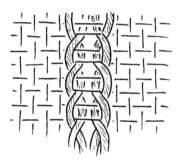

CROSSED, * *the left gimp is lifted, the workers passed through them and the gimps crossed.** Repeat from * to * and from ** to ** every time the workers meet the gimps, lifting the thread on the same side each time. Exchanging the twisting and crossing movements makes the 'chain' face the other way (figure). Also called corded chain, herringbone and interlocking V gimp. *See also* CABLE GIMP, HERRINGBONE BRAID.

chain lace (bobbin) A BRAID LACE, the FILLINGS of which are often made using just two pairs of bobbins, as made in Russia and other eastern European countries.

chain of rings (needle) A series of small BUTTONHOLED RINGS, as found in point de gaze, with their FOUNDATION THREADS linked in one of three ways. Twist the foundation thread according

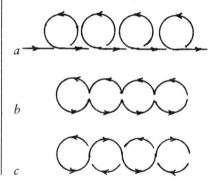

a

b

c

to its twist and as it makes a small loop, COUCH it down. (The direction of the twist will depend on the twist of the thread – i.e., S or Z.) Repeat for all the rings (figure a). Alternatively, couch the thread round the upper parts of the rings, follow round the end ring and couch the lower parts on the return (figure b). The third way is to couch an undulating thread, follow round the end ring and couch the missing parts of the circles on the return (figure c).

chain stitch (bobbin) *See* CHAIN CORD-ING/GIMP/STITCH.

chain stitch picot (needle) Pass the needle through the last buttonhole stitch and bring through its loop, pull up the loop, placing the needle through it before tightening is complete and bring through its own loop again. Continue as required, then continue buttonholing (figure).

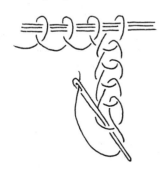

changing the pinhole side of a rib (bobbin) The PINHOLE SIDE of a Honiton RIB is usually on the outside of the curve and, if the curve of the rib changes direction, the pinhole side may need to change sides. At this point the RUNNERS work to the PLAIN EDGE where both they, and the edge DOWNRIGHTS are TWISTED three times and an EDGE STITCH made and pinned. The runners return

to the other side, now the plain edge, and continue as usual, the three twists being left on the former edge pair as it becomes the edge downright pair (figure).

changing workers (bobbin) When the workers are exchanged for another pair, the roles of the two pairs being reversed. Typical situations are (1) where the workers are exchanged for the edge pair

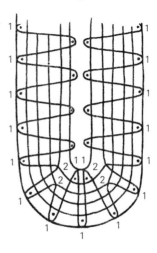

when working the FOOT(SIDE), also called exchanging pairs/workers, and (2) where the workers are exchanged for a pair of passives when working a fairly tight curve in braid lace (figure). Also called gaining on a pin and turning stitch.

check (tambour) A Coggeshall FILLING consisting of parallel lines of stitches, three holes apart, running diagonally in two directions. The resulting diamonds may have spots worked within them (figure).

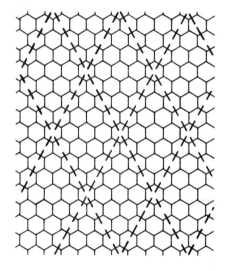

checked paper (general) *See* GRAPH PAPER.

chemical lace (machine) In a process developed in the 1880s, machine embroidery in cotton yarn was worked on a woollen or silk fabric, and the fabric was then chemically removed by being treated with caustic soda or chlorine to leave the cotton embroidery. Today, fabrics that are designed to dissolve in water or to be removed by a blast of hot air are used as a temporary support for the embroidery. Also called burnt-out lace.

chequered filling (needle) Used to fill large, sometimes irregularly shaped, spaces. A SQUARE FOUNDATION of threads is stretched across the space; over this diagonals may be superimposed (figure) and the resulting grid embroidered. Also called grid filling. *See also* BAR ROSETTES, CHEQUERED RINGS, CHEQUERED SPIDERS.

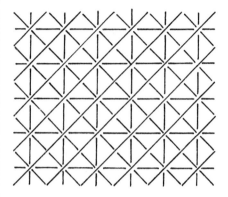

chequered rings (needle) A CHEQUERED FILLING. After stretching a SQUARE FOUN-DATION, BUTTONHOLE STITCHES are worked along the side of the threads with ten stitches per section. Large buttonhole stitches are worked from one corner to the centre of an adjacent side, to the next corner and so on until the one in the

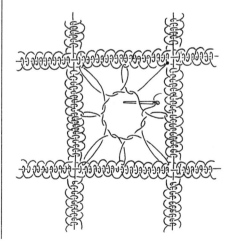

centre of the last side is worked. These stitches are whipped around the centre (figure) and drawn into a ring that is whipped a further two or more times. The central ring is buttonholed, with the same number of stitches worked along each section. When the ring is complete the thread is taken along the single thread towards the remaining incomplete corner, thus completing the first square.

chequered spiders (needle) A CHEQUERED FILLING. After stretching a SQUARE FOUNDATION, BUTTONHOLE STITCHES are worked along either side of the threads, with ten stitches per section. Threads, for the web, are stretched across each square starting from one corner and laying to the opposite one, then whipping along the buttonhole stitches to the centre of one side, across the centre of the square to the opposite side, whipping to the next corner and laying the other diagonal, then whipping to the centre of the side and laying the final thread. The working thread is then whipped along one of the web threads to the centre where a knot is made to control the threads. (Alternatively a tacking stitch can be made to control the crossing point.) The centre is worked in back stitch – i.e., the needle is taken under two threads and back over one (figure). When the spider has reached the required size (count the number of rounds so that subsequent spiders will be the same size), make a stitch into the back of the spider and whip down another of the legs to the next section.

chip-carved bobbin (bobbin) *See* PENKNIFE BOBBIN.

chubby pricker (bobbin) A PRICKER with a bulbous handle, originally designed for those with hand problems (figure).

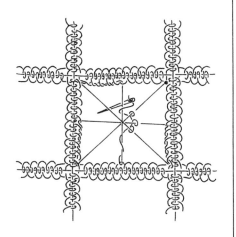

church window bobbin (bobbin) A bobbin with a hollow shank that has slots, occasionally sloping but usually vertical like church windows, in sets of two or four with pairs opposite each

church window bobbin

other (figure). *See also* BABY BOBBIN, LANTERN BOBBIN, PORTHOLE CHURCH WINDOW BOBBIN, TWISTED CHAMBER BOBBIN.

cigarette (bobbin) A motif found in torchon lace that can be worked in CLOTH or HALF STITCH (figure).

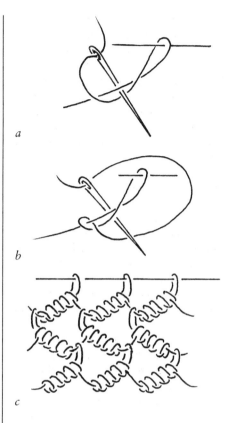

a

b

c

cinq point de Venise (needle) A variant of POINT DE VENISE. (1) A single BUTTON-HOLE STITCH is taken into a preceding row and the thread taken back to cross the loop it has made. A stitch is made over the loop (figure a) and tensioned carefully; this is the stitch that determines the size and position of the cluster. The next buttonhole stitch is worked over the double thread (figure b), as are the remaining three stitches of the cluster of five (figure c). This cluster may contain four to six stitches. Also called cinq point ground, corn stitch, point de grain(s), point de Venise, purl filling, seed stitch as well as shell stitch. (2) Rows of clusters may be worked alternately with rows of single buttonhole stitches worked between the clusters. Also called purl filling (Branscombe). *See also* PURLING.

cinq point ground (needle) *See* CINQ POINT DE VENISE.

cinq trous ground (bobbin) *See* FLANDERS GROUND.

circle (tatting) *See* RING.

circles in darning stitch (needle and netting) *See* BAR ROSETTE.

circular netting (netting) *See* WORKING IN THE ROUND.

cleaning bobbins (bobbin) Wooden bobbins can be cleaned by carefully using a polish made from bees wax and turpentine, but polish should not be used where it may come into contact with the

thread. Avoid using polish on coloured decoration. Bone bobbins may be cleaned using an uncoloured, unperfumed toilet soap. Use both soap and water sparingly, applying and rubbing gently with a sponge or soft brush. Rinse thoroughly and dry with a soft cloth. Do not allow to remain wet any longer than necessary and avoid wetting any wood, metal or coloured decoration.

cleaning lace (general) Modern lace can be washed by hand at the temperature recommended by the yarn manufacturers. Most modern washing powders and liquids contain bleaches, whiteners and perfumes that may destroy natural fibres in as little as twenty years, so choose carefully. Powders and liquids that are recommended for woollens and silk are less likely to cause damage but cleaning agents specially prepared for museums are to be preferred. Pure cotton and linen may be boiled. Never rub or wring and always rinse thoroughly. Wet lace should be supported when lifted (a piece of white sheeting makes a suitable support), and pressed gently between towelling to remove most of the moisture. Pull lace gently into shape, BLOCK OUT and leave to dry. Lace that has been well pinned out will not need pressing. Small pieces of lace may be pinned, around their edges, to a polystyrene block and cleaned by squeezing a soft sponge against it. The lace can be rinsed and allowed to dry before being removed. (Polystyrene can be boiled safely.) Always check that there is no reaction between pins and the washing agent. Antique lace requires professional treatment. *See* DRYING-BOTTLE.

climbing in (tatting) A RING is made on a CHAIN, separated from the chain by a space equal to the size of PICOTS on it, so

that the threads leading to and from the chain simulate a picot (figure).

climbing out of a ring (tatting) A method of starting at the centre where a RING is surrounded by a CHAIN. Using a CONTINUOUS THREAD make a RING having one fewer PICOTS than the total number required. CLOSE the ring and REVERSE the work. Surround the ring with a chain starting with a LOCKING STITCH followed by the second half of a DOUBLE STITCH. These are made at such a distance from the ring that the two threads simulate the missing picot (figure). Return work to the original side and continue as required. Also called simulated picot.

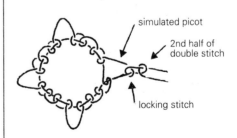

reverse side

Clones crochet (crochet) A form of Irish crochet, from the areas around the town of Clones in County Monahagen, that has CLONES KNOTS made on the CHAINS forming the FILLINGS between the motifs.

Clones knot (crochet) An ornamental knot, used in Irish crochet, said to have been invented in the Clones region of Ireland. After working the required number of CHAIN stitches, *YARN OVER HOOK, bring the hook down in front of the chain and back under it, yarn over hook while it is behind the chain and bring a loop to the front* (figure a). Repeat from * to * about nine times, but count so that all your knots, for one piece, are the same. Yarn over hook and draw this loop through all those on the hook. Secure by making a slip stitch to the second chain from the hook (Count from the other end!) (figure b). To make it easier to draw the hook through the loops: (1) do not keep too tight a tension while making the loops, (2) keep the hook facing the chain, with its back pressed against the loops and (3) hold the bunch of loops where they pass round the chain gently, but firmly, between your finger and thumb, steadying them as the hook passes through.

a

b

close (in) (bobbin) *See* COVERING A PIN.

close (needle) When this word precedes the name of a needle lace stitch or filling, it indicates that the stitches are worked closely, in many cases without leaving spaces between them.

close (tatting) After the required number of stitches has been made for a RING,

the SHUTTLE THREAD is pulled with a steady tension until the ring closes with all the stitches touching one another and the shuttle thread cannot be seen between them.

close buttonhole filling *See* CORDED BRUSSELS/BUTTONHOLE STITCH.

close running (needle) A NEEDLERUN FILLING in which, after making running stitches from one hole to the next, the thread is taken back through the same holes, but passing through the net in the opposite direction (figure).

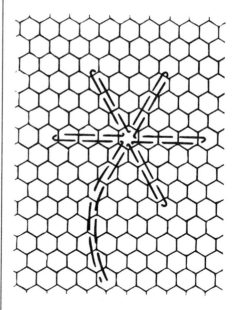

close stitch (needle) The simplest needle lace filling, consisting of rows of BUTTONHOLE STITCHES each worked into the space between stitches of the previous row. The stitches are so close that hardly any space can be seen between them. Also called point noné. *See* BRUSSELS STITCH.

close work (general) *See* CLOTH WORK.

closed check (bobbin) A variant of ROSE GROUND in which the centre of each 'rose' is closed by working a stitch with the centre pairs (figure). The variation illustrated is worked:

pairs 1 & 2 and 3 & 4 half stitch and twist

*centre pairs half stitch and twist, pin A, half stitch

pairs 1 & 2 half stitch, twist pair 1, pin B

pairs 3 & 4 half stitch, twist pair 4, pin C

pairs 2 & 3 half stitch

pairs 1 & 2 half stitch, twist pair 1

pairs 3 & 4 half stitch, twist pair 4

pairs 2 & 3 half stitch and twist, pin D, half stitch and twist

pairs 1 & 2 and 3 & 4 half stitch and twist

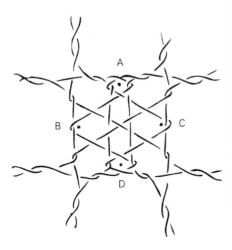

closed edge (bobbin) *See* FOOT(SIDE).

closed pin stitch (bobbin) *See* TWISTED HALF STITCH GROUND.

closed stitch (bobbin) *See* HONEYCOMB STITCH.

closing (bobbin) *See* COVER(ING) A PIN.

closing a braid (bobbin) Joining a braid end to beginning to form a circle.

closing bead (bobbin) *See* TOP BEAD.

closing stitch (bobbin) A stitch worked after the pin when COVER(ING) A PIN. Also called ending stitch.

cloth and twist (bobbin) A stitch where two pairs of bobbins, NUMBERED from the left after every movement (figure). Work:

2 over 3
2 over 1 and 4 over 3
2 over 3
2 over 1 and 4 over 3

Also called complete stitch, double, double half stitch, double passing, double stitch, Downton whole stitch, twisted cloth stitch and WHOLE STITCH.

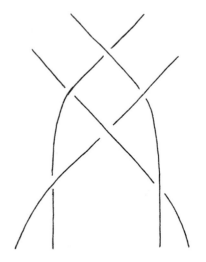

cloth and twist edge (bobbin) The WORKERS have one TWIST before making a CLOTH STITCH with the edge PASSIVES, they are TWISTED twice as they pass round the EDGE PIN and work a cloth stitch and twist with the edge passives before continuing across the row. Can

a

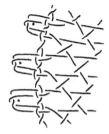

b

be worked at the edge of cloth stitch (figure a) or HALF STITCH (figure b). *See also* TWIST PAIR.

cloth and twist fan (bobbin) *See* SPANISH FAN.

cloth stitch (bobbin) A basic stitch of bobbin lace in which two pairs of bobbins, numbered from the left after every movement work (figure):

    2 over 3
    2 over 1 and 4 over 3
    2 over 3

Also called bandage stitch, full stitch, linen stitch, one-two-three stitch, point de toile (Fr.), weaving stitch and WHOLE STITCH.

cloth stitch (general) *See* CLOTH WORK.

cloth stitch (needle) Stitch, that when worked closely, forms a solid area and fulfils the same function as the stitch of the same name in bobbin lace. *See also* BRUSSELS STITCH, CORDED BRUSSELS/ BUTTONHOLE STITCH.

cloth stitch (netting) *See* POINT DE TOILE.

cloth stitch circle (bobbin) *See* BEDFORDSHIRE CIRCLE.

cloth stitch crossing (bobbin) *See* WINDMILL.

cloth stitch footside (bobbin) A FOOTSIDE where the PASSIVES are worked in plain CLOTH STITCH without any TWISTS.

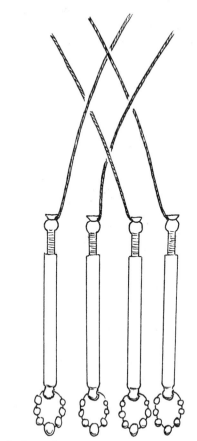

cloth stitch

Also called whole stitch footside. *See also* BEDFORDSHIRE FOOTSIDE, TWISTED FOOTSIDE.

cloth work, clothwork (general) Those parts of lace that have a cloth-like appearance regardless of the technique used to make them. Also called clothing, mat, matt, matte, plain work and toile. *See* CLOTH STITCHES of various types.

clothing (bobbin) This term applies particularly to Honiton lace. *See* CLOTH WORK.

clove hitch (knotting) A knot composed of two facing HALF HITCHES (figure). Also called double stitch (tatting) and lark's head.

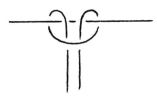

cluster (netting) Make a SIMPLE KNOT into the loop where the cluster is to be made. Wind the thread around the MESH STICK the required number of times, bringing the NETTING SHUTTLE forwards through the loop each time. Finish the cluster with a simple knot (figure a).

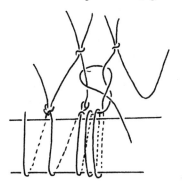

a

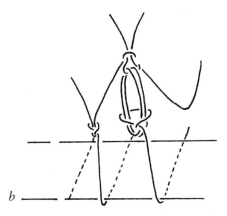

b

When this point is reached, when working the next row, make one simple knot through all the cluster loops (figure b).

coarse pair (bobbin) A Honiton term for the DOWNRIGHT PAIR, consisting of a COARSE THREAD and its FINE PARTNER, frequently used to outline WHOLE or HALF STITCH. Under most circumstances the coarse pair is used as any other downright pair.

coarse thread (bobbin) A Honiton term for the thicker thread that is frequently used to outline WHOLE or HALF STITCH. *See also* COARSE PAIR.

coarse thread(s) crossing (bobbin) In Honiton lace. (1) When a COARSE THREAD weaves across the DOWNRIGHTS, passes right round the coarse thread on the other side and returns to its original side (figure a). (2) When one coarse thread weaves through the downrights to the other side and the other weaves back (figure b). Method 1 causes the side from which the coarse thread weaves and returns to be constricted slightly; method 2 causes this to happen on both sides. The amount of constriction can be controlled by careful tension applied to the coarse threads and their

FINE PARTNERS. *See also* Appendix for indicator.

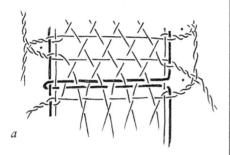

a

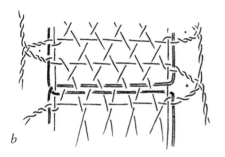

b

cobweb (bobbin) A decoration for a small space made using three or more pairs. The pairs are sewn in at equal

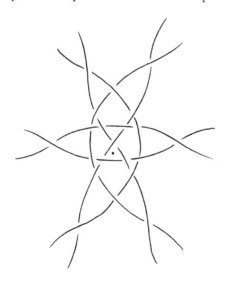

distances half way round the space and TWISTED as many times as required for the distance to the centre. For a three-pair cobweb work (figure):

> HALF STITCH pairs 1 & 2, 2 & 3, 1 & 2
>
> set up a pin with three pairs either side
>
> half stitch pairs 2 & 3, 1 & 2, 2 & 3

Cobwebs with even numbers of pairs are worked better as a SPIDER, while those with an uneven number of pairs are better in half stitch. The cobweb can be surrounded with one or more rings of CROSS THREADS.

cobweb (needle) *See* RAISED RIB COBWEB, SORRENTO WHEEL, SPIDER (WEB), WEB.

cold ironing (needle) Using an AFFICOT to smooth needle lace.

coil stitch (crochet) *See* ROLL STITCH.

collar (bobbin) The wider band immediately below the neck of a BOBBIN.

coloured bobbin (bobbin) Traditionally bobbins were coloured by soaking in dye. Modern paints have led to bobbins being painted.

coloured dots on bobbins (bobbin) Small depressions were made in wooden or bone bobbins, usually in a decorative pattern or in the form of an inscription, and then coloured with powdered colour mixed with gum arabic, or sometimes possibly with sealing wax dissolved in methylated spirits, bobbins with this type of decoration are sometimes referred to as piquéd. *See also* DOMINO BOBBIN/SPOTS.

column (needle) (1) *See* BAR STITCH. (2) *See* SIUNASHAR.

combination edge (needle) An edging for Tenerife lace produced by a combination of loops and PICOTS. The threads are grouped into fours, with the centre two being supported by a single pin and the outer threads coming from adjacent pairs (figure). *See also* LOOPED EDGE, PICOT EDGE.

combining braids/trails (bobbin) *See* BRAIDS/TRAILS COMBINING.

commemorative bobbin (bobbin) A bobbin that bears an inscription or picture, ENGRAVED, INSCRIBED, painted or in pyrography, to commemorate a particular event. This may be an event that is of personal importance to the owner – e.g., the birth of a child – or of international importance – e.g., the Queen's Silver Jubilee. *See also* HANGING BOBBIN.

common work (bobbin) A term used by Honiton workers for the simpler, easier FLAT work, to distinguish it from very fine, high quality RAISED HONITON.

complete stitch (bobbin) *See* CLOTH AND TWIST.

compound inlay bobbin (bobbin) A BOBBIN that has more than one type of inlay that is used separately in the BUTTERFLY, LEOPARD and TIGER BOBBINS. *See also* LEPTIG.

compound spider (bobbin) *See* SPIDER GROUND.

connecting stitch (bobbin) *See* SEWING.

continental bar (bobbin) A technique normally used in BRAID lace. A pair, usually the WORKERS, is TWISTED several times, laid across a space and SEWN to an existing part of the work. The pair is then twisted one or more times and sewn across the bar (figure). The process of twisting and sewing is repeated until the pair arrives at its starting place, where it resumes its original role. Also called false braid, false plait, laying pair across gap, sewing and sewing across the pair on the return/way back. *See also* EXTENDED JOIN.

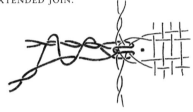

continental bobbin (bobbin) An unspangled bobbin of the kind used in most countries. *See also* BELGIAN BOBBIN, DANISH BOBBIN, ITALIAN BOBBIN, MALTESE BOBBIN, SPANISH BOBBIN, SWEDISH BOBBIN.

continental picot (bobbin) *See* CAUGHT PICOT.

continuous circles/rings filling (needle)

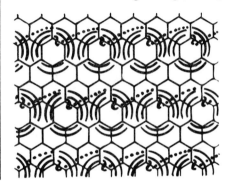

A NEEDLERUN FILLING in which the thread is taken a number of times around a single MESH (sufficient to fill the mesh) before passing onto the next-but-one (figure). Usually worked in a thread thicker than that of the net.

continuous filament (yarn) A yarn with the filaments running continuously through the ball or spool – e.g., SILK and SYNTHETIC YARNS – numbered in DENIER. *See also* YARN.

continuous (thread) lace (bobbin) BOBBIN LACE made in one piece in one direction. The bobbins work different parts of the lace at different times – CLOTHWORK, GROUND and FILLINGS – passing freely from one to the other as required. Bobbins may be added to, or removed from, the work as required to maintain the density. Called trolly lace by Honiton workers. Also called fil continu, one-piece lace, straight lace, strip lace and yard lace/work. *See also* PART LACE.

continuous row (bobbin) In Bucks point HONEYCOMB GROUND, in which a pair travels down a diagonal row working a HONEYCOMB STITCH with each pair in turn (figure). Also called long row. *See also* GAP ROW.

continuous thread (tatting) When the work is to be of one colour the SHUTTLE can be wound and left continuous with the ball thread, thus avoiding a join at the start of the work. *See also* BALL AND SHUTTLE.

continuously wound (bobbin) *See* LINKED BOBBINS.

conversion factor (yarn) A method of comparing the THREAD COUNTS produced by different systems by equating them with the TEX SYSTEM. *See* Appendix for Table of Conversion Factors.

cookie pillow (bobbin) American term for a slightly domed, circular pillow. *See also* MUSHROOM PILLOW.

copying patterns (bobbin) *See* RUBBING.

cord (yarn) A yarn made by twisting two or more PLY yarns together. *See also* YARN.

cord stitch (needle) *See* CORDED BUTTONHOLE STITCH.

cord stitch outline (needle) In NEEDLERUN LACE when the outline is worked in loosely whipped running stitch (figure).

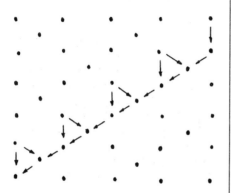

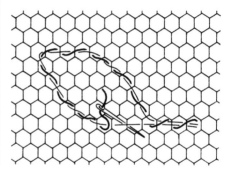

corded bar (needle) A CORE of three threads is laid across a space and overcast, closely, back to the original side. The laid threads should be completely hidden by the overcasting (figure). Also called bar in cording and bound bar. Not to be confused with TWISTED BAR.

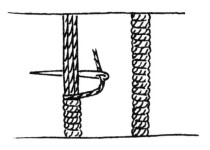

corded buttonhole/Brussels stitch/ filling (needle) A FOUNDATION ROW of BUTTONHOLE STITCH is worked and the thread whipped into the edge of the work at that point. A RETURNING THREAD is laid along the lower edge of the row of stitches and whipped into the edge of the work just below the start of that row. A row of buttonhole stitches is worked into the previous row of stitches with each stitch enclosing the laid thread (figure). Also called close buttonhole filling, cloth stitch, cord(ed) filling, cord(ed) stitch, flat point, flatwork, linen stitch, point d'entoillage, single corded Brussels/ Bruxelles/buttonhole stitch and Venetian cloth stitch. *See also* FIL DE RETOUR, POINT D'ANVERS.

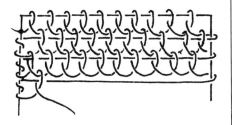

corded gimp (bobbin) *See* RAISED GIMP.

corded net stitch (needle) *See* POINT FESTON DOUBLE.

corded stitch (needle) *See* CORDED BUTTONHOLE STITCH.

cording (bobbin) *See* RAISED GIMP.

cording (needle) Process of COUCHING the FOUNDATION THREAD of Carrickmacross lace.

cordonet/cordonnet (needle) *See* FOUNDATION THREAD.

cordonnette (needle) *See* TOP STITCHING.

core (thread) (needle) A group of threads around which stitches are made – e.g., CORDED BAR.

Cork crochet (crochet) A form of Irish crochet that has no network of crochet lace GROUND. The work is simply connected with BARS, occasionally worked in BUTTONHOLE STITCH, but usually in crochet. Designs have to be accurately drawn and accurately worked to fit the drawing.

corking pin (bobbin) A large brass pin used to secure equipment, such as BOBBIN BAG, PINCUSHION, PRICKING and so on, to the PILLOW.

corn stitch (needle) *See* CINQ POINT DE VENISE.

coronet fan (bobbin) A FAN worked between the pinholes of the curved headside and another curved row within the pattern. Usually worked in CLOTH STITCH with various TWISTS (figure, p.62). Also called scallop fan. *See* Appendix for guideline.

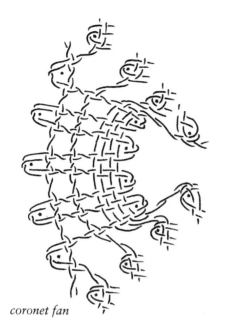

coronet fan

cotton (yarn) A yarn spun from the seed head fibres of plants of the genus Gossypium. This yarn was not suitable for lacemaking until the process of spinning was improved and was first used by lacemakers only in the 1830s.

cotton count system (**continental**) (yarn) A system of estimating SINGLES thickness, expressed as the number of 1,000 metre hanks per 500 gram – i.e., if the yarn is 50s then 50 hanks will weigh 500 grams. *See also* CONVERSION FACTOR, INDIRECT SYSTEM, YARN COUNT.

cotton count system (**Ne**) (yarn) The traditional English system of estimating SINGLES thickness, expressed as the number of 840 yard hanks (LEAS) per pound weight – i.e., if the yarn is 50s (Ne) then 50 leas will weigh 1lb; also used for spun silk. *See also* CONVERSION FACTOR, INDIRECT SYSTEM, YARN COUNT.

couching (needle) Small, usually SPACED,

stitches used to secure a thread against a BACKING (figure).

couching thread (needle) This is the thread that COUCHES another thread to a BACKING.

count (yarn) *See* YARN COUNT.

counterchange (general) In lace design, exchanging the solid for the net.

counting bobbins (bobbin) Always count from the left, unless otherwise instructed, either singly or in pairs. Both bobbins and pairs are renumbered after every movement.

couple (bobbin) *See* PAIR.

coupled/coupling bobbins (bobbin) *See* LINKED BOBBINS.

couronne (needle) A decorative BUTTONHOLED LOOP, BUTTONHOLE(D) RING and so on, used to embellish the TOP STITCHING and buttonholed grounds, particularly of Venetian point laces. These items are sometimes made separately and attached to the otherwise finished lace. Also called crown. *See also* FLEURES VOLANTES, FLOWER COURONNE, THREADED COURONNE.

couronne ring with scallops/couronne with looped cordonette (needle) *See* FLOWER COURONNE.

couronne stick (needle) *See* RING STICK.

cover cloth (general) Pieces of fabric,

preferably pure cotton, that are used (1) to keep the PILLOW clean and protect it from wearing; (2) to protect lace made on the pillow and keep it clean; (3) to keep the pricking in place and protect it from being worn by the bobbins (4) to protect the thread from wearing on the pricking; and (5) to cover the lace being made when the pillow is not being used. The form of cover cloths used depends largely on the style of the pillow. *See* BACK CLOTH, HELLER, PILLOW CLOTH, WORKER.

cover(ing) a pin (bobbin) Working a stitch, possibly with TWISTS, after SETTING UP A PIN. Sometimes, but not always, this is the same stitch as was worked before the pin was set. Also called close (in), closing and enclosing a pin. *See also* CLOSING STITCH, INTERMEDIATE PIN.

covering cloth (bobbin) *See* HELLER.

cow-and(in)-calf (bobbin) A wooden or bone bobbin in two parts, joining with a screw or push fit and having a hollowed SHANK containing a MINIATURE BOBBIN, the calf, attached to the lower part of the bobbin (figure). Sometimes called JACK-IN-THE-BOX. *See also* BABY BOBBIN.

coxcombs (general) *See* BAR (general). An old English term.

crackle stitch (needle) A ground of irregularly spaced bars.

craft laces (general) *See* MINOR LACES.

crin (le) (needle) Horse hair PADDING THREADS over which the TOP STITCHING of Alençon lace was worked. *See also* FOUNDATION THREADS.

crinkle plaiting (bobbin) In Honiton lace a long plait that is doubled over and SEWN OUT close to its origin. Often used as a stamen.

crochet fork (crochet) *See* HAIRPIN.

crochet hook (crochet) An implement used for making crochet. *See* CROCHET NEEDLE.

crochet hook join (bobbin) *See* SEWING.

crochet needle (crochet) The name used in Irish crochet for what is more commonly known as a crochet hook, the tool used for crocheting. It is a useful distinction in instructions where the hook part of the tool needs to be mentioned separately from the whole tool, which is the crochet needle.

crochet prong (crochet) *See* HAIRPIN.

crochetage (bobbin) An old French term for a SEWING.

cross stitch (bobbin) *See* POINT DE LA VIERGE.

cross strands/threads (bobbin) After making a COBWEB, the centre may be surrounded by one or more rings of cross strands. With pairs from A, B and C make the cobweb in the ordinary way and SEW OUT pairs D and E. A pinhole is made where the cross strand will meet each pair. The remaining pair is twisted

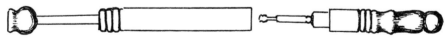

cow-and (in)-calf

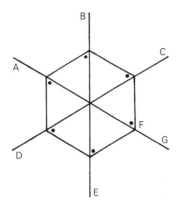

several times, taken round the outside of the pin at F and sewn to the next pair. This is repeated until the cross strand returns to its original position, at F, where it is sewn close to the pin, twisted and sewn out at G (figure). *See also* WHEEL (bobbin).

cross with closed centre (bobbin) A FILLING for a small space. Four pairs are SEWN IN, TWISTED three times and two LEADWORKS made, each supported by a pin, and each pair is twisted three times. Work cloth stitch with the following pairs: 2 & 3, 1 & 2, 3 & 4 and 2 & 3, twist each pair three times. Pin between pairs 1 & 2 and 3 & 4. Work leadworks

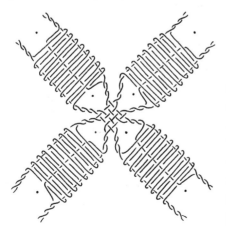

with pairs 1 & 2 and 3 & 4, twist all pairs three times and sew out (figure). *See also* CROSS WITH OPEN CENTRE.

cross with open centre (bobbin) A FILLING for a small space. Four pairs are SEWN IN, TWISTED three times and two LEADWORKS made. Each is supported by a pin and each pair is twisted three times. Work WHOLE STITCH and twist three times with the following pairs: 2 & 3, 1 & 2, 3 & 4 and 2 & 3. Pin between pairs 1 & 2 and 3 & 4. Work leadworks with pairs 1 & 2 and 3 & 4, twist all pairs three times and sew out (figure). *See also* CROSS WITH CLOSED CENTRE, DIAMOND FILLING/GROUND, PLAITED GROUND.

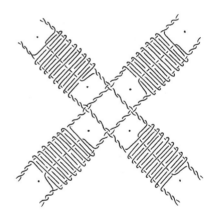

crossing (bobbin) When multiple pairs meet and cross each other. In some cases the name refers to the number of pairs being crossed; at others to the total number of those arriving and leaving. *See also* EIGHT PAIR/PLAIT CROSSING, SIX PAIR/PLAIT CROSSING, WINDMILL.

crossing of eight pairs (bobbin) *See* EIGHT PAIR/PLAIT CROSSING.

crossing of six pairs (bobbin) *See* SIX PAIR/PLAIT CROSSING.

crossing braids (bobbin) In Honiton lace work the second braid until it reaches the first braid and, when the RUNNERS have completed a row, SEW the runners and EDGE PAIR on that side to the first braid (A) (figure). Sew the edge pair, on the other side of the second braid, to the first braid (B). If the braid is narrow, the pairs can be kept tidy with a BUNCH AND TIE. Alternatively, the runners can make one or more rows of WHOLE STITCH, exchanging with the edge pair at the end of each row (unpinned), The runners and one edge pair are sewn at one side of the continuing braid (C) and the other edge pair at the other (D). *See also* CROSSING TRAILS.

crossing gimps

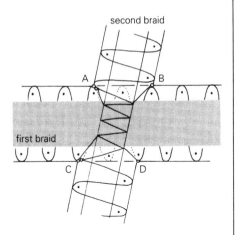

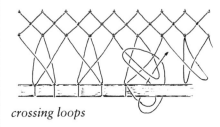

crossing loops

crossing gimps (bobbin) When gimps meet they are usually TWISTED right over left, although they can be CROSSED the other way, with all such movements being kept in the same direction in one piece of work (figure).

crossing loops (netting) Make a row of loops with a wide MESH STICK and return to a narrower one for the next row where the alternate loops are slotted through the adjacent one and stitches made, through the loops (figure).

crossing one line with another (tatting) *See* UNDER AND OVER JOIN.

crossing plaits (bobbin) *See* WINDMILL.

crossing ribs (bobbin) In Honiton lace the second RIB stops, with the runners at the plain side, when it meets the first rib. The EDGE PAIR and the RUNNERS both make SEWINGS, TOP OR EDGE as appropriate, followed by knots. These pairs then continue making the rib (figure p.66).

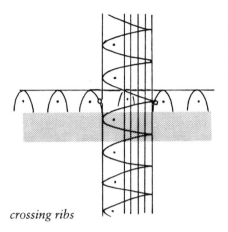

crossing ribs

crossing trails (bobbin) (1) In traditional Bedfordshire lace this should be treated as BRAIDS/TRAILS COMBINING AND BRAIDS/TRAILS DIVIDING (figure a). (2) In Cluny lace the WORKERS meet, make a CLOTH STITCH AND TWIST, a pin is SET between them and they return across the trails to be pinned at the outer edges.

a

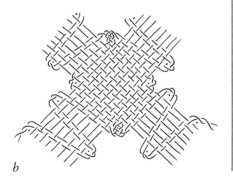

b

The PASSIVES cross each other as working half a SPIDER and the workers work towards each other, make a cloth and twist, a pin is set between them and they continue making the trails (figure b). *See also* CROSSING BRAIDS.

crown (bobbin) *See* BUCKINGHAMSHIRE ROUND.

crown (needle) *See* COURONNE.

crumb bead (bobbin) A bead, used to weight BOBBINS, that has been rolled in tiny glass chips, of many colours, while it was being made. *See also* IMPRESSED CRUMB BEAD, RAISED CRUMB BEAD.

crystal bead (bobbin) A glass bead with numerous ground facets, usually regular in design, used to weight BOBBINS (figure).

ctc stitch (bobbin) The initials stand for CROSS, TWIST, cross. This is a CLOTH STITCH.

cucumber foot (bobbin) An East Midland FOOT(SIDE) in which wide, short TALLIES are made at alternate pinholes where the footside joins the rest of the work (figure, p.67).

cucumber stitch/tally (bobbin) An East Midland term for a TALLY that is wider

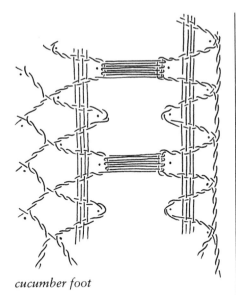

cucumber foot

than its length. It is used in CUCUMBER FOOT (figure). *See* Appendix for indicator.

Cumberland foot(side) (bobbin) The FOOT(SIDE) used in Tønder lace. The WORKERS twist twice after CLOTH STITCHING through the PASSIVES and work HALF STITCH with the EDGE PAIR. The edge pair is twisted twice (making a total of three twists), and the returning workers are given a single extra twist to make

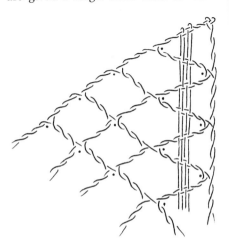

the two required when returning. The workers make the CATCH PIN STITCH, with the pair returning as workers only having a total of two twists, the pair continuing the ground having a total of three (figure). Early Tønder lace can be found with a single twisted passive pair.

cup (bobbin) The wooden socket, in a CANDLE BLOCK/STOOL, that supports a FLASH.

curtsying the pin (bobbin) The technique of leaning out the HEADPINS and FOOTPINS, which helps to counteract the tendency for lace and pattern to rise off the pillow.

cushion (bobbin) *See* PILLOW.

cushion (netting) A firmly stuffed, heavily weighted, large pincushion, to which netting is attached while it is made.

cut bead (bobbin) *See* SQUARE CUT.

cut-off day (tradition) The day on which the lace buyer visited the lacemakers to buy lace, about once every four or five weeks. It also led to a halfday holiday for children of the local lace school.

cut off in couples (bobbin) *See* BOW OFF.

cut spider (bobbin) A torchon GROUND made by uniting two pairs at a time with CLOTH STITCHES with pins SET between them, taking the WORKERS from one side to the other in cloth stitch, setting a second row of pins directly below the first and uniting the same pairs with cloth stitches. Each pair is TWISTED before uniting with the pair on the other side to start the next repeat (figure, p.68). *See also* FISHES, ITALIAN FILLING.

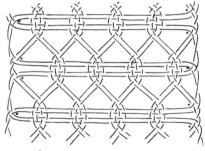

cut spider

cutwork (bobbin) *See* SQUARE-ENDED TALLY.

cutwork (needle) A technique that involves embroidering a woven fabric and cutting away parts of the original fabric to form a lacy effect. Also called point coupé.

cylindrical netting (netting) *See* WORKING IN THE ROUND.

cylindrical pillow (bobbin) *See* ROUND PILLOW.

D

daisy winder (needle) A circular implement with retractable prongs around its edge over which a thread may be wound. The centre is stitched, and the prongs are retracted to release the motif. Motifs may be joined by knotting a thread through the outer loops or by crochet (figures a and b). *See also* MULTI-NEEDLE.

a

b

Danish bobbin (bobbin) Usually made of wood, although occasionally of bone, it has a spherical, bulbous end to provide weight. Although usually plain, these bobbins may be decorated with horizontal bands of beads threaded on wire and inset into the bulb (figure).

darned band (needle) A band of darning worked around the web in Tenerife lace. Two rounds of KNOT STITCH are worked on the same web threads and darning worked between them. The darning may be worked around the web (figure a) or radially between the two rounds of knot stitches (figure b).

a

b

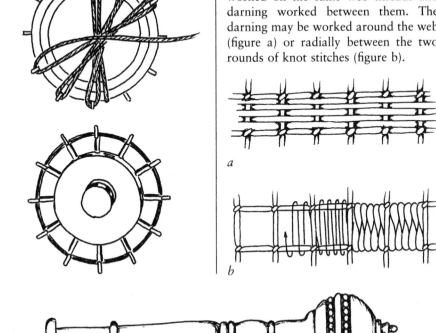

Danish bobbin

darned bar (needle) *See* WOVEN BAR.

darned blocks (needle) In Tenerife lace. (1) Work four rounds of KNOT STITCH over the same threads forming a series of squares, darn blocks across these squares (figure a). (2) Blocks can be darned without intervening rounds of knot stitch (figure b). (3) Blocks can be darned radially across the squares (figure c).

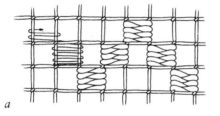

a

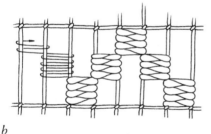

b

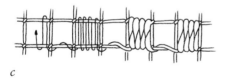

c

darned centre (needle) *See* CENTRE.

darned circles (needle) *See* BAR ROSETTE.

darned netting (netting) *See* FILET LACE.

darned point (netting) Lay two diagonal threads over the mesh in the form of a V (figure) and fill the triangular space closely with rows of darning. *See also* DARNED TRIANGLES.

darned rosette (needle) *See* BAR ROSETTE.

darned semi-circle (needle) Threads are knotted to make five spokes radiating from a point and the working thread darned across four to form a semi-circular area (figure). Also called festons in darning stitch.

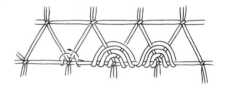

darned triangle (needle) In Tenerife lace these can be worked (1) by darning

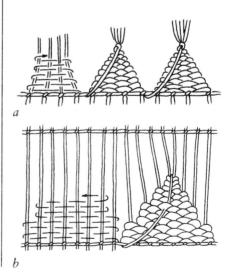

a

b

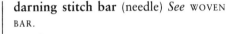
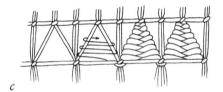

c

across a group of threads and pulling a little tighter at the end of each row until the threads are drawn together (figure a); (2) darning across a group of threads and discarding the outer ones at intervals until a point is reached (figure b); (3) knotting the web threads so as to make triangles and darning across them (figure c). Also called point de reprise. See also DARNED POINT.

darning away (bobbin) (1) When lace has been JOINED END TO BEGINNING and the pairs knotted; they are then darned away for neatness – i.e., each thread sewn into the fabric of the lace. Two small stitches may be worked through the CLOTHWORK, the thread may be sewn through a GIMP thread, a thread may be whipped up the leg of SPIDER, following the direction of the twists and fastened off into the centre using two oversewing stitches. All ends are trimmed off closely. (2) See ROLL.

darning stitch (needle and netting) Passing a needle under and over threads to imitate weaving. Also called armaletta, basket stitch, in-and-out stitch, needle-weaving, and weaving stitch (figure). See also POINT DE TOILE, POINT DE REPRISE.

darning stitch bar (needle) See WOVEN BAR.

darning stitch web (needle) See SORRENTO WHEEL.

decitex system (yarn) Yarn thickness expressed as the weight in grams of 10 kilometres of yarn, if the yarn is 50 dtex then 10 kilometres will weigh 50 grams. See also DIRECT COUNT SYSTEM, CONVERSION FACTOR AND YARN COUNT

decorated crossing (bobbin) When a crossing of single pairs and/or plaits is accomplished in an elaborate fashion so that it becomes a feature in the lace – e.g., SPIDER.

decorated lines (bobbin) A narrow strip of lace having a straight edge each side and a simple repetitive design, often used as BEADING.

decorated netting (netting) See FILET LACE.

decorated pin (bobbin) A pin decorated with beads, goose grass seeds or sealing wax as HEADPINS and/or FOOTPINS. See also BUGLE, BUR(R) HEAD, DIVIDER, STRIVER.

decreasing (stitch) (netting) Work one

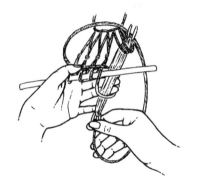

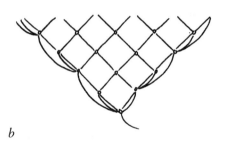

b

netting stitch into two loops (figures a and b).

denier (YARN) Yarn thickness expressed as the weight in grams of 9000 metres of yarn, if the yarn is 50 denier then 9000 metres weighs 50 grams, used for CONTINUOUS FILAMENT YARN. *See also* DIRECT COUNT SYSTEM, YARN COUNT.

dentelle (general) French for lace. Originally the term was used for any indented edging but quickly became used for all laces.

detached buttonhole stitch (bobbin) *See* BRUSSELS STITCH.

detached leaf, petal etc. (general) *See* APPLIED PIECE.

Devon cartwheel (bobbin) *See* CARTWHEEL (bobbin).

Devonshire cutwork (bobbin) *See* SQUARE-ENDED TALLY.

diagonal filet (netting) *See* PLAIN NETTING.

diamond (bobbin) Areas of CLOTH or HALF STITCH, with or without added TWISTS, worked within an area bounded by a diamond of pinholes (figure). Also called LOZENGE. *See also* Appendix for guideline.

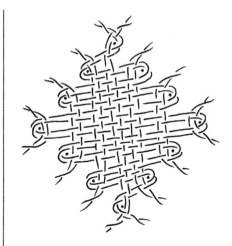

diamond/diamond filling (needle) (1) *See* FLY (STITCH). (2) An area of BRUSSELS STITCH in which spaces, usually of two missed stitches, are left at intervals resulting in a diamond-shaped pattern (figure). Also called escalier lace and gros point diamonds.

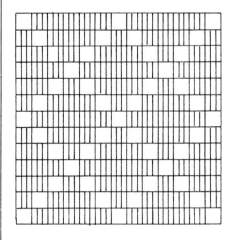

diamond filet (netting) *See* PLAIN NETTING.

diamond filling/ground (bobbin) (1) Honiton filling. Sew in pairs as required and TWIST three times. Make two LEAD-

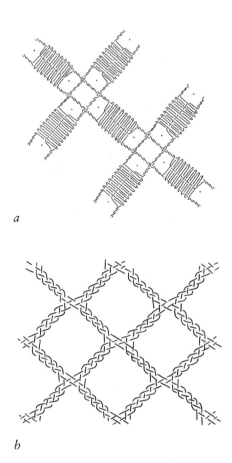

a

b

WORKS, support each with a pin and twist THREE times. Work WHOLE STITCH and twist three times with the following pairs – 2 & 3, 1 & 2, 3 & 4, 2 & 3. Pin between pairs 1 & 2, and 3 & 4. Work leadworks with pairs 1 & 2 and 3 & 4, twist all pairs three times and sew out (figure a). Called plaited ground by Bedfordshire workers. *See also* CROSS WITH CLOSED CENTRE, CROSS WITH OPEN CENTRE. (2) Valenciennes ground. The pairs are PLAITED, CLOTH STITCH plus four REVERSE HALF STITCHES (the number of reverse half stitches is adjusted to the space available) Where the plaits meet, adjacent pairs work a cloth stitch. This ground is UNPINNED (figure b). Also

called Valenciennes square ground. *See also* ROUND GROUND.

diamond net (netting) *See* PLAIN NET-TING.

dick/dicky pot (bobbin) *See* FIRE POT.

Dieppe ground (bobbin) One of the TORCHON GROUNDS worked HALF STITCH, pin, HALF STITCH, TWIST (figure). Also called point de Dieppe.

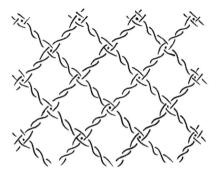

direct count system (yarn) Yarn thickness expressed as the weight of a fixed length of yarn, the number increases as the thickness increases. Direct systems in use include DENIER and DECITEX SYSTEM, LINEN SYSTEM (dry spun), SILK SYSTEM and TEX SYSTEM. *See also* CONVERSION FACTOR, YARN COUNT.

disappearing couronne (needle) *See* THREADED COURONNE.

discarding pairs/threads (bobbin) *See* THROW(ING) BACK.

dishcloth lace (bobbin) *See* RAG LACE.

divided braid/trail (bobbin) One that has the WORKERS TWISTED each time they pass between the same pairs of PASSIVES, characteristic of Cluny lace (figure p.74).

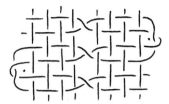

divided braid/trail

divided leaf (bobbin) Honiton or other PART LACE leaf worked in two halves, joining them with SEWINGS along the central vein (figure a). Usually one side is worked in WHOLE STITCH and the other in HALF STITCH. One half may be worked from the base towards the tip, the point turned and the second half worked towards the base taking sewings along the vein (figure b). The leaf may be started from the tip and divided at the start of the vein when one set of threads is set aside while one half of the leaf worked, then the second half is worked, TAKING SEWINGS along the vein (figure c).

divided tally (bobbin) A TALLY having a central division where the WORKING THREAD is returned to its original position and makes four twists with the thread at that side while the other threads twist twice. A pin is usually inserted to support the first half while the second half of the tally is made (figure).

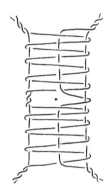

divider (pin) (bobbin) A long pin, usually highly decorated, used to separate bobbins on a pillow. *See also* STACKING PIN.

dividing braid (bobbin) *See* BRAID DIVIDING.

dominant trail (bobbin) In Bedfordshire lace the TRAIL, usually the widest, that continues through the design, carrying the eye forwards and to which the SECONDARY TRAILS join. Also called main trail.

domino bobbin/spots (bobbin) Bobbin decoration consisting of recessed, coloured spots arranged as on a

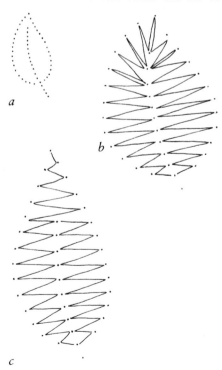

a

b

c

domino bobbin/spots

domino. Usually red, dark blue or black (figure). *See also* COLOURED DOTS ON BOBBINS.

dot (needle) *See* PICOT.

double (bobbin) *See* CLOTH AND TWIST.

double (tatting) *See* DOUBLE STITCH.

double Brussels/buttonhole/loop stitch (needle) *See* POINT DE SORRENTO. *See also* BRUSSELS STITCH, TREBLE BRUSSELS STITCH.

double buttonhole stitch bar (needle) *See* BAR IN DOUBLE BUTTONHOLE STITCH.

double caught/knotted picots (bobbin) CAUGHT PICOTS on both sides of a PLAIT. Make the right picot first, then TWIST right pairs, CROSS centre pairs, twist left pairs to close the centre before the left picot is made (figure). If the left picot is made first follow by twisting the left pair, crossing the centre pairs and twisting the right pair to close the centre. *See* Appendix for indicator.

double chain (crochet) Work two chain, insert the hook into first stitch, * YARN OVER HOOK and draw a loop through, yarn over hook and draw a loop through both loops on hook. Continue

by inserting hook into left loop and repeating from * (figure). Also called double foundation chain.

double circles of pins (needle) In Tenerife lace there can be two concentric circles of pins, the inner circle having half the number of pins around the outer circle. The web is laid first between the pins of the inner circle and alternate pins

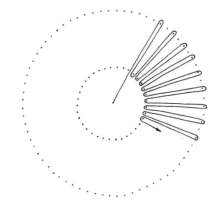

of the outer (figure), using the remaining pins of the outer circle in the usual manner. A round of KNOT STITCH must be worked just outside the inner circle of pins. This technique reduces the bulk where the web threads cross in the centre.

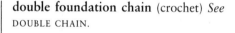
double corded Brussels/buttonhole stitch (needle) Made as CORDED BRUSSELS STITCH but with two buttonhole stitches worked into each loop of the previous row (figure).

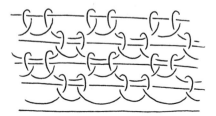

double crochet (crochet) *Miss one stitch or CHAIN, insert hook under the top two loops of the next stitch, YARN OVER hook (figure) and draw a loop through, two loops on the hook, yarn over hook and draw a loop through both loops on hook, repeat from *. Make one chain to turn, also called plain crochet (old name).

double darned centre (needle) Centres of Tenerife lace medallions may be darned by taking the needle under and over pairs of threads (figure). *See also* CENTRE.

double foundation chain (crochet) *See* DOUBLE CHAIN.

double(d) gimps (bobbin) When GIMPS run parallel with several pairs crossing before they go their several ways, there are rarely twists between the gimps (figure). *See also* RAISED GIMP.

double ground (bobbin) *See* KAT STITCH.

double half stitch (bobbin) *See* CLOTH AND TWIST.

double head (bobbin) A HEAD that is divided in two parts by a chamfered groove called the SHORT NECK in which the HITCH should rest, typical of EAST MIDLAND'S BOBBINS but not used for HONITON BOBBINS (figure). Also called THISTLE HEAD. *See also* SINGLE HEAD.

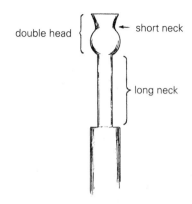

double head { — short neck

— long neck

double knot net stitch (needle) *See* FILET STITCH (needle).

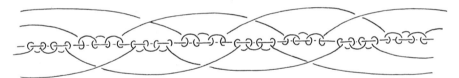

double pearl chain

double loop join (crochet) Method for joining strips of HAIRPIN CROCHET, made as SINGLE LOOP JOIN but picking up two loops from the side instead of one, passing the hook through front to back for each, and pulling both through the previous two loops. *See also* LOOP JOIN.

double loop stitch (needle) *See* POINT DE SORRENTO.

double neck (bobbin) A bobbin with a long narrow section, the LONG NECK, where the thread is wound, and a chamfered groove, the SHORT NECK, around the HEAD where the HITCH rests (figure). *See also* DOUBLE HEAD.

double passing (bobbin) *See* CLOTH AND TWIST.

double pearl chain (tatting) With four shuttles and one AUXILIARY THREAD knotted together work a CHAIN using each shuttle in turn with the auxiliary thread. Make DOUBLE STITCHES, singly or in pairs, using each shuttle in turn, allowing plenty of thread so that picots form over the opposite stitches. Arrange the stitches so that those from two shuttles face one way and those of the other two shuttles, used alternately with the first, face the other (figure). *See also* SINGLE PEARL CHAIN.

double picot (bobbin) (1) TWIST the pair three, five or seven times, according to the thickness of the thread, place the point of a pin under the thread nearest the work, point towards you, and pass the point over the bobbin head and into the pinhole in the pricking (figure a). Do not allow the thread to pull tight around the pin at this stage. Take the second thread around the pin in the same direction (figure b). Take up the slack, gently at first with a see-sawing motion, then more firmly. Twist one, two or three times (figure c). *See also* HONITON PURL, LEFT-HAND PURL, PICOT (general), RIGHT-HAND PURL, TURN PIN.

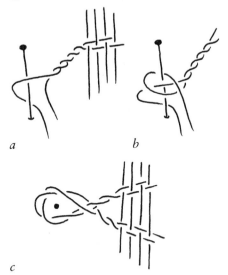

a   *b*

c

(2) Picots on both sides of a PLAIT, the higher picot is made first, a CLOTH or HALF STITCH made with the two pairs and then the second picot is made (figure p.78). *See also* DOUBLE CAUGHT PICOT and Appendix for indicator.

double picot

double plait (bobbin) A PLAIT made using pairs as single threads, very useful in Bedfordshire and other laces where the number of pairs in use must be reduced at the point where the plait leaves a CLOTH or HALF STITCH. Single threads, from the pairs can be thrown out at intervals along the PLAIT if required (figure). *See also* MULTIPLE-PAIR PLAIT.

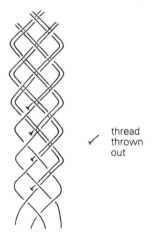

✓ thread thrown out

double point de Venise (needle) A variant of POINT DE VENISE. Make two BUTTONHOLE STITCHES then make another into the loop leading to the first (figure a). Increasing the number of stitches worked

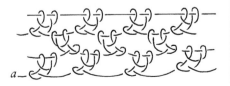

a

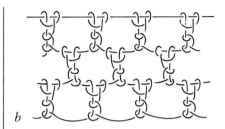

b

into the loop results in further variations (figure b).

double rose ground (bobbin) *See* POINT DE MARIAGE.

double rounds of interlacing (needle) In Tenerife lace pre-group the WEB by working one round with threads knotted in pairs, and the next with the pairs regrouped – i.e., one thread from each of two adjacent pairs knotted together, thus forming triangular spaces. A round of INTERLACING is worked near the inner round of knot stitch then another between this round and the outer round of knot stitch (figure).

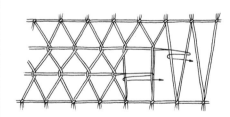

double running stitch foundation (needle) In Tenerife lace a double circle

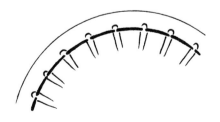

of running stitches – i.e., circle of running stitches with a second circle filling the spaces – that supports the WEB. The web is STRETCHED by passing the needle out through one stitch and back through the next (figure).

double sewing (bobbin) (1) SEWING when both threads of a pair are drawn through, making a double loop through which a second pair is passed (figure a), and if they are to make a plait, the latter bobbins drawn through are placed to the left and between those that made the loop, helping to counteract any tendency for the plait to twist (figure b). This is sometimes preferred to making two separate sewings as it can produce a neater and stronger result. (2) TOP

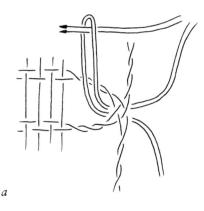

a

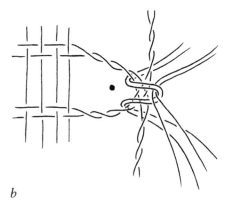

b

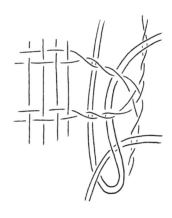

c

SEWING made around both BARS at a PIN-HOLE (figure c).

double side loop (needle) In Armenian lace a loop projecting from the side of a stitch into a row of loops. *Make a large loop (figure a) and a PICOT (figure b), make a loop to its top (this is the side loop) (figure c). *See also* SINGLE SIDE LOOP.

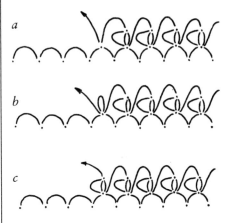

a

b

c

double-sided buttonhole bar (needle) *See* BAR IN DOUBLE BUTTONHOLE STITCH.

double spider (bobbin) SPIDERS with a large number of 'legs' can look clumsy, by adding an extra pair of pinholes the cloth stitch area can be split (figure p.80).

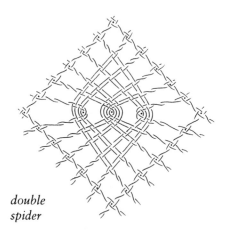

double spider

double stem stitch bar (bobbin) Narrow braid having a TURNING STITCH on both sides (figure). *See* TURNING STITCH (1).

double stitch (bobbin) *See* CLOTH AND TWIST.

double stitch (crochet) *See* DOUBLE CROCHET.

double stitch (tatting) The basic stitch of tatting, composed of two parts PLAIN and PURL, also called clove hitch and lark's head (figure).

double treble (crochet) Take the thread around the hook twice, insert the hook into the next chain, thread around the hook and draw through a loop (four loops on the hook), thread around the hook and draw a loop through two loops (three loops on the hook), thread around the hook and draw a loop through two loops (two loops on the hook), thread around the hook and draw a loop through the remaining two loops (figure). Also called long treble. *See also* LONG STITCH.

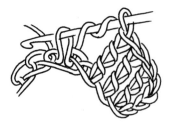

double twist bar (bobbin) After SETTING THE PIN, twist the WORKERS as many times as necessary, sew where the bar is to meet existing work, twist as necessary to return to the starting point and continue (figure).

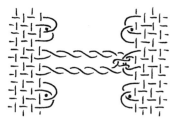

double twisted ground (bobbin) *See* SPANISH GROUND.

double twisted net stitch (needle) *See* TWISTED NET STITCH.

doubling up (bobbin) Suitable in most cases for joining a thread. A new thread is laid alongside of the offending thread and the two twisted 25 times. The doubled thread is worked as the single thread until there is no chance of it pulling out when the lace is in use, then the remaining twists are removed and the offending thread THROWN BACK.

down (bobbin) (1) *See* PRICKING. (2) A DOWN has been completed when one length of the pricking has been worked.

downright (bobbin) Honiton term for PASSIVE.

Downton bobbin (bobbin) Straight, unspangled bobbin used in the Downton area, near Salisbury, sometimes decorated with inscribed bands and designs, similar to but larger than a HONITON BOBBIN (figure).

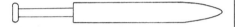

Downton whole stitch (bobbin) *See* CLOTH AND TWIST.

draft (bobbin) *See* PATTERN DRAFT.

drawback stitch (tambour) A stitch frequently used for eyelets and around the edge of the item. Insert the hook into hole A and draw through a loop, *insert the hook into a hole several meshes

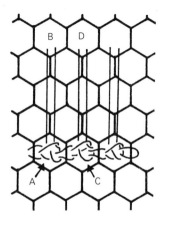

higher, B, draw a loop through the hole and the thread on the hook, allowing the thread to remain loose (loosen at the back if necessary), and draw the loop down to A, insert the hook into A again and draw a loop through the hole and the loop on the hook, make a tambour chain stitch into the next hole, C. Repeat from * for holes C and D (figure).

drawn bead (bobbin) Plain cylindrical beads produced by blowing an air bubble into glass and drawing it out into a tube. After annealing the tube is cut into beads, used to weight SPANGLES (figure).

drawter (bobbin) Folded COVER CLOTH pinned across the pillow behind the pins to cover the lace as it is made (figure). *See also* BACK CLOTH.

dressing a pillow (bobbin) Process of getting a pillow ready for working – i.e. pinning on the COVER CLOTHS, the PRICKING, SLIDER, BOBBIN BAG, PINCUSHION and so on – according to the lace to be made. *See also* SETTING UP A PILLOW.

drilled wheel (needle) Tenerife lace wheel, made from a stiff material, with a circle of holes drilled through it. Pins may be inserted through these holes and into a pincushion, or a line of backstitches can be worked through the holes and the web stretched across these stitches. *See also* STITCHED FOUNDATION, STRETCHING THE WEB.

drizzling (yarn) Removing precious metal from metal thread lace, which happened when the lace went out of fashion. Also called parfilage.

droschel ground (bobbin) A hexagonal GROUND used for Brussels and early Honiton PART LACES where it was worked between the finished motifs, later on it was made in strips, which were joined by RACROC STITCH, and to which motifs, bobbin or needle lace, were applied. Each hexagon consists of two vertical PLAITS of six or seven HALF STITCHES, followed by an extra TWIST on each pair so that the diagonal pairs linking the plaits have a total of two twists (figure). The term is some-

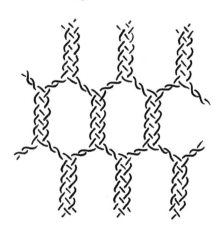

times erroneously applied to MECHLIN GROUND, a lace with similar ground although having shorter plaits. Also called POINT D'ANGLETERRE GROUND/NET, vrai droschel/réseau and, confusingly, sometimes called Brussels bobbin mesh, a term that is also applied to MECHLIN GROUND.

drying-bottle (general) A straight-sided bottle covered with flannel or similar material, around which lace is wound and stitched prior to washing and drying, a method that both protects the lace and reduces the necessity for ironing. The bottle can be inverted over a stick for drying. *See also* CLEANING LACE.

duchesse braid (needle) A machine-made tape for TAPE LACE with a 'FOOT(SIDE)' down each edge, sometimes with an openwork design through the centre.

dump (bobbin) *See* SOUTH BUCKS BOBBIN.

Dutch lace braid (needle) Plain machine-made braid for TAPE LACE.

dyed bobbins (bobbin) A form of decoration where a finished bobbin is coloured by immersion in dye. Sometimes dyed bone bobbins would have some of the dyed material removed by further turning, revealing the white bone beneath.

dyke side (bobbin) A deeply scalloped HEADSIDE.

E

East Midlands bobbin (bobbin) A slender bobbin, typical of the East Midlands area, with a DOUBLE HEAD and SPANGLE, used for making the CONTINUOUS (THREAD) LACES of the area (figure). Also called Bucks bobbin and Midlands bobbin. *See also* BOBBIN, SOUTH BUCKS BOBBIN.

eche (bobbin) The linen or cotton tab sewn to each end of a pricking, particularly PARCHMENT prickings. These protected the ends of the patterns and made it easier to pin them tightly to the pillow.

edge (bobbin) *See* STITCH ABOUT A/THE PIN.

edge couple/pair (bobbin) The pair lying at the footside that will exchange with the workers when next EDGE STITCH is made (figure). Also called resting bobbins/workers. *See also* FOOTSIDE.

edge pin (bobbin) A pin on the outside edge of the lace.

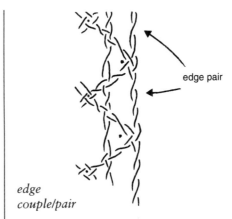

edge pair

edge couple/pair

edge sewing (bobbin) A Honiton term for a SEWING over the EDGE STITCH (figures a and b, p.84). Also called flat sewing, ordinary sewing and side sewing. *See also* NEEDLEPIN SEWING.

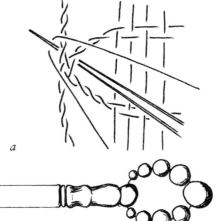

a

East Midlands bobbin

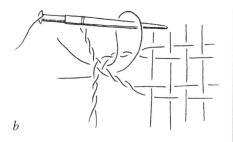

b

edge stitch (bobbin) (1) *See* STITCH ABOUT A/THE PIN. (2) A Honiton term for the TWISTS and STITCH worked at the edge of a braid. When the RUNNERS have worked a WHOLE STITCH with the last but one pair the work is FIRMED UP, the runners twisted three times and a pin set beneath them. The RUNNERS and EDGE PAIR work a whole stitch and both pairs are twisted three times (figure).

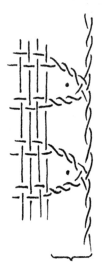

edging (general) A strip of lace designed to be attached to the edge of a piece of fabric. Usually with a FOOT(SIDE) along the edge that is to be attached. The HEADSIDE is usually decorated. *See also* BORDER.

edging-stitch *See* FOOT(SIDE).

eight pair/plait crossing (bobbin) Where eight pairs, usually from PLAITS or LEAVES, cross. Using the pairs as single threads work:
    centre pairs: half stitch
    right pairs: half stitch
    left pairs: half stitch
    centre pairs: half stitch
    right pairs: half stitch
    left pairs: half stitch
    pin
    centre pairs: cloth stitch
    pass 2 over 3, 6 over 7
(figure). Also called four plait crossing. *See also* CROSSING AND APPENDIX FOR INDICATOR.

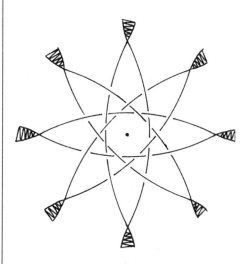

Eis ground (bobbin) *See* MECHLIN GROUND.

elshing (bobbin) Making a HITCH WITH EXTRA TURN.

embroidered net (needle/tambour) Hand- or machine-made net, decorated using a needle or tambour hook.

embroidery frame (needle/tambour) A circular, square or rectangular frame

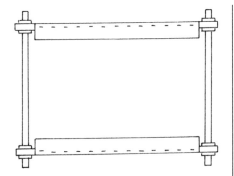

for holding net or another fabric taut while it is being stitched (figure). *See also* STRETCHING FABRIC IN A FRAME.

emerald foundation (crochet) Tough, green fabric, specially produced as a BACKING for assembling Irish crochet sprigs and to which they are tacked while the GROUND or other connections are made.

emery pincushion (general) A PINCUSHION containing emery powder, or a mixture of emery powder and sand, an abrasive powder that helps keep pins polished as they are pushed in and taken out.

enclosing a pin (bobbin) *See* COVER(ING) A PIN.

end pin (bobbin) *See* HEAD PIN.

ending stitch (bobbin) *See* CLOSING STITCH.

English stitch (needle) Sometimes used to make hollie point lace, similar to HOLLIE POINT but made with the needle pointing away so that the twists occur in the other direction (figure).

English wheel (needle) *See* RAISED RIB COBWEB.

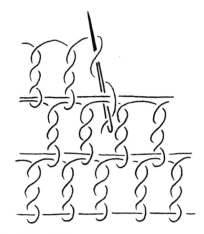

English stitch

engraved bobbin (bobbin) Bobbins decorated by engraving designs, names etc. in the surface. *See also* COMMEMORATIVE BOBBIN.

engrêlure (general) *See* BEADING.

entoilage (needlepoint) GROUND as applied to needle lace.

escalier lace (needle) *See* DIAMOND/DIAMOND FILLING (NEEDLE).

eternelle (bobbin) *See* EVERLASTING LACE.

everlasting lace (bobbin) A narrow edging of EVERLASTING STITCH with a footside on one side and the pairs taken around pins on the headside (figure p.86).

everlasting stitch (bobbin) A ground that is worked as alternate CONTINUOUS and GAP ROWS with each stitch worked half stitch, pin, half stitch (figure). A variant of KAT STITCH with a similar thread arrangement but with the pins set below the junctions of the pairs of threads instead of within them, resulting

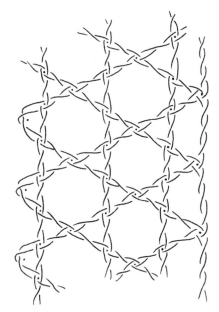

everlasting lace

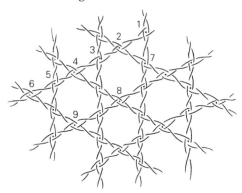

everlasting stitch

in a slightly different final appearance. Also called fond à la marriage and simple round stitch.

evil eye (bobbin) (1) *See* SNAKE BEAD. (2) An AMULET BEAD decorated with an eye, used to weight bobbins. *See also* FLUSH SPOT EYE, RAISED EYE BEAD.

exchanging pairs/workers (bobbin) *See* CHANGING WORKERS.

extended corner (bobbin) When a corner is larger than the edging that accompanies it (figure).

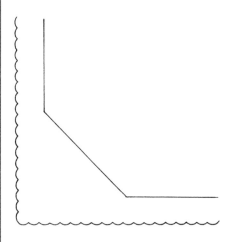

extended join (bobbin) A short CONTINENTAL BAR used when two edges being SEWN together are slightly apart.

extra pairs (bobbin) *See* ADDING PAIRS.

eye (needle) Small BUTTONHOLED RING.

eye bead (bobbin) *See* EVIL EYE BEAD, FLUSH SPOT EYE, HORNED EYE, KITTY FISHER'S EYE BEAD, RAISED EYE.

eyelet (bobbin) A hole produced in CLOTH STITCH by dividing the pairs, working both sides independently and recombining (figure). Also called hole in clothwork. *See also* HOLE IN CLOTH STITCH.

eyelet-hole (needlerun) Thread is run around the mesh, which is enlarged using a stiletto, and the edge whipped closely.

eyelet lace (bobbin) Narrow Bucks Point insertion, having a series of holes

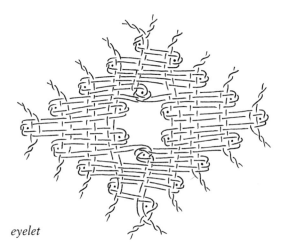

eyelet

through which narrow ribbon is threaded. Also called aglet lace and trou trou.

eyes out (bobbin) *See* LAZY SUSAN.

F

faceted bead (bobbin) A CANE BEAD ground to make extra facets, usually irregular in shape, used to weight BOBBINS (figure).

facing buttonhole stitches (needle) A BUTTONHOLE STITCH followed by another worked with the needle facing in the opposite direction (figure).

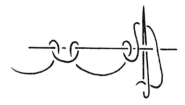

faggoting/faggoting stitch (needle) Decorative stitches forming a very narrow insertion between the two pieces of fabric they join. There are many variants, one of the simplest is illustrated (figure).

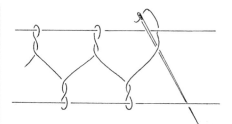

fairing (bobbin) A BOBBIN, usually made of bone, with one, or more, spiral grooves in which narrow strips of tinsel have been stuck (figure). Also called tinsel inlay.

false braid (bobbin) *See* CONTINENTAL BAR.

false foot(ing)/footside A method of starting whereby the start has the

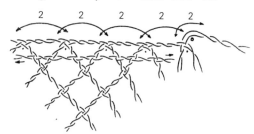

appearance of a FOOTSIDE lying horizontally across the piece. Two sets of two pairs placed on TEMPORARY PINS work a

fairing

CLOTH STITCH AND TWIST and a pin is set between them; the temporary pins can then be removed. Each outer pair TWISTS three times, being an EDGE PAIR (figure), and two other pairs work cloth stitch and twist across the inner pairs to form the passive pair of the 'footside'. Also called mock footside and simulated footside.

false picot (bobbin) A Bucks point technique for adding two pairs at the headside by introducing them as a PICOT. Hang two pairs over a pin, STRADDLE WISE, TWIST the pair on one side of the pin as for a picot and enclose with a CLOTH STITCH and twist both pairs as for leaving a picot, the numbers of twists being the same as for the rest of the picots (figure).

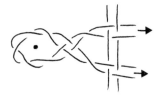

false picot (tatting) A chain starts at a picot, make a PURL LOCKING STITCH followed by an ordinary PURL stitch, the two counting as the first DOUBLE STITCH (figure). Also called starting with a picot.

false pinhole (bobbin) When a BACK-STITCH is required on the other side of a braid from picots an extra hole may be made for a pin to support the loop; this pin is removed when the next EDGE STITCH is made on this side.

false plait (bobbin) See CONTINENTAL BAR.

fan (bobbin) Motifs having a fan shape, typical of torchon lace. *See also* CORONET FAN, FRENCH FAN, SPANISH FAN, TORCHON FAN.

fan grouping (crochet) A method of collecting the loops along a strip of HAIRPIN CROCHET. Holding the strip with the loops uppermost and starting from the left, insert a crochet hook through a series of loops with the hook passing from front to back and secure together by finishing as a DOUBLE CROCHET, the loops remaining untwisted (figures a and b). *See also* BUD GROUPING.

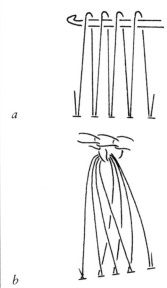

a

b

fan stitch (needle) *See* BUTTERFLY STITCH.

fancy hole (bobbin) *See* FOUR-PIN BUD.

fast crossing (bobbin) A Cluny technique for joining a single pair to a PLAIT. Use pairs as single threads. The single pair and the closest pair of the plait CROSS, pin between the pairs, TWIST the single pair with the other pair of the

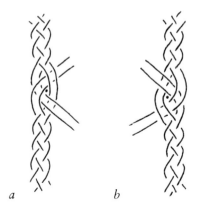

a   *b*

plait and cross the plait pairs. Single pair approaching from the right (figure a), single pair approaching from the left (figure b).

fat hen (bobbin) (1) *See* PILLOW. (2) *See* TALLY.

faulty stitch (bobbin) A method of exchanging bobbins between pairs by making an extra TWIST or CROSS when working a CLOTH STITCH. Usually used to exchange a WORKER thread with a PASSIVE thread when the worker thread is running out. Examine both pairs and select the best thread of the other pair to exchange with the thread running out. Make the stitch slowly and, when the two identified bobbins work together, repeat the movement. The movement repeated may be a twist or a cross. Only one of the possible four variations is illustrated (figure).

feather (bobbin) (1) a variation of the FIR TREE FAN (figure) also called palm.

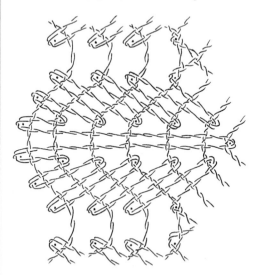

See Appendix for guideline. (2) A bead decorated around the centre with a swirling design, sometimes having more than one colour (figure). Also called plume.

feather (tatting) A chain of picots, separated by the usual double stitches, with the chain reversed at regular intervals. The picots of each section are graded in size.

feston, la (needle) *See* TOP STITCHING.

festons in darning (needle) *See* DARNED SEMI-CIRCLES.

festoon stitch (bobbin) A series of HALF HITCHES worked around a group of bobbin threads, used as a method of fastening off (figure, p.91).

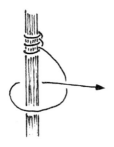

feuille bar (needle) *See* WOVEN BAR.

fil (general) Thread (Fr.).

fil attaché (bobbin) *See* ADDING BOBBINS.

fil continu (bobbin) *See* CONTINUOUS (THREAD) LACE.

fil coupé (bobbin) *See* THROW(ING) BACK/OUT PAIRS.

fil de crin (needle) *See* FOUNDATION THREAD.

fil de retour (needle) *See* RETURNING THREAD/CORD.

fil de trace (needle) *See* FOUNDATION THREAD.

filet (general) Lace that has a design of squares of close work against a background of open squares.

filet (netting) (1) Hand-knotted net. *See* FISHERMAN'S KNOT. (2) *See* FILET GUIPURE/LACE/WORK.

filet circles (netting) *See* WORKING IN THE ROUND.

filet crochet (crochet) Blocks made of three TREBLE CROCHET (tr), one into each of the next three tr or, if above a space (sp), 2 tr into sp, 1 tr into next tr. Open squares or spaces worked (2 CHAIN (ch), miss 2 tr (or 2 ch if over a sp), 1 tr into next tr). *See also* FILET (GENERAL).

filet ground (bobbin) *See* BOBBIN FILET.

filet guipure (netting) *See* LACIS.

filet guipure / lace / work (netting) SQUARE NET ground embroidered with DARNING STITCH and other stitches. Also called darned netting, decorated netting, filet, guipure d'art, lacis and point conté. *See also* GUIPURE D'ART.

filet stitch (needle) A needle-made GROUND imitating the FISHERMAN'S KNOT of netting (figure). Also called double knot net stitch, knot stitch, net (groundwork) stitch and point de filet. *See also* KNOTTED MESH.

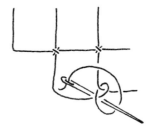

filling (general) Fancy stitches used to fill spaces between heavier parts of the design. Also called jours (Fr.) and modes (Fr.).

fine joining (bobbin) *See* POINT DE RAC(C)ROC.

fine partner (bobbin) In Honiton lace the fine thread that accompanies the COARSE THREAD to make the COARSE PAIR.

finger (bobbin) In Bucks point, when a gimp passes through pairs, around a pin

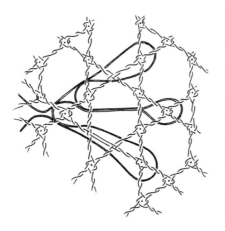

and back through the same pairs. Sometimes pinholes of the ground, or filling, are not used. If the gimps follow a pair there will be no twist between the pair and the gimps (figure). Fingers in HONEYCOMB.

finger (general) A unit of length of approximately 11cm (4½in), formerly used by lacemakers.

finishing at a point (bobbin) In Honiton lace to throw pairs back when

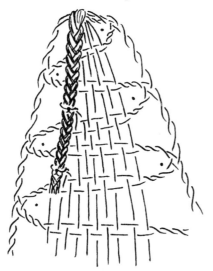

the lace narrows as it approaches the point MAKE UP THE EDGE at the point and make a BUNCH AND TIE with the remaining pairs. Add the tie pair(s) to the bunch, divide into three parts and make a THREE PART PLAIT. Turn the pillow around and lay the plait down over the lace. Twist the thrown back pair nearest the point and separate the bobbins, *lay the plait between the two bobbins, tie a REEF KNOT AND A HALF over them and add this tie pair to the plait. Twist the next thrown back pair and then repeat from *. Trim the ends closely (figure).

finishing on a straight line (bobbin) When all the bobbins are neatly cast off along a line at right angles to the final line of work.

finishing over a completed piece of work (bobbin) In Honiton lace when the pairs are sewn into an existing part and then secured by bunching and tying.

fir tree fan (bobbin) See SPANISH FAN.

fire pot (bobbin) An earthenware pot, similar to a chamber pot but with holes for ventilation, which was filled with hot ashes, embers etc. and used to keep lacemakers warm. Also called chad pot and dick/dicky pot.

firming up (bobbin) The process of tensioning a stitch and removing any slack present in the threads. Also called pulling up.

fish bone (bobbin) Thought to have been used by poor lacemakers as a substitute for pins; possibly the origin of the term BONE LACE.

fisherman's knot (netting) Hold the MESH STICK horizontally in the V

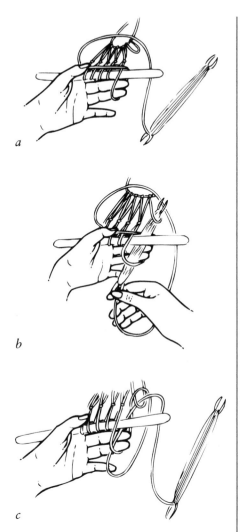

a

b

c

behind the left fingers and back to the front. Pass the shuttle upwards, through the left hand, the loop held by the fingers, over the thread held by the thumb and through the foundation loop, or the loop of the previous row. This loop is retained in place by curling the left little finger (figure b). Gradually ease up the thread. Release the loop held by the thumb first (figure c), then the loop held by the third finger. Then, when all the slack has been taken up, release the loop held by the little finger. This makes the arrangement of threads as the SIMPLE KNOT but, because of the way it is formed, it always locks correctly. Also called fishnet knot. *See also* SIMPLE KNOT.

fishes (bobbin) Milanese braid (figure). *See also* CUT SPIDER, ITALIAN FILLING.

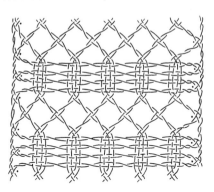

between the thumb and first finger so that it lies immediately below the knot of the FOUNDATION LOOP. With the SHUTTLE in the right hand, take the thread down in front of the mesh stick, under and round to the back between the third and fourth fingers of the left hand. Continue taking it up behind the fingers, over the first finger and towards the left, where it is held by the left thumb (figure a). Take the thread backwards over the left first finger, down

fishnet knot (netting) *See* FISHERMAN'S KNOT.

five hole ground/mesh (bobbin) *See* FLANDERS GROUND.

five-pin bud (bobbin) A decorative hole, typical of Honiton lace, made as a FOUR-PIN BUD with the runners coming in to one side (from the right in the illustration), exchanging with the pair waiting at the centre and returning to the same

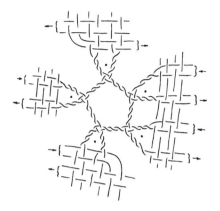

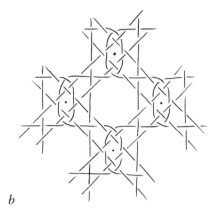

b

side before returning to the centre and completing the bud (figure). *See also* FOUR-PIN BUD.

fixed length system (yarn) *See* DIRECT COUNT SYSTEM.

fixed weight system (yarn) *See* INDIRECT COUNT SYSTEM.

fixing (bobbin) Temporary pins used by beginners to hold bobbins out of the way while working.

Flanders ground (bobbin) The traditional ground of Flanders lace. Each

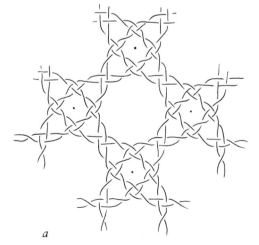

a

unit of the ground surrounding a single pinhole, called a packet, is worked using four pairs of bobbins. The early version was worked entirely in CLOTH STITCH AND TWIST. Using four pairs of bobbins for each unit work:

> pairs 1 & 2 and 3 & 4,
> pairs 2 & 3*
> set up a pin between pairs 2 & 3
> pairs 1 & 2 and 3 & 4*
> pairs 2 & 3
> pairs 1 & 2 and 3 & 4 (figure a)

(Note: the pin can be set up any time *–*.)

The modern version in a mixture of HALF STITCH and cloth stitch and twist. Using four pairs of bobbins for each unit work:

> pairs 1 & 2 and 3 & 4 half stitch
> pairs 2 & 3 cloth stitch and twist*
> set up a pin between pairs 2 & 3
> pairs 1 & 2 and 3 & 4 half stitch*
> pairs 2 & 3 cloth stitch and twist
> pairs 1 & 2 and 3 & 4 half stitch
> (figure b)

(Note: the pin can be set up any time *–*.)

Also called cane ground, cinq trous ground, five-hole ground/mesh, fond à cinq trous and square ground/mesh. *See also* HALF PACKET.

flap (needle) *See* APPLIED PIECE.

flash (bobbin) A glass flask, containing water, which was used to focus light from a candle. Also called flask. *See also* CANDLE BLOCK/STOOL, LACEMAKER'S LAMP.

flash cushion (bobbin) A wisp of straw bound into a ring, used for supporting FLASHES.

flash stool (bobbin) *See* CANDLE BLOCK/STOOL.

flask (bobbin) *See* FLASH.

flat (bobbin) When applied to Honiton lace, indicates the absence of RAISED WORK.

flat cutwork (needle) In Branscombe lace a SORRENTO WHEEL, made with an uneven number of spokes (figure).

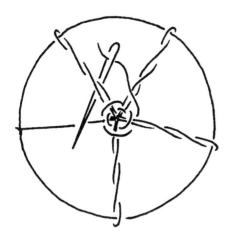

flat pillow (bobbin) A term which is applied to all pillows where the lace is worked flat on the pillow as opposed to a ROUND PILLOW that rotates. *See also* BLOCK PILLOW, MUSHROOM PILLOW, U-SHAPED PILLOW.

flat point (needle) (1) *See* CORDED BUTTONHOLE STITCH. (2) *See* FLATWORK.

flat sewing (bobbin) *See* EDGE SEWING.

flat spool/stick (netting) A flat MESH BOARD/GAUGE/STICK (figure). *See also* ROUND SPOOL.

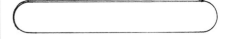

flatwork (needle) (1) Needle lace made without raised or surface decoration and without the usual raised edge. Also called flat point and point plat. (2) *See* CORDED BUTTONHOLE STITCH.

flax (general) An annual plant (*Linum usitatissimum*) of the family Linacaceae. *See also* LINEN.

Flemish pillow (bobbin) *See* BLOCK PILLOW.

fleures volantes (needle) *See* FLYING FLOWERS.

flies (bobbin) Point de Paris FILLING with pairs travelling across each other mainly in CLOTH STITCH, based on a square grid (figure a). There are several variants, one of which is illustrated (figure b, p.96). Similar fillings are used in Flanders lace, where they are known as SMALL SNOWFLAKE.

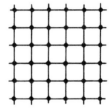

a

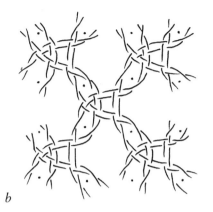

b

floating threads/floats (general) Threads that lie across a wide space, mostly used in freestyle lace.

floral Bucks (bobbin) Bucks point lace having a freestyle design and the pin-holes within the motifs not regular with the grid but following the design. Also called FREE FLOWING BUCKS as the design does not necessarily contain flowers.

Florentine knot (bobbin) *See* RAISED TALLY.

flour bag (bobbin) In some lacemaking areas workers would have a bag of flour, or starch, to dry their hands. In other areas it was not considered good practice. *See also* GET UP.

flower couronne (needle) A couronne having BUTTONHOLED LOOPS made around it, like petals around a flower's centre. Also called couronne ring with scallops and couronne with looped cordonnette.

flower loom (needle) An implement, usually circular, with two circles of prongs over which thread may be wound. The centre is stitched and the motif eased off. Motifs may be joined by

knotting a thread through the outer loops or by crochet (figure).

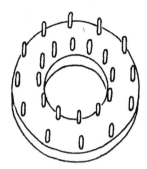

flush spot eye (bobbin) A bead decoration of 'eye' spots made so that they do not protrude from the surface (figure). *See also* EVIL EYE BEAD, KITTY FISHER'S EYE, RAISED SPOT EYE.

fly (bobbin) A very small Honiton motif.

fly (**stitch**) (needle) Four decorative holes worked in CORDED BUTTONHOLE STITCH (figure).

row 1: for the top 'hole'* whip the RETURNING CORD through two stitches and miss these two spaces when working the covering line of button-hole stitches

row 2: for the two side 'holes'* whip the returning cord through the two stitches preceding the long loop, twice through the long loop and through the following two stitches (when working the covering line of button-hole stitches miss the stitches that have been whipped and make two

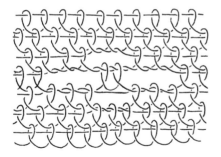

close buttonhole stitches in the centre of the long loop)

row 3: for the lower hole*, whip the long loops twice (when working the covering line of stitches make three in each long loop)

row 4: *whip the returning cord twice through the long loop and, when working the covering line of stitches, make three in the long loop

(The sequence can be followed omitting whipping through the stitches by simply laying the thread instead of whipping at *. Also called diamond, four hole bud, four-pin bud and pinwork.

flying flowers (needle) Small, three-dimensional, flower-like motifs attached to needle-made lace. The stitches attaching them are deliberately loose so that the 'flowers' can move. Also called fleures volantes.

fold (yarn) (1) The number of SINGLES units from which a yarn is made, also called the ply number. A 2-fold yarn has two single units twisted together and is also called 2-ply. This is represented by the '2' in 2/60 where the 60 refers to the SINGLES NUMBER, the whole number being sometimes referred to as the fold number. *See also* YARN COUNT. (2) The number of threads over which another is darned backwards and forwards. *See also* LEAF IN TWO-FOLD DARNING.

fond (general) *See* GROUND.

fond à cinq trous (bobbin) *See* FLANDERS GROUND.

fond à la marriage (bobbin) *See* EVERLASTING STITCH.

fond à la vierge (bobbin) *See* POINT DE LA VIERGE.

fond chant (bobbin) *See* KAT STITCH.

fond clair (bobbin) *See* POINT GROUND.

fond de mariage (bobbin) *See* POINT DE MARIAGE.

fond double (bobbin) *See* KAT STITCH.

fond simple (bobbin) *See* POINT GROUND.

footing (bobbin) *See* FOOTSIDE.

footpin/foot pin (bobbin) A pin used at the FOOTSIDE.

foot(side) (bobbin) The reinforced EDGE made to be attached to fabric. There is usually at least one PASSIVE pair and the pair working out to the edge exchanges function with the pair lying at the edge. Also called closed edge, edging stitch, four-about-the-pin, margin stitch, pin after two, pin under four, reinforced foot, straight edge and torchon edge. *See also* BEDFORDSHIRE FOOT(SIDE), BUCKS FOOT(SIDE), EDGE (Honiton), EDGE STITCH, TORCHON FOOT(SIDE), TWISTED FOOTSIDE.

footside passive (bobbin) one or more pairs that run the length of the FOOTSIDE and retain the shape – i.e., prevent the edge from stretching. They may be

TWISTED or untwisted according to the style of lace being made. *See also* BED-FORDSHIRE FOOT(SIDE), BUCKS FOOT(SIDE), EDGE (HONITON), EDGE STITCH, TORCHON FOOT(SIDE).

forgotten purls (bobbin) SEW in a pair at the PINHOLE before the start of the PURLS. * Make a purl, removing the pin from the required hole in the braid and replacing under the edge of the braid. Make a sewing to the braid PINHOLE and tie. Repeat from * as required, sew out into the next pinhole and TIE (figure).

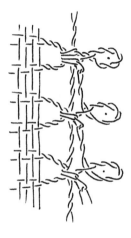

fork (crochet) *See* HAIRPIN.

fork crochet (crochet) *See* HAIRPIN CROCHET.

formulae (tatting) A diagrammatic method of representing a pattern. The start is indicated by an arrow, single threads by fine lines, CHAINS by thicker ones, RINGS by circles and ovals, PICOTS by short lines projecting from them, the length of the line indicating the length of the picot and a JOIN indicated by the projection crossing the line of the ring or chain. Large numbers inside the rings or by the chains indicate the order in which

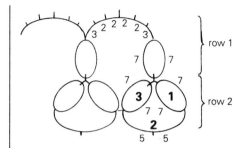

they are made and small numbers at the sides of the circles and lines indicate the numbers of DOUBLE STITCHES between picots and joins. A single pattern repeat lies between the dotted lines. The figure illustrates these different symbols. This, written out, would read:

> row 1: * ring of 7 ds, p, 7 ds, cl, rw, chain of 5 ds, p, 5 ds, cl, rw, ring of 7 ds, join to previous ring, 7 ds, cl. Repeat from * as required.
> row 2: **ring of 7 ds, join to join of rings of row 1, 7 ds, cl, rw, chain of 3 ds, sm p, 2 ds, p, 2 ds, lp, 2 ds, p, 2 ds, sm p, 3 ds, rw. Repeat from ** as required.

foundation cord (needle) *See* FOUNDATION THREAD.

foundation (fabric) (needle) *See* BACKING.

foundation grid (needle) A squared grid of threads on which reticella is made.

foundation loop (netting) A loop of thread, usually about 15cm (6in) long, pinned to a WEIGHTED CUSHION, or tied to a secure support, and used to support the work when netting; it can be longer if required. Also called head-rope. *See also* STIRRUP.

foundation row (needle) The first row of stitches when working a FILLING, not always repeated when the pattern repeats.

foundation stitches (bobbin) The basic stitches of bobbin laces, namely CLOTH STITCH and HALF STITCH.

foundation thread (needle) The thread (usually doubled) laid, and couched, around the design and from which the CLOTHWORK and fillings are suspended. Also called bâti, fil de crin, cordon(n)et, fil de trace, le brodé and la feston.

four-about-the-pin (bobbin) *See* FOOT-SIDE.

four hole bud/diamond (needle) *See* FLY (STITCH).

four pair crossing (bobbin) *See* WIND-MILL.

four-pin bud (bobbin) (1) A small hole found in Honiton clothwork. After working the runners to one side select the three pairs immediately above the top pinhole, A, work the pair, of the three, on the same side as the runners to the other side and make up the edge. Taking the remaining two pairs, of the three, *twist three times, set a pin between them, whole stitch and twist three times. Bring both pairs of runners through the downrights until they meet the centre group and twist three times. Set the side pins, B and C, under their respective runners, whole stitch each with nearest pair from pin A, twist three times and whole stitch to the outer edges. Whole stitch the centre two pairs and set a pin (D) between them *. Make up the edges and return to the centre group. The pair returning, from the side where the original runners were left, works through the centre pairs and is

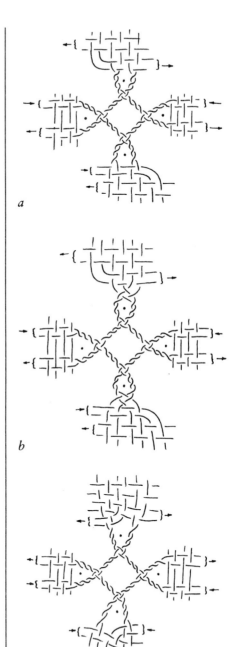

a

b

c

left. The other runners continue (figure a). (2) Work as (1) but work a whole stitch at * (figure b). (3) Work as (1) using the centre pair of the three selected as runners and returning them so that they lie between the centre pairs, this reduces the division that sometimes appears (figure c). (4) Work as (2) using the centre pair of the three selected as runners and returning them so that they lie between the centre pairs, also called fancy hole. (5) *See* FOUR-PIN HONEYCOMB RING.

four-pin bud (needle) *See* FLY (STITCH).

four-pin honeycomb ring (bobbin) In Bucks point lace four HONEYCOMB STITCHES surrounded by a GIMP (figure). Also called four-pin bud.

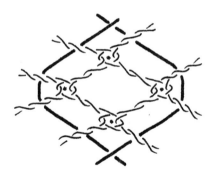

four plait crossing (bobbin) *See* EIGHT PAIR/PLAIT CROSSING.

four-sided stitch (mounting) A method of attaching lace to fabric. Tack lace to the right side of the fabric, work one row of four-sided stitch – fasten on the thread at A, below the lace,* insert

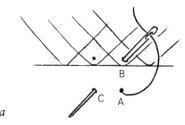

a

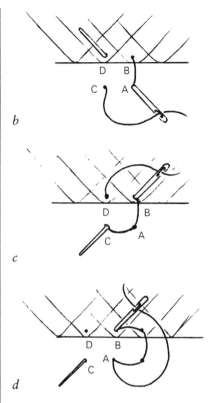

b

c

d

needle through the lace at B and bring out at C (figure a), inset needle into A again and bring out through the lace at D (figure b), insert into B again and bring out at C (figure c). Repeat from * relettering the points so that C and D become the A and B of the next group of four (figure d). When the row is complete remove the tacking thread and fold fabric along the base of the lace. Work another line of stitches over the first, or below the first with its top stitches over those of the first row.

fours (bobbin) Olney term for ROSE GROUND.

frame (needle) *See* EMBROIDERY FRAME, NETTING FRAME, STRETCHING FABRIC IN A FRAME, TAMBOUR FRAME.

free edge (bobbin) *See* PLAIN EDGE.

free end (netting) The end of a thread that is unattached as opposed to the STANDING END.

free flowing Bucks (bobbin) *See* FLORAL BUCKS.

free lace (bobbin) (1) *See* PART LACE. (2) Lace that is an amalgam of techniques taken from different laces and invented by the maker in order to make lace to a freestyle design.

free stitching (needle) Using any combination of stitches and tension.

front (bobbin) The part of the pillow facing you when you work.

French eyelet (needle) *See* BULLION PICOT.

French fan (bobbin) A torchon fan having a curved headside and a single pin just inside the V. The WORKERS alternate between the HEADSIDE pins and the single pin in the V (figure a). There are various methods of working the inner pin. For the simplest the worker does not make a stitch with the innermost pair but the worker wraps around it at the same time as it passes around the pin

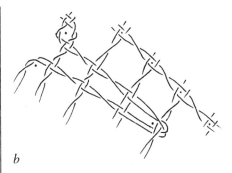

b

(figure b). The pin should be removed after the fan has been completed and before the inner passive is used again. Also called Paris fan, shell fan and toad's foot. *See* Appendix for guideline.

French ground (bobbin) *See* KAT STITCH.

French knot picot (needle) While making a TWISTED BAR, the point of the needle is placed under the bar and the

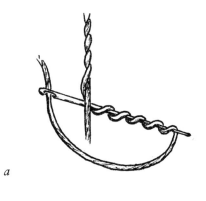

a

b

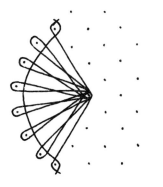

a

thread wound several times around it (figure a). The needle is then carefully pulled through (figure b). Also called simple picot and single picot. *See also* BULLION PICOT.

French pillow (bobbin) A rectangular pillow having a ROLLER, set at the rear, and with a downward sloping area at the FRONT, convenient for making lengths of lace, because the pattern can be joined in a continuous loop, and the sloping front is comfortable for spreading bobbins while working (figure). Also called torchon pillow.

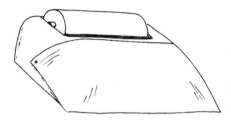

fringe (needle) Developed from Tenerife lace, a thread is passed back and forth across two lines of pins. The upper section is decorated using KNOT STITCH and other stitches typical of the lace, finally the lower loops are trimmed off (figure).

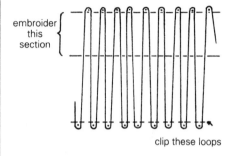

embroider this section

clip these loops

full stitch (needle) *See* CLOTH STITCH.

fuseau (general) French for BOBBIN.

fuselli (general) Italian for BOBBIN.

G

gaining on a pin (bobbin) (1) *See* BACK STITCH. (2) *See* CHANGING WORKERS (2).

gamourch (needle) An Armenian lace technique. Make a tall loop (three times as high as a normal loop), bring the thread up and make an ARMENIAN KNOT STITCH at the top of the loop, into the next loop of the previous row make a taller loop (figure a), make a knot around the previous three tall threads (figure b), make a knot in the upper loop (figure c). (The first half of the first tall loop may be cut away or incorporated

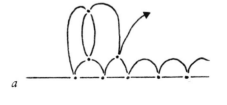

a

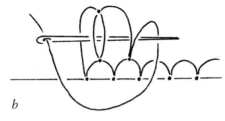

b

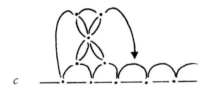

c

into the row.) Also called bow-tie, bridge and lovers' knot.

gap row (bobbin) A row in Bucks point HONEYCOMB GROUND where each two pairs, independently, make a HONEYCOMB STITCH without any pair moving on to make another stitch (figure). Also called short row. *See also* CONTINUOUS ROW.

gardening (bobbin) The process of improving the appearance of a finished piece of work by tweaking with a pin, stitching with a needle and so on.

garter stitch (bobbin) A method of attaching the ROLL. Using the TIE PAIR, prior to THROWING UP THE ROLL, make a SEWING in the first available pinhole noting which bobbin passes through the loop and use this bobbin to make the next loop – i.e., the threads that make

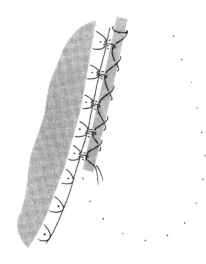

the loop and pass through the loop alternate when progressing up the roll (figure). It is not necessary to knot after each sewing when using this method. *See also* ROLL AND TIE.

gassed thread (yarn) A cotton yarn treated by a process invented in 1817 by Samuel Hall. The fine, fluffy fibres around the cotton yarn have been removed by passing it through a gas flame pulled upwards by a partial vacuum; the resulting yarn has a dull finish.

gate (bobbin) A SQUARE-ENDED TALLY with the WEAVING THREAD not returning to the side from which it came, one of

the other pair crossing the tally to take its position (figure). *See also* LADDER.

gauge (netting) *See* MESH STICK.

gauze point mesh (needle) *See* TWISTED BUTTONHOLE STITCH.

gauze stitch (bobbin) *See* HALF STITCH.

gauze weave *See* LENO WEAVE.

geometric bobbin lace (bobbin) Lace made on a pricking that follows a geometrical grid, with the possible exception of the HEADSIDE. With a few exceptions, this results in there being an exact route for each thread.

German spider (bobbin) An OPEN-CENTRED SPIDER worked as an ordinary SPIDER but the last pairs entering from each side cross in the centre, work out to the sides, return and cross in the centre and work out. It then finishes as an ordinary SPIDER (figure). Also called spider with eye, there are many variations.

get up (bobbin) *See* GOT UP.

Ghiordes knot (needle) One or more threads are used to make 'tufts' on existing work. A needle or crochet hook may be used to pass the thread down through one space (A), up through the one next to it (B), across the first space and down through the one on the other side (C), then back up through the first space (figure).

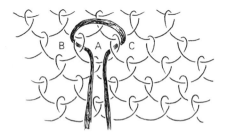

ghost stitch (needle) A method used for filling consisting of successive rows of INTERLOCKING LACE STITCH (figure). Also called point d'esprit (netting). *See also* INTERLACING (I).

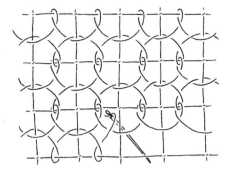

gimp (bobbin) Also spelt gymp. Originally meaning a thick thread bound with silk or metal or lace made using such thread. Today it denotes a thicker thread used to form designs within the ground, often outlining CLOTH or HALF STITCH; this thread does not take part in the formation of stitches but passes between the threads of the pairs between stitches; there are often twists separating the gimp from an adjacent stitch. Although the method used for passing the gimp through the pairs varies with the lace made, often the gimp is passed under the left thread and over the right thread of the pair, the pair then being TWISTED one or more times (figure a shows gimp passing left to right and figure b right to left). *See also* CABLE GIMP, CHAIN CORDING, DOUBLE(D) GIMPS, PAIRED GIMPS, RAISED GIMP and Appendix for indicator.

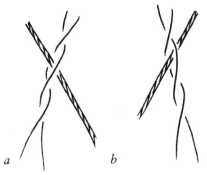

a　　　　　　*b*

gimp stitch (bobbin) A narrow CLOTH STITCH braid made using ten pairs of bobbins. The WORKERS travel across the row, make a TURNING STITCH with the last pair, are supported by an AUXILIARY PIN placed inside the TURNING STITCH.

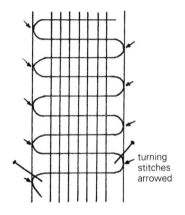

turning stitches arrowed

gingle

The inner pair become the workers for the next row. As each row is pinned the pin supporting the previous row is removed, resulting in a firm edge. The edges of the braid can be decorated with an occasional PICOT (figure).

gingle (bobbin) Also spelt jingle. (1) A ring that fits loosely into grooves around a bobbin so that it will rattle as the bobbin is used. Sometimes used for a bobbin decorated with such rings. The rings are usually made of pewter but can be found made of bone or wood (figure). (2) *See* SPANGLE.

glass bobbin (bobbin) Formerly hand-made glass bobbins were used as prizes and not used for making lace as they were so fragile but today, with tougher glass available, they are being used for making lace.

glossing (needle) Smoothing out and polishing the CLOTHWORK of needle lace with an AFFICOT to impart a gloss.

glum (bobbin) A pause in a LACE TELL when children working in the lace schools would work a set number of pins. In some areas the first to set a required number of pins would shout out 'My glum's done' or say a rhyme.

got up (bobbin) A colloquial phrase for lace that has been whitened by using flour or starch.

grafting off (bobbin) Primarily used in Bedfordshire lace, a means of casting off pairs along a horizontal line. After working the last row of CLOTH STITCH

the WORKERS are TWISTED two or three times, a pin set under them and they are then worked through several pairs of PASSIVES before being LAID BACK. A pin is set in the first pinhole along the horizontal line, separating the first pair of passives from the second; these are twisted two or three times before becoming the workers working through several pairs before being laid back. The routine of separating off and twisting a pair of passives, which then work through several pairs of passives before being laid back, is continued as far as possible. The remaining pairs can frequently be used to make a plait. If this is not possible they can be tied off and the tuft of threads tidily sewn to the back of the work after it is finished (figure). Also called basket edge and bottoming out.

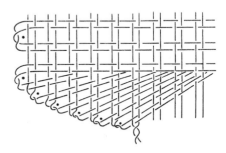

grand bride ground (needle) The hexagonal buttonholed ground of Argentan lace. Also called Medici ground. *See* ARGENTAN GROUND, BRIDE(S) CLAIRE(S). *See also* BRIDE(S) BOUCLÉE(S), BRIDE(S) D'ÉPINGLE(S), BRIDE(S) TORTILLÉE(S).

grandmother bobbin (bobbin) A BABY BOBBIN containing a MINIATURE BOBBIN also having a hollow shank in which lies a smaller bobbin. Also called three-in-one bobbin.

graph paper (general) Paper printed with an all-over grid, usually square, used for PATTERN DRAFTING. Also called checked paper and sectional paper. *See also* ISOMETRIC PAPER, POLAR CO-ORDINATE PAPER.

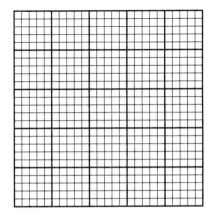

Grecian point (needle) A FILLING consisting of blocks of three TWISTED BUTTONHOLE STITCHES with the blocks of each succeeding row worked between the blocks of the previous row (figure), can be worked with a RETURNING THREAD, the thread whipping once

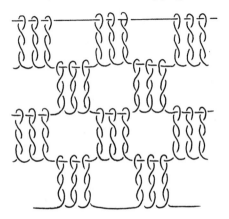

through each stitch. Also called point de Grecque; not to be confused with GREEK NET STITCH OR GREEK STITCH.

Greek net stitch (needle) A FILLING consisting of blocks of three BRUSSELS STITCHES with the blocks of each succeeding row worked between the blocks of the previous row (figure). Can be worked with a RETURNING THREAD, the thread whipping once through each stitch. Also called treble Brussels stitch and triple Brussels stitch. Not to be confused with GRECIAN POINT OR GREEK STITCH.

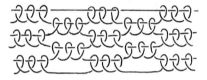

Greek stitch (needle) *See* ALENÇON GROUND/MESH. Not to be confused with GRECIAN STITCH OR GREEK NET STITCH.

grenadine (yarn) A matt black silk thread formerly used for laces such as Chantilly.

grid (bobbin) A regular arrangement of points upon which a particular lace is based and typical of that lace.

grid filling (needle) *See* CHEQUERED FILLING.

grillé (bobbin) *See* HALF STITCH.

grommet (netting) Make a SLIP KNOT with a loose TAIL, thread a FOUNDATION LOOP through the loop and make secure. Cast on the required number of SIMPLE KNOT STITCHES, passing the shuttle up through the slip knot loop and making the knot over both threads (figure a).

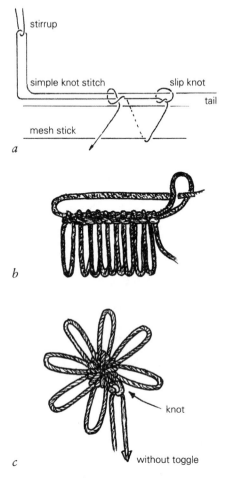

a

b

c

stirrup

simple knot stitch

slip knot

tail

mesh stick

knot

without toggle

Remove the foundation loop and pass the tail through the slip knot loop (figure b), place around a TOGGLE and pull up, tie a REEF KNOT with the tail and WORKING THREADS (figure c). Used for starting WORKING IN THE ROUND. Also called grummet.

gros point diamonds *See* DIAMOND/ DIAMOND FILLING (needle).

ground(ing) (general) The background net of lace, worked between the various parts of the overall design, the different laces having their own special varieties. Also called fond (Fr.) mesh, net and réseau (Fr.). *See also* ALENÇON GROUND, ARGENTAN GROUND, POINT GROUND, ENTOILAGE, TORCHON GROUND and so on.

grounded lace (bobbin) Lace having a GROUND, as opposed to GUIPURE.

grounding (bobbin) *See* GROUND.

groundwork pair (bobbin) A pair used to work the GROUND.

groundwork pin (bobbin) A pin supporting a groundwork stitch.

groundwork stitch (bobbin) One of the stitches composing the GROUND.

group darned centre (needle) The centre of a Tenerife lace medallion made by taking the needle under and over several pairs of threads at a time, this causes the threads to be divided into groups for subsequent decoration (figure). *See also* CENTRE.

grummet (netting) *See* GROMMET.

guard (bobbin) A shaped piece of ACETATE used to protect underlying work by sliding it between the layers. Used when making a sewing into the top layer of several pieces that have been worked over each other (figure, p.109). Also called lazy Susan and shield.

guard   real size

guideline (bobbin) A line drawn on a PATTERN DRAFT and transferred to the PRICKING, which indicates how the pattern is to be worked. It often represents the path of the WORKERS or some feature – e.g., SIMPLE FAN (figure). Not to be confused with SCHEMATIC DIAGRAM or THREAD DIAGRAM. *See also* INDICATOR, INKING IN *and* Appendix.

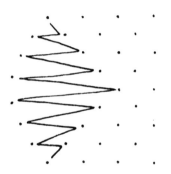

guipure (general) (1) In the sixteenth and seventeenth centuries a thick thread wound with silk or metal wire and lace made using it. (2) In the nineteenth century darned netting and other heavy laces e.g. for furnishing. (3) Today, lace in which the designs are held in place by BARS rather than a net-like GROUND.

guipure d'art (netting) Typically having LEAVES in TWO- or THREE-FOLD DARNING incorporated into the design. *See also* FILET LACE.

gum arabic (general) A powder, obtainable from chemists, which was mixed with pigment and used to colour the spots on bobbins.

gymp (bobbin) *See* GIMP.

H

hairpin (crochet) A semi-rigid, U-shaped implement with rounded ends about 13cm (5¼in) long, with the prongs varying from 12mm (½in) to several centimetres (inches) apart, for making HAIRPIN CROCHET. The bend of the implement may be semi-circular or flattened as illustrated (figure). Also called crochet fork and crochet prong.

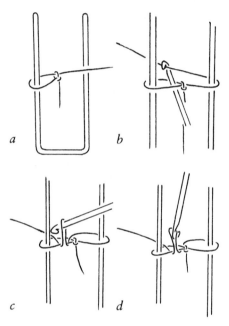

a   b

c   d

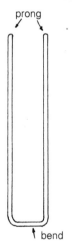

prong

bend

hairpin crochet (crochet) A crochet braid with loops on both sides incorporated into crochet work or connected to other similar braids by drawing one or more loops of one braid through the loop(s) of the next. To make the braid, form a SLIP KNOT at the end of a thread, hold the HAIRPIN in the left hand between the forefinger and thumb and slip the loop over the right prong, holding the thread around the left

fingers as usual for crochet, rotate the prong through 180 degrees, pushing right prong forwards with the finger. The knot of the slip knot should lie centrally between the prongs (figure a). From the front, insert a crochet hook upwards through the loop on the left prong, YARN OVER HOOK (figure b), and draw through a loop (figure c). Make one chain. **Bring the hook forwards over the loop on the prong, YARN OVER HOOK and draw through the loop on the hook. *Lift the tail of the crochet hook until it is almost vertical (figure d), turn the prong as before and bring the crochet hook down into the working position, work a DOUBLE CROCHET passing the hook upwards through the top loop on the left prong. Repeat from * as required. When the hairpin is full, slide off the loops, replacing the last three or four made on their correct prongs, and continue. The braid can be made with the hairpin held with its bend uppermost. In this case, each time it is rotated the crochet hook must be taken out of its loop, just before it is rotated, and reinserted immediately after. (If difficulty is experienced in keeping the original loop in the central position when starting, use a larger loop placed over both prongs, bring the TAIL over the loop and make a knot with the WORKING THREAD and continue from **.) Also called fork crochet. *See also* LOOP JOIN, SURFACE SPINE STITCH.

hair-pin stitch (bobbin) *See* KAT STITCH.

half hitch (general) Looping a thread round to secure it. *See also* HITCH.

half hitch with extra turn (bobbin) *See* HITCH WITH EXTRA TURN.

half packet (bobbin) A modified FLANDERS GROUND stitch used to exchange pairs between ground and CLOTH STITCH motif or FOOTSIDE (figures a and b). Also called joining stitch.

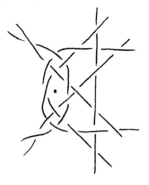

a

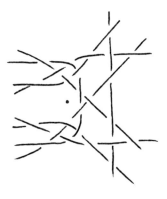

b

half passing (bobbin) *See* REVERSE(D) HALF STITCH.

half-ring (tatting) *See* SCALLOP.

half stitch (bobbin) One of the basic stitches of bobbin lace; with two pairs that CROSS the centre bobbins 2 over 3, TWIST the outer pairs 2 over 1 and 4 over 3 (figure). Also called gauze stitch, grillé, half throw, lace stitch, lattice stitch, net stitch and no stitch. *See also* PASS *and* Appendix for indicator.

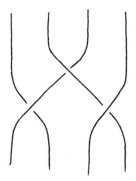

half stitch (tatting) One half of a DOUBLE STITCH. *SEE ALSO* PLAIN, PURL.

half stitch bar (bobbin) *See* PLAIT.

half straddled (bobbin) *See* HANGING ON HALF STRADDLED.

half treble crochet (crochet) YARN OVER HOOK, insert the hook into the next chain, yarn over hook and draw through a loop (three loops on the hook), yarn over hook and draw a loop through all loops on hook (figure).

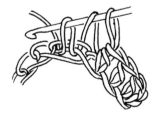

haloed spider (bobbin) Made as the ordinary SPIDER but with the outer pairs of the CLOTH STITCHED centre making a CLOTH STITCH AND TWIST with each pair working through them (figure). Also called spider in/with a ring.

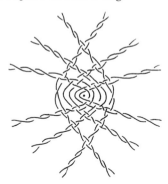

halse (bobbin) A Midlands term for winding a bobbin.

handbag pillow (bobbin) A pillow that folds up for travelling. See also TRAVEL-LING PILLOW.

handle (bobbin) See SHANK.

hanging bobbin (bobbin) A BOBBIN that bears an inscription commemorating the hanging of a criminal.

hanging in bobbins/pairs (bobbin) See ADDING BOBBINS/PAIRS.

hanging in pairs for later use (bobbin) A Honiton term when one, or occasion-ally two, pairs are slipped onto the RUNNERS before and/or after working the EDGE and LAID BACK, out of the way, for use later, usually after TURNING THE PILLOW when BACKING or for a section branching off (figure). Also called laying back/in pairs.

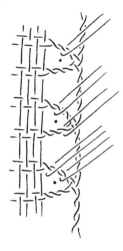

hanging on half straddled (bobbin) Placing LINKED BOBBINS over a pin so that each bobbin lies to the same side, right or left, of the pair previously placed over the pin (figure). The pairs remain linked together when the pin is removed. See also HANGING ON IN

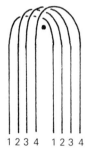

1 2 3 4   1 2 3 4

numbers indicate order in which pairs are placed over pin

hanging on in order (bobbin) (1)
Placing LINKED BOBBINS over a pin so
that the bobbins of each pair lie adjacent
to each other and in the order in which
they are placed over the pin; the pairs
separate when the pin is removed
(figure). (2) *See* HALF STRADDLED, HANG-
ING ON STRADDLE WISE/STRADDLED.

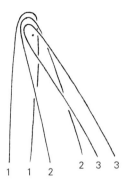

hanging on pairs (bobbin) Starting a
piece of lace.

hanging on pairs open (bobbin) *See*
HANGING ON STRADDLE WISE/STRADDLED.

hanging on pairs side-by-side (bobbin)
See HANGING ON IN ORDER.

hanging on straddle wise/straddled
(bobbin) Placing LINKED PAIRS over a pin

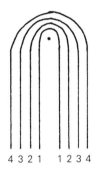

4 3 2 1   1 2 3 4   numbers indicate
order in which pairs
are placed over pin

so that each pair is placed with one
bobbin on either side of those previously
placed over the pin, also called hanging
on pairs open and straddling a pin
(figure). *See also* HALF STRADDLED, HANG-
ING ON IN ORDER.

hardhead (bobbin) *See* BUR(R) HEAD.

hariffe pin (bobbin) *See* BUR(R) HEAD.

hazel (general) The process of leaving to
dry lace that had been washed and
rinsed while wound around a bottle, by
inverting the bottle over a stick stuck
into the ground.

head (bobbin) This is the bulbous top of
a BOBBIN that prevents the thread from
sliding off. *See also* DOUBLE HEAD, SINGLE
HEAD.

head-rope (netting) *See* FOUNDATION
LOOP.

heading (general) *See* (1) BEADING. (2)
HEADSIDE.

headpin/head pin (bobbin) (1) A pin
placed at HEADSIDE. *See also* FOOT PIN.
(2) A Bedfordshire term for PICOT.

headside/head side (bobbin) The side
of an edging that is not attached to
fabric. It is usually more decorative,
frequently with an undulating edge, and
may be decorated with FANS or PICOTS.
Also called heading and turnside.

head(side) passives (bobbin) In Bucks
point lace there are usually at least two
pairs of PASSIVES, lying immediately
inside the PICOTS (figure p.114).

heart-shaped pincushion (bobbin) *See*
STRAWBERRY PINCUSHION.

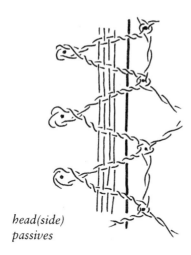

head(side)
passives

heelball (bobbin) A wax bar, usually black or brown, produced for boot and shoe menders for colouring damaged heels. Used by lacemakers for TAKING RUBBINGS. *See also* RUBBING, RUBBING WAX.

heller (bobbin) The COVER CLOTH that is placed over the lace-in-the-making to protect it and keep it clean while the pillow is not being used. Also called covering cloth.

help(er) thread (bobbin) A thread laid through the edge of a piece of work, as it is made, that is later used to assist in taking sewings. Wind an extra bobbin with a finer, strong coloured thread and pin approximately 10cm (4in) behind the pattern. Start the lace in the usual way and when a pin is used, where there will later be a sewing, bring the coloured thread over the workers, round the pin, out under the workers, round a temporary pin some way from the edge, about 2.5cm (1in), back under workers (figure a), round the pin again and out over the workers. The same help thread can be used along row of sewings (figure b). Do not cut the help thread off

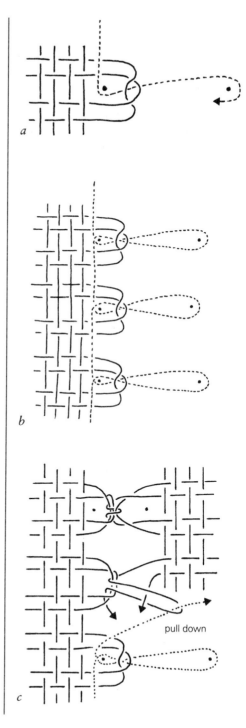

a

b

pull down

c

short. It is useful to tie its end to a pin to prevent it from being pulled through too soon. When the work returns along the other side of the pins the temporary pin supporting the help thread is removed and a bobbin passed through its loop. This thread is pulled through the lace by the help thread and the SEWING can be completed as usual by passing the other bobbin through the loop (figure c). *See also* LAZY LOOP.

herringbone (bobbin) *See* CHAIN CORDING.

herringbone braid (bobbin) CLOTH STITCH BRAID with a CHAIN GIMP through the centre.

hexagonal mesh (bobbin) *See* POINT GROUND.

hiller (bobbin) *See* HELLER.

hind cloth (bobbin) *See* BACK CLOTH.

hinged spangle (bobbin) A shaped piece of bone that fits across a narrowed TAIL of a BOBBIN and to which it is attached by a pin passing through both, usually with a bead within a hole again held in

place by a pin passing right through (figure a). Sometimes made by a narrow projection from the spangle fitting into a slot in the tail of the bobbin and being retained by a pin passing through both (figure b).

hitch (bobbin) A HALF HITCH used to secure the thread wound around a bobbin. One method of making this is to hold the bobbin in the left hand and the thread with the right thumb and middle finger. Place the right index finger in front of the thread, bringing the thread forwards over it to make a loop (figure a), and place the bobbin head behind the portion of thread between the

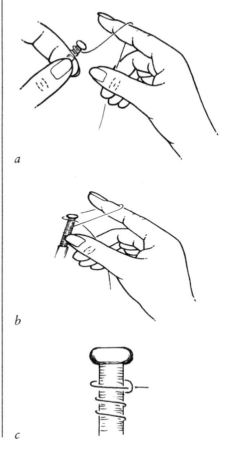

a

b

c

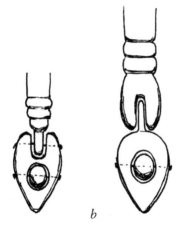

a   *b*

thumb and index finger. Bring the bobbin head forwards and upwards through the loop (figure b). When it is correctly made, the thread doubles back, forming a loop, its TAIL passing round the neck of the bobbin and through the loop (figure c). Also called half hitch and noose. *See also* HITCH WITH EXTRA TURN, WINDING BOBBINS.

hitch with extra turn/twist (bobbin) When the ordinary HITCH does not hold the thread sufficiently in the SHORT NECK

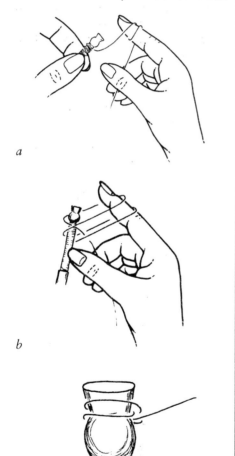

a

b

c

of a DOUBLE HEADED bobbin, an extra TURN can be added. The extra turn is made round the index finger (figure a) before passing the head of the bobbin through (figure b), making an extra turn round the short neck (figure c). A half hitch can be made with three turns if the bobbin is particularly slippery and the thread difficult. Also called elshing. *See also* WINDING BOBBINS.

hitching a bobbin (bobbin) Securing the bobbin thread with a HITCH or HITCH WITH EXTRA TURN. Also called elshing.

hole board (bobbin) The top of a CANDLE BLOCK/STOOL with holes in which the NOZZLE and CUPS are placed.

hole in cloth stitch/clothwork (bobbin) Sometimes indicated by a dot or circle on the pattern, this can be worked by TWISTING the WORKERS up to three times then, on the return row, twisting the PASSIVES either side of the hole and the workers between them the same number of times (figure). Also called pinhole and plain hole. *See also* EYELET, FOUR-PIN BUD, PLAIN HOLE *and* Appendix for indicator.

hole in half stitch (bobbin) work to the pinhole, where the hole is to be made, and set up the pin under the WORKERS.

Continue with the same workers, leaving the pin in place until the work is finished (figure). Several pins may be used for a larger hole. Also called pinhole.

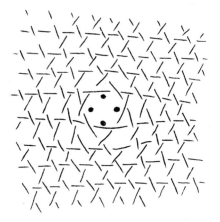

hole side (bobbin) In Honiton lace. (1) *See* PIN (HOLE) SIDE. (2) The side of a raised leaf on which the pinholes are used, as opposed to the PLAIN SIDE.

hollie point (needle) A solid ground where the design is produced by holes left within it. Place the left thumb on the thread, take the thread up, in front of the thumb, and down the back to be held as well. Pass the needle downwards behind the FOUNDATION THREAD and downwards under the loop over the left thumb nail (figure a). Draw the thread through so that the twists roll almost on top of each other. At the end of each row of stitches, throw the thread back to the starting side and pass the needle downwards behind this thread as well as through the stitch of the previous row. The holes are produced by whipping once through the stitch immediately above the required position; these spaces are missed when the next row of stitches is worked, the RETURNING THREAD being whipped twice through the space. Two

stitches are worked into this space when the next row is worked (figure b). *See also* ENGLISH STITCH.

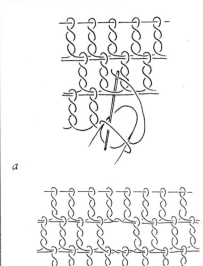

a

b

hollie stitch (needle) TWISTED NET STITCH pulled up as HOLLIE POINT.

holy point (needle) *See* HOLLIE POINT/ STITCH.

honeycomb chain (bobbin) A line of honeycomb stitches worked between two gimps. When they occur diagonally, a pair travels from one stitch to the next; when horizontally and vertically,

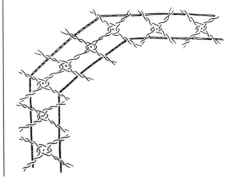

two pairs enter across the GIMPS and leave after making the stitch (figure). Also called honeycomb stem.

honeycomb filling/ground (bobbin) A Bucks point filling of alternate CONTINUOUS and GAP ROWS of HONEYCOMB STITCHES. Also called rose net ground and rose point. *See also* BRABANT GROUND.

honeycomb ring (bobbin) A group of HONEYCOMB STITCHES surrounding a space, in turn being surrounded by a GIMP. *See also* FOUR-PIN HONEYCOMB RING, SEVEN-PIN HONEYCOMB RING, SIX-PIN HONEYCOMB RING.

honeycomb stitch (bobbin) With two pairs make a HALF STITCH and TWIST, pin, half stitch and twist (figure). *See also* HONEYCOMB FILLING/GROUND.

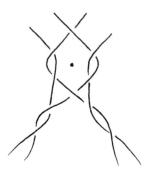

Honiton bobbin (bobbin) A small, SINGLE HEADED bobbin without a SPANGLE used to make Honiton lace. The end of the SHANK is finished with a blunt point to facilitate the taking of SEWINGS (figure). Also called lace stick.

Honiton braid (needle) A machine tape of connected ovals and leaf shapes, some of which could be gathered into flowers and others cut apart to make petals or leaves which are assembled using a needle. *See also* HONITON POINT, TAPE LACE.

Honiton pillow (bobbin) A circular PILLOW, approximately 35cm (14in) across and 15cm (6in) deep, used for making Honiton lace. The height brings the work closer to the eyes, reducing the need to bend over, and it is relatively small in diameter as the individual motifs are usually small and the pillow needs to be rotated as they are made. Traditionally, such a pillow would be made from two 33–35cm (13–14in) circles and a strip of pillow ticking, 7.5 × 91cm (3 × 36in), the strip being sewn as a gusset between the circles and, after turning it right side out, this CASING would be stuffed with straw (preferably barley) until it weighed 1.5kg (3½lb) (figure).

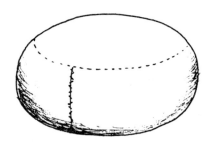

Honiton point (needle) TAPE LACE using HONITON BRAID that imitates Honiton bobbin lace.

Honiton purl (bobbin) *See* FORGOTTEN PURLS, LEFT-HANDED PURL, RIGHT-HANDED PURL.

hooded bobbin (bobbin) A SINGLE HEADED bobbin, used in Austria and Germany, with a narrow SHANK on which the thread is wound (figure a). This is protected by a shaped, hollow,

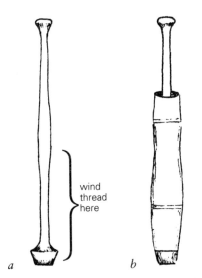

wind
thread
here

a   *b*

wooden tube, or hood, which slides down covering the thread, being retained by the bulbous end of the shank, which is carefully shaped so that the hood remains steady in use (figure b). Also called sheathed bobbin.

hook (crochet) An abbreviation of CROCHET HOOK.

horizontal shading (needle) Thread a needle with the next shade of thread and fasten on, working in CORDED BRUSSELS STITCH, * lay the new thread across and

stitch over with the original shade, proceed to work two more rows in this way. Work three rows using the original shade laid across and the new shade to make the stitches. Fasten off the original thread and then proceed to work three rows using the new thread. Fasten on another thread of the next shade down and repeat as required.

hooking (bobbin) *See* SEWING.

hooking in (bobbin) *See* SEWING IN.

horn slider (bobbin) *See* SLIDER.

horned eye/spot (bobbin) *See* RAISED EYE.

horse (bobbin) A piece of equipment that supports the pillow when in use. Also called lady (Midland term), maid (Midland term) and (pillow) horse/stand. *See also* BOWED HORSE, SINGLE HORSE.

horse hair (bobbin) Used to support the PICOTS in Alençon lace. Also sometimes used to pad the TOP STITCHING.

hutch (bobbin) A rush basket used to store spare FLASHES.

I

ice ground (bobbin) *See* MECHLIN GROUND.

impressed crumb bead (bobbin) A CRUMB BEAD with the tiny chips being pressed flush with the surface.

in-and-out stitch (needle) *See* DARNING STITCH.

in order (bobbin) *See* HANGING ON IN ORDER.

incised decoration (bobbin) A BOBBIN decoration that has been produced by scoring, cutting or otherwise making holes and/or grooves in the bobbin.

increasing (netting) Working twice into the same MESH to increase the number of meshes in the next row (figure a).

When making a square or rectangle this only happens in the last mesh of the row (figure b).

indicator (bobbin) A GUIDELINE drawn on, or holes in, the PRICKING that indicate how the lace is to be made, these holes are not usually used for making the lace and, if a pin is inserted in the hole, it is removed soon afterwards. Also called marker pin. *See* Appendix.

indirect count system (yarn) Yarn thickness expressed as the number of hanks of a given length made from a fixed weight, the number decreases as the thickness increases. Indirect systems in use include COTTON COUNT SYSTEM (Ne), COTTON COUNT (CONTINENTAL), LINEN SYSTEM (wet spun), METRIC SYSTEM, (Nm), SPUN SILK SYSTEM. *See also* CONVERSION FACTOR, YARN COUNT.

inking in (bobbin) Drawing in both

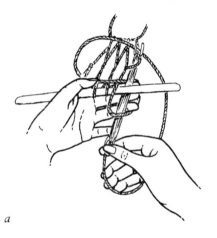

a

GUIDELINES and INDICATORS with a fine waterproof pen. Also called lining up.

inlaid bobbin (bobbin) A BOBBIN design produced by removing part of the bobbin and replacing it with similar material of a different colour or a different material. *See also* BITTED BOBBIN, BUTTERFLY BOBBIN, COMPOUND BOBBIN, LEOPARD, LEPTIG, SPIRAL PEWTER, TIGER.

inner purl (bobbin) A SNATCH PIN or WINKIE PIN edge to a hole within CLOTHWORK.

inscribed bobbin (bobbin) A BOBBIN that bears an inscription, message, saying, name and so on as a decoration, the letters being formed by a series of coloured, burnt or painted dots. *See also* COMMEMORATIVE BOBBIN.

insertion (general) A length of lace designed to be inserted between two pieces of lace, fabric, net and so on; if of bobbin lace, usually with a FOOTSIDE on both sides. *See also* SEAMING LACE.

interlacing (needle and netting) (1) SURFACE STITCHING on netting and Tenerife lace where the web threads have been pre-grouped to form squares, see GHOST STITCH and INTERLOCKING LACE STITCH. (2) In Tenerife lace two rounds of knot stitch pre-group the same threads and

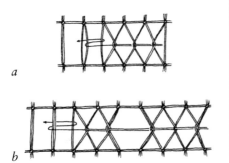

a

b

the intervening threads are split with one or more threads of one group crossed over one or more threads of the adjacent group (figures a and b).

interlocking lace stitch (needle) SURFACE STITCHING on netting and Tenerife lace where the web threads have been pre-grouped to form squares (figure). *See also* INTERLACING.

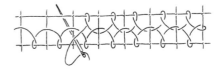

interlocking V gimp (bobbin) *See* CHAIN GIMP.

interlocking webs (needle) When the webs of two adjacent Ñanduti or Tenerife webs are joined by passing the thread of the second through two adjacent spokes of the first (figure).

intermediate pin (bobbin) A pin used in GROUND and FILLING STITCHES THAT CONSIST OF A STITCH BEFORE THE PIN IS SET UP and another COVERING IT.

inverted pyramid stitch (needle) *See* BUTTERFLY STITCH.

inward facing corner (bobbin) A corner that has been designed with the HEAD-SIDE to the inside (figure).

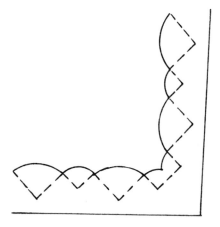

Irish chain (bobbin) A design in GIMPS to form a shamrock (figure).

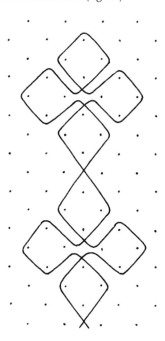

Irish gimp (bobbin) *See* RAISED GIMP.

ironing lace (general) It is generally considered better not to iron lace because the process flattens it, removing the undulations produced when it is made that give lace much of its character. However, should it be necessary, it is better to press lace while it is damp and covered with a cloth (preferably a semi-transparent one so that the lace can be seen). Use the lowest possible temperature setting on the iron. *See also* AFFICOT, BLOCKING OUT, CLEANING LACE.

isometric graph paper (general) GRAPH PAPER with an all over triangular pattern without any bold lines, used for preparing SCHEMATIC DIAGRAMS, particularly useful for Bucks point motifs as it has a 60° angle (figure). *See also* TRIANGULAR GRAPH PAPER.

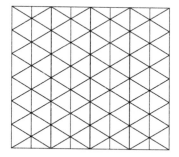

Italian bobbin (bobbin) A BOBBIN with a DOUBLE HEAD and a bulbous SHANK tapering to a point (figure, p.123).

Italian filling (bobbin) An unpinned Honiton filling. Make a WHOLE STITCH and three TWISTS with each two pairs and repeat, taking one pair from each two of the previous adjacent whole stitches, make whole stitches with one pair from each two of the previous adjacent whole stitches, with another pair work three rows of *whole stitches,

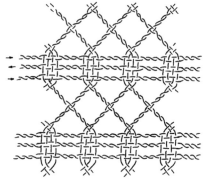

Italian bobbin

Italian filling

with two pairs that have just been joined with a whole stitch, and three twists, repeat from * to the end of the row (figure). *See also* CUT SPIDER, FISHES.

Italian picot (bobbin) *See* CAUGHT PICOT.

ivory point/stitch (needle) *See* PUNTO AVORIO.

J

Jack-in-the-box (bobbin) A wooden or bone BOBBIN in two parts joining with a screw or push fit, and having a hollowed shank containing a loose MINIATURE BOBBIN that jumps (falls) out when it is opened (figure). Sometimes called COW-AND(IN)-CALF.

jetted lace (bobbin) Coarse black bobbin lace on to which jet beads have been sewn.

jewel (bobbin) *See* TALLY.

jingle (bobbin) *See* GINGLE.

jinkum (bobbin) A corruption of the term JINGLE.

join (bobbin) *See* SEWING.

join(ing) (tatting) Insert a tatting, or crochet, hook through the existing tatting, or fabric to which the current tatting is to be joined, draw through a loop of AUXILIARY or RING THREAD. Pass the shuttle through the loop and CAPSIZE the knot as usual. This acts as the first half of the following DOUBLE STITCH (figure).

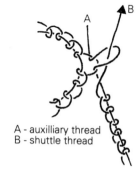

A - auxilliary thread
B - shuttle thread

join(ing)

joined circles (bobbin) Series of cloth stitch circles lying one below the other (figure). Treat each 'join' as COMBINING and DIVIDING TRAILS or CROSSING TRAILS.

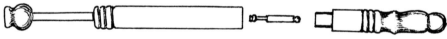

Jack-in-the-box

joining end to beginning (bobbin) When the finishing point of the lace meets the start. The starting end should be pinned to the PRICKING and each pair at the finish is cut in turn, one thread is passed through the starting loop of the pair in the position to which it points, or joined to it by a SEWING, the pair is tied in a REEF KNOT AND HALF and all ends darned away.

joining-on-a-leg (bobbin) A Cluny technique for joining a PLAIT to a BRAID. With the WORKERS from the braid CLOTH STITCH across the two plait pairs, set a

pin between the plait pairs and COVER with a cloth stitch. Leave the two outer pairs for the following plait and continue with the remaining pair as workers (figure). Also called three stitch join. *See also* FAST CROSSING.

joining stitch (bobbin) *See* HALF PACKET.

Josephine knot (tatting) Make six-eight single stitches, all either PLAIN or PURL, and CLOSE THE RING (figure).

jours (general) *See* FILLINGS.

K

kat/kattern stitch (bobbin) One of the GROUNDS of Bucks point lace worked in CLOTH AND TWIST STITCH. Work diagonally downwards across the ground in cloth stitch and twist and SET UP a pin after each two pairs (figure a). Work a cloth stitch and twist with each two pairs as grouped by the pins, these pins being left uncovered (figure b). Also called double ground, fond chant, fond double, French ground, hair-pin stitch, Paris ground, Parisian ground, point de Paris, point de six, point double, six-pointed star ground, star mesh and wire ground. *See also* EVERLASTING STITCH.

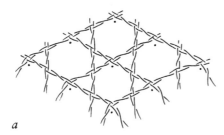

a

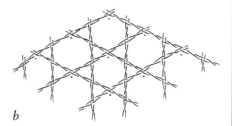

b

kat stitch edge/footside (bobbin) Worked entirely in CLOTH STITCH AND TWIST, the FOOTSIDE may have one or two pairs of PASSIVES (FIGURE).

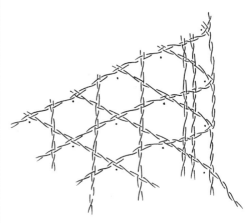

key pattern join (crochet) A method of joining hairpin crochet strips. Holding two strips side-by-side, start at the lower edges by passing the hook from front to

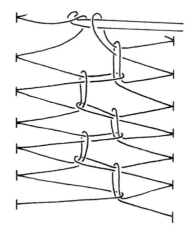

back through the first loop of the left strip then front to back through the first loop of the other strip. Pull the first loop through the second. *Pick up the next loop of the same strip and pull through the loop on the hook. Pick up the next loop of the other strip and pull through the loop on the hook. Repeat from * picking up two successive loops from each strip, pulling each loop through the one on the hook as it is picked up. Usually worked with groups of two or more loops (figure). *See also* LOOP JOIN.

kingpin (bobbin) A Bedfordshire term for a decorated pin. Until 1824 pin heads were separate rings of wire fixed around the end of a pointed wire and, as these could be removed, beads could be pushed onto one pin and retained in place by the head removed from another pin. Now glue is used to fix the beads in place. *See also* BUGLE, LIMMICK, STRIVER.

kiss (bobbin) When two WORKER pairs meet, are TWISTED and make a CLOTH STITCH followed by the same number of twists. The workers then continue as workers for the opposite sections (figure). *See* Appendix for indicator.

Kitty Fisher's eyes (bobbin) A grey bead decorated with RAISED EYE spots of white each having a small blue spot in the centre, said to represent the beautiful eyes of the eighteenth-century actress after whom they are named. Sometimes there are pink spots, to represent her mouth, sometimes the blue is replaced by red (figure).

knot (tatting) *See* DOUBLE STITCH.

knot stitch (needle) (1) A needle-made stitch involving a knot. *See also* ARMENIAN KNOT STITCH, BAR STITCH, FILET STITCH, RODI STITCH. (2) In Tenerife lace the knot used to secure the working thread to the web threads (figure).

knot stitch (tambour) Used for fastening the thread on and off, the last CHAIN is enlarged and another loop brought through, the hook is inverted to catch the end of the enlarged chain stitch which is brought through the following loop (figure) and the thread tightened around the chain stitch loop. The remainder of the loop may be taken to the back of the work.

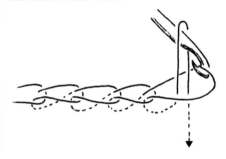

knotted buttonhole stitch (needle) Any stitch that starts by looping the thread

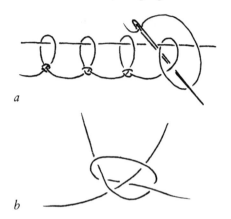

a

b

through, as a BUTTONHOLE STITCH, and ends by making a knot that locks the stitch, of which this is the simplest version (figures a and b).

knotted mesh (needle and netting) Net made using FILET STITCH, FISHERMAN'S KNOT or SIMPLE KNOT STITCH.

knotted picot (bobbin) *See* CAUGHT PICOT.

knotted picot (needle) *See* VENETIAN PICOT. *See also* BULLION PICOT, FRENCH KNOT PICOT.

L

lace board (bobbin) *See* PRICKING BOARD.

lace card (bobbin) The card around which lace was wound as it was made.

lace chest (bobbin) A container for storing equipment not currently in use.

lace pillow (general) *See* PILLOW.

lace stick (general) (1) A Honiton name for HONITON BOBBIN. (2) A yardstick used by dealers to measure lace they were buying.

lace stitch *See* HALF STITCH.

lace tell (bobbin) A song sung by lacemakers to help them keep a good rhythm and help maintain speed when they found the repetitious work monotonous. Some would give an immediate goal of a set number of pins to work during a pause in the song. *See also* GLUM.

lace token (general) Special coins produced for dealers and used for paying lacemakers. They were redeemable only in certain shops.

lacemaker's lamp (bobbin) A stand topped with a round, hollow glass container that, when filled with water, will focus light from a candle (figure). *See also* FLASH.

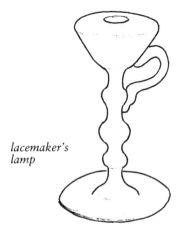

lacemaker's lamp

lacemaker's pincushion (bobbin) *See* STRAWBERRY PINCUSHION.

lacet (**braid**) (general) A tape for making TAPE LACE, can be bobbin or machine made.

lacis (netting) *See* FILET LACE.

ladder (bobbin) A SQUARE-ENDED TALLY

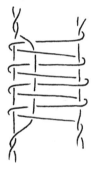

with the WEAVING THREAD returning to the side from which it came (figure). *See also* GATE.

ladder braid/trail (bobbin) *See* TWISTED VEIN.

ladies' work (needle) *See* TAPE LACE.

lady (bobbin) *See* HORSE.

laminated bobbin (bobbin) When one or more very thin sheets of wood have been glued between thicker pieces and the bobbin turned from the resulting 'sandwich', the thin layers appearing as stripes that may occur along the length of the bobbin or slantwise across it (figure).

lantern bobbin (bobbin) A BOBBIN with a hollow SHANK having slots occasionally sloping but more commonly vertical, usually in sets of two or four, with pairs opposite each other, through which beads, lead shot or bone balls can be seen. The contents are often thought to be inserted through the slots, but the centre can be hollowed out by drilling upwards from the end of the bobbin, and after the contents have been inserted the end is plugged with a small wooden dowel (figure). *See also* BABY BOBBIN, CHURCH WINDOW BOBBIN, PEPPER POT, TWISTED CHAMBER BOBBIN.

lap frame (general) A square EMBROIDERY FRAME that can be held on the lap or, more usually, propped on the arms of a chair.

large snowflake (bobbin) A Flanders filling with pairs travelling across each other, based on a diamond grid (figure a), there are several variants, one of which is illustrated (figure b). *See also* SMALL SNOWFLAKE, SNOWBALL.

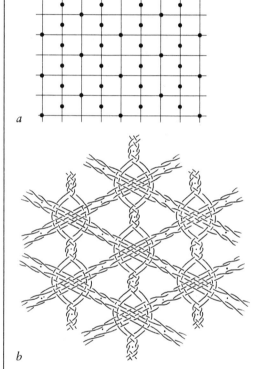

a

b

lark's head (knotting) *See* CLOVE HITCH.

lark's head (tatting) *See* DOUBLE STITCH (tatting).

lattice filling (needle) (1) An open version of TREBLE CORDED BRUSSELS STITCH (figure a, p.131). (2) A needlerun

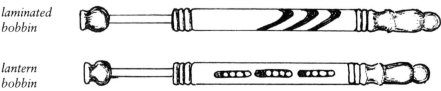

laminated bobbin

lantern bobbin

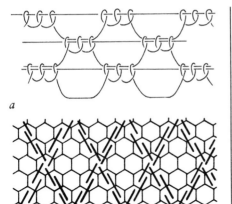

a

b

filling made by stitching double lines of running stitches, passing through every mesh, in two directions so that they cross leaving diamonds of four meshes in the spaces. When the running stitches cross an existing pair the needle passes up or down between the two lines being crossed (figure b).

lattice stitch (bobbin) *See* HALF STITCH.

laying a cord/thread (needle) *See* FIL DE RETOUR.

laying a pair across a gap (bobbin) *See* CONTINENTAL BAR.

laying back pairs (bobbin) *See* HANGING IN PAIRS FOR LATER USE.

laying in pairs (bobbin) A Honiton term. (1) *See* ADDING PAIRS. (2) *See* HANGING IN PAIRS FOR LATER USE.

laying out pairs (bobbin) A Honiton term. *See* THROWING OUT PAIRS.

laying pairs along a gimp (bobbin) *See* CARRYING PAIRS ALONG A GIMP.

lazy loop (bobbin) When a SEWING has to be made through the loops of several pairs, a separate loop of thread may be used instead of a NEEDLEPIN or hook; the loop may be temporarily attached to the top of the pin with a CLOVE HITCH (figure a) or just laid through by the pin (figure b) as the WORKERS pass round the pin. To make the sewing, remove the thread from the pin and open the loop, pass one bobbin, making the sewing, through it and draw through a loop for the other bobbin to pass through. Release one thread of the lazy loop and gently remove it. Also called magic thread. *See also* HELP THREAD.

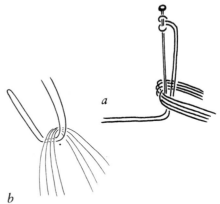

a

b

lazy Susan (bobbin) (1) A needle, sometimes curved, set into a handle with the eye protruding (figure), used for making sewings. The needle is threaded and the ends tied in a knot. Pass the eye, and thread, through the lace leaving loop when the eye is withdrawn, pass one bobbin, making the sewing, through it and use the lazy Susan threads to draw through a loop for the other bobbin to pass through. Also called eyes out. (2) *See* GUARD.

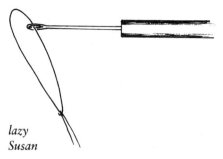

lazy Susan

lea (general) A unit of measurement on which the numbering of some yarns, particularly cotton and linen, is based, one lea being 840 yards for the COTTON COUNT SYSTEM (Ne) and 300 yards for the LINEN SYSTEM (wet spun).

lead(ing) bobbin/thread (bobbin) The bobbin and thread that pass diagonally through POINT GROUND, at any time this bobbin and its thread are to be found at the furthermost point of the row.

leader (bobbin) *See* WORKER.

lead (bobbin) A sheet of lead formerly used by pattern makers, placed below the PATTERN DRAFT and PRICKING to protect the surface beneath while not blunting the PRICKER but still allowing its point to penetrate sufficiently for the pricker to make a hole of the correct size. When the surface of the lead sheet became too pitted it was melted and rolled, to make it smooth.

lead carbonate (general) In the past this poisonous, white powder was used to whiten lace. Motifs were placed in the packet of powder and beaten by hand or shoe heel. When the motifs were dusted off they were startlingly white. However, they would turn black because

of sulphurous compounds in the air. It is difficult to remove.

leadwork (bobbin) A Honiton term for SQUARE-ENDED TALLY.

leaf (bobbin) A leaf-shaped TALLY produced by working a CLOTH STITCH then weaving a single thread across the other three and traditionally finishing with a cloth stitch (figure a). Alternatively, it can be finished by knotting any two adjacent PASSIVE threads (figure b) or making a HALF HITCH round the passive thread with the WORKING THREAD (figure c). Also called pointed tally and wheatear. *See* Appendix for indicator.

a

b   *c*

leaf (needle) Work a BAR IN DOUBLE BUTTONHOLE STITCH to A, the end of the leaf (omitting any stem) on the second side (figure a). Take the needle through to the other side of the bar, work a row of BRUSSELS STITCH for the length of the leaf, take the thread through to the other side of the bar, work back to the starting point along the other side of the bar and continue stitching one or more rows all round (figure b). Finish by working the incomplete section of the bar for the stem. The outer row may be decorated with several picots. This bar may be worked from a WOVEN BAR foundation and be worked in CORDED BUTTONHOLE STITCH.

leaf in three-fold darning (needle and netting) A foundation of four threads is stretched between the two ends of the 'leaf'. SUPPORT THREADS are looped round each side thread of the four and secured so that the side threads are pulled out slightly to make the shape of the leaf. The shape is darned with the tension carefully controlled, so that the shape is not distorted (figure). Remove

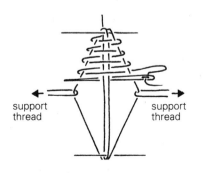

support thread   support thread

the support threads when the leaf is finished. If a more substantial leaf is required, the number of threads laid down and darned over can be increased. *See also* THREE-FOLD DARNING.

leaf in two-fold darning (needle and netting) Lay an even number of threads across the work and take the needle down between them and out to each side in turn. An increased tension, towards the ends, will produce points (figure). *See also* TWO-FOLD DARNING.

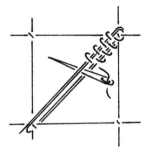

leaf with raised rib (bobbin) (1) *See* LEAF WITH RAISED VEIN. (2) *See* RAISED RIB LEAF.

leaf with raised vein (bobbin) A Honiton leaf with a RAISED EDGE, made by working a RIB up one side, from its base to the tip, TURNING THE PILLOW and then BACKING the leaf to its base, making SEWINGS into the rib (figure a).

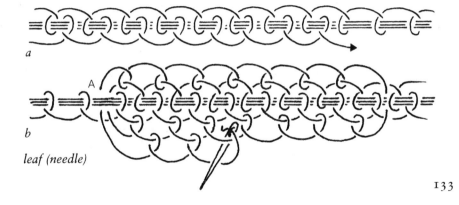

a

b

leaf (needle)

Alternatively, made with a rib down the vein, starting at its top. The pillow is turned and one side of the leaf is backed, sewings being made into the rib, the pillow is turned again at the tip and the second side is backed, again with sewings made into the rib (figure b). *See also* RAISED RIB LEAF.

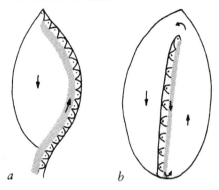

a   b

learning a lace (bobbin) Trying out a new pattern, particularly where judgement is required regarding the numbers of pairs needed in the different parts, and making sure that all the parts balance as regards density of work.

left-handed purl (bobbin) Honiton PURL worked on the left hand side of a braid or RIB. When the RUNNERS reach the left side, TWIST them seven times, place the point of a pin under the thread farthest

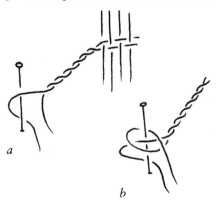

a

b

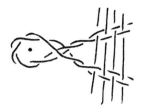

c

from the work, point towards you and pass the point over the bobbin HEAD and into the pinhole in the pricking (figure a). Do not allow the thread to pull tight around the pin at this stage. Take the second thread around the pin in the same direction (figure b). Take up the slack, gently at first with a see-sawing motion, then more firmly. Make two REVERSE TWISTS (figure c).

leg (bobbin) (1) A Bedfordshire term for PLAIT. (2) *See* BAR (general).

lengthening bobbin thread (bobbin) Holding the bobbin horizontally, gently rotate it to unwind the required amount then tighten the hitch by sharply reversing the twist (figure, p.135). *See also* SHORTENING THREAD.

leno weave (weaving) A basic weaving technique where the WARP threads are first twisted one way and then the other, in order to keep the WEFT threads apart. The resulting net has a square mesh suitable for decorating with a needle (figure). It is used as the foundation for BURATO. Also called gauze weave.

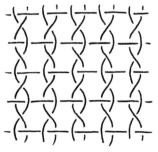

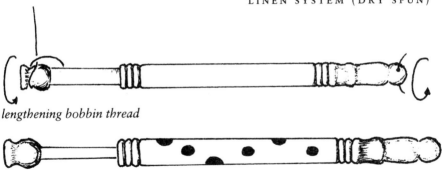

lengthening bobbin thread

leopard

leopard (bobbin) (bobbin) An INLAID BOBBIN having spots produced by inserting metal rods or contrastingly coloured wooden dowels into holes drilled through the SHANK and smoothing them off flush with the surface (figure). Can be used with other forms of inlay. *See also* LEPTIG, PEWTER INLAY.

Leptig (bobbin) A COMPOUND INLAY bobbin having a combination of spots as for a LEOPARD BOBBIN and bands as for a TIGER BOBBIN.

lifter (bobbin) *See* PIN LIFTER.

lifter (needle) A rod, pencil or large-diameter knitting needle used under the COVER CLOTH of a NEEDLE LACE PILLOW to raise the work, making it easier to insert the needle.

lifting lace (bobbin) *See* MOVING UP.

Lille ground/mesh (bobbin) *See* POINT GROUND.

lill(s) pins (general) Short brass pins, approximately 0.55mm in diameter and 14mm long, used for BLOCKING OUT lace.

limmick (bobbin) A North Bucks term for a decorated pin. Until 1824 pin heads were separate rings of wire fixed around the end of a pointed wire and, because these could be removed, beads could be pushed onto one pin and retained in place by the head removed from another pin. Now glue is used to fix the beads in place. *See also* BUGLE, KINGPIN, STRIVER.

line (tambour) Working tambour CHAIN stitch backwards and forwards over one or more lines of MESHES, working into every mesh along the two sides or alternate ones (figure).

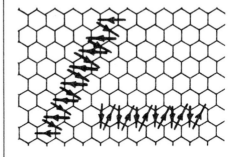

linen (yarn) Yarn spun from fibres obtained from the stem of the FLAX plant.

linen stitch (bobbin) *See* CLOTH STITCH.

linen stitch (needle) *See* CORDED BUTTONHOLE STITCH.

linen system (dry spun) (yarn) Yarn thickness expressed as the weight in pounds of 14,4000 yard of yarn. If the yarn is no. 50, 14,4000 yards will weigh 50lb. *See also* CONVERSION FACTOR, INDIRECT SYSTEM, THREAD COUNT.

linen system (wet spun) (yarn) SINGLES expressed as the number of 300yd hanks (LEAS) per pound weight – i.e., if the yarn is 50s, 50 leas will weigh 1lb. *See also* CONVERSION FACTOR, INDIRECT SYSTEM, YARN COUNT.

lining up (bobbin) *See* INKING IN.

link loop/picot (tatting) A very small PICOT, only sufficiently large to make a JOIN and so avoiding a large amount of 'play' between the sections being joined.

link (stitch) (bobbin) When making ROSE GROUND, the unpinned stitches, coupling the bobbins in pairs, worked between the sets of four pinned stitches.

linked bobbins (bobbin) Two bobbins wound from different ends of the same thread (figure). Also called continuously wound bobbins and coupled/coupling bobbins.

little point (needle) *See* PUNTO AVORIO.

little snowflake (bobbin) *See* SMALL SNOWFLAKE.

little Venice point (needle) *See* POINT DE VENISE.

loading a needle/shuttle (netting) (1) Make a SLIP KNOT at the end of the thread and loop over the TONGUE, take the thread down the SHUTTLE and between the prongs to the other side (figure a). *Turn the shuttle, bring the thread up round the tongue, back down the same side and between the prongs to the other side (figure b). Continue from * as required. (2) For a fine shuttle, pass the end of the thread through the hole and tie, pass the thread through the split in one eye, down the shaft and through the eye at the other end, continue winding as required (figure c).

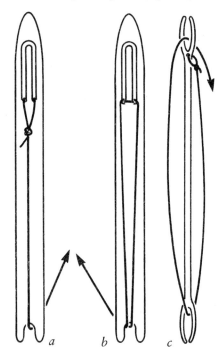

a   *b*   *c*

locking stitch/knot (tatting) One or two single stitch(s), either PLAIN or PURL, that are not CAPSIZED (figure a) and therefore prevent the stitches sliding along the RUNNING THREAD, resulting in the chain turning through a right angle. Use one stitch if the angle is internal (figure b), two if it is external.

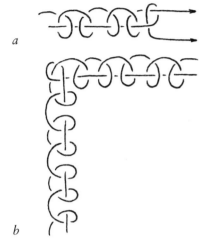

a

b

long loop (netting) The size of the MESH may be increased either by using a wider MESH STICK resulting in all meshes being longer, or by passing the thread twice round the mesh stick (figure). When only selected meshes need be longer, make these by passing the thread twice around the stick, the remainder being made in the usual manner.

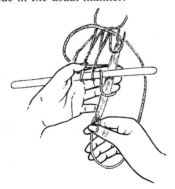

long neck (bobbin) The narrow section of the BOBBIN where the thread is wound.

long picot (tatting) The longer the space left before the second DOUBLE STITCH when making a PICOT, the longer the picot.

long row (bobbin) *See* CONTINUOUS ROW.

long stitch (crochet) In Irish crochet the old name for DOUBLE TREBLE.

long Toms (bobbin) Fine brass pins that were specially made for lacemaking. Also called yellow pins.

long treble (crochet) *See* DOUBLE TREBLE.

loome lace (needle) A term used in the sixteenth and seventeenth centuries, possibly referring to BURATO.

loop join (crochet) A method of joining strips of hairpin crochet by interlocking the loops. *See also* DOUBLE LOOP JOIN, KEY PATTERN JOIN, MULTIPLE LOOP JOIN, SINGLE LOOP JOIN.

loop ornament (netting) Make three meshes into selected meshes. When working the next row, use only the first of the three meshes, leaving the others free.

loop stitch (needle) *See* BUTTONHOLE STITCH. Usually used by embroiderers.

loop(ed) picot (needle) Bring the thread down, round a SUPPORT PIN, back over the FOUNDATION THREAD and down under it. Pass the needle, from right to left, behind the threads supported by the pin and the thread emerging from

under the foundation thread; take this thread back under the needle (figure). Also called simple picot, single picot and Venetian loop picot. Not to be confused with VENETIAN PICOT.

looped cordonnette (needle) BUTTON-HOLED LOOPS worked along the edge while TOP STITCHING. Also called flower couronne and scalloped cordonnette.

looped edge (needle) An edging for Tenerife lace, produced by making a KNOT STITCH on each web thread (figure).

looped interlacing (needle) SURFACE STITCHING on netting and Tenerife lace where the web threads have been pre-grouped to form squares (figure). *See also* INTERLACING.

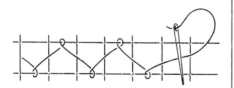

looping a bobbin (bobbin) *See* HITCH-ING A BOBBIN.

loose leaf (needle) Lay a small loop,

returning the needle through the point where the thread emerged and using a SUPPORT THREAD to hold the loop in place. Darn across the two sides of the loop to the end to make the leaf (figure). Sew the thread back through the leaf and remove the support thread. A motif found in reticella.

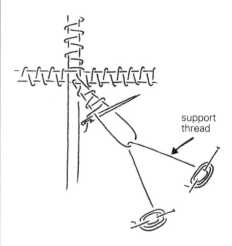

support thread

lovers' knot *See* GAMOURCH.

lozenge (bobbin) *See* DIAMOND.

lucet (knotting) A lyre-shaped imple-ment for making a square cord or lace. Hold between left forefinger and thumb and pass the end of the thread through the hole from back to front, holding it in place with the left thumb. Pass the working thread forwards between the prongs, round the right prong, forwards between them, round the left prong, forwards between them and to the right (figure a). Holding the thread in the left hand as for crochet, loosen the lower loop, on the right prong, and pass over the prong (figure b). * Turn the lucet, right prong towards you, until it faces the other way, lay the thread over the right prong (figure c) and then

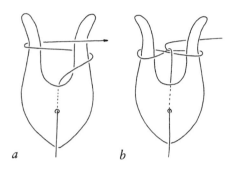

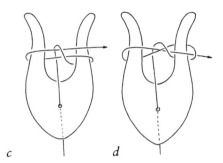

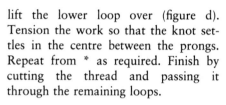

a   b   c   d

lift the lower loop over (figure d). Tension the work so that the knot settles in the centre between the prongs. Repeat from * as required. Finish by cutting the thread and passing it through the remaining loops.

ludwork (bobbin) *See* SQUARE-ENDED TALLY.

lysopol (general) A very mild washing agent, which is used by some conservationists.

M

macro gauze/lace (general) Wall hangings and other items that, while made using lace techniques, are monumental in size and texture, usually used to decorate large spaces such as conference centres.

magic thread (bobbin) *See* LAZY LOOP.

maid (bobbin) *See* HORSE.

maiden's net (bobbin) *See* POINT DE LA VIERGE.

main trail (bobbin) *See* DOMINANT TRAIL.

making a pricking (bobbin) *See* PRICKING (OUT).

Maltese bobbin (bobbin) Unspangled bobbins used in Malta, about 10.5cm (4¼in) long, with a SINGLE HEAD and straight SHANK tapering towards the end where it suddenly widens and ends in a short, straight-sided section. Decoration consists of incised rings (figure).

Maltese pillow (bobbin) *See* SPANISH PILLOW.

manilla card (bobbin) A glazed card produced for electrical insulation, used as a substitute for parchment for making PRICKINGS. *See also* PARCHMENT, PRICKING CARD.

Manlove's thread (yarn) Yarn specially manufactured for Irish crochet. Some references say that it was made of cotton, others that it was of linen. It was of high quality and available in various thicknesses, including very fine.

margin stitch (bobbin) *See* FOOT(SIDE).

Marie Antoinette braid (needle) Machine-made tape with a plain or looped edge, produced for making TAPE LACE.

marker pin (bobbin) A Bedfordshire term for a pricked hole used as an INDICATOR, not as a pinhole, to indicate, for example, a KISS. *See* Appendix.

mat, matt, matte (le) The solidly worked areas of the design. *See also* CLOTH WORK.

matting stitch *See* TALLY.

Mechlin ground/réseau (bobbin) A hexagonal, bobbin-made GROUND, used

Maltese bobbin

in Mechlin lace. Each hexagon consists of two vertical PLAITS of four HALF STITCHES, followed by an extra TWIST on each pair so that the diagonal pairs linking the plaits have a total of two twists (figure). Also called Eis ground, ice ground and, confusingly, sometimes called Brussels bobbin mesh, a term that is also applied to DROSCHEL GROUND.

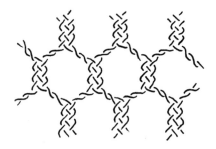

medallion (general) A circular item, where the design is developed by dividing it into a number of equal segments in which the same design, sometimes with alternate sections reversed, is repeated. Frequently made in the round. Particularly used for circular Tenerife lace motifs, when it is also called rosette.

Medici stitch (needle) *See* ARGENTAN GROUND, BRIDES(S) CLAIRE(S).

mending net (general) *See* REPAIRING NET.

mercerized yarn (yarn) A process, developed by John Mercer in 1844, of treating cotton with caustic soda to make it softer, stronger and able to absorb dyes more readily. When carried out while the yarn is under tension, the process imparts a lustrous quality.

merging braids/trails (bobbin) *See* BRAIDS/TRAILS COMBINING.

mesh (general) (1) Individual spaces of an openwork GROUND or net that are typical of that ground or net, its stated size being the length of one of its sides. (2) An area of ground. (3) An abbreviation of MESH GAUGE/STICK. (4) A gauge size for BOSSES.

mesh board /gauge /stick (netting) A flat or cylindrical implement that regulates the size of the mesh when netting is being made. Also called board, gauge, mesh, netting gauge and spool. *See also* FLAT SPOOL/STICK, FISHERMAN'S KNOT, ROUND SPOOL/STICK, SIMPLE KNOT, STICK.

mesh ground (general) A regular GROUND within which motifs are set.

metric system (**Nm**) (yarn) A system of estimating yarn thickness, SINGLES expressed as the number of 1000 metre hanks per kilogram – i.e., if the yarn is 50s (Nm) then 50 1,000m hanks will weigh 1kg. It is used for NATURAL YARNS. *See also* CONVERSION FACTOR, INDIRECT SYSTEM, METRIC NUMBER, YARN COUNT.

metric ticket number (yarn) Yarn thickness expressed as the METRIC SYSTEM (Nm) three-fold equivalent – e.g., 3/60s Nm is metric ticket no. 60; 2/40s is metric ticket no. 60. That is, the metric ticket number is the equivalent SINGLES (Nm) number of the finished yarn multiplied by 3. It is used for SYNTHETIC YARNS. *See also* CONVERSION FACTOR, YARN COUNT.

mezza/mezzo mandolina (netting) Netted lace in which the mesh varies in size.

mezzo punto (needle) An early BOBBIN TAPE LACE.

Midlands bobbin (bobbin) *See* EAST MIDLANDS BOBBIN, SOUTH BUCKS BOBBIN.

midrib (general) A central vein through a leaf.

mirror ground (bobbin) *See* BRABANT GROUND.

miniature bobbin (bobbin) A tiny bobbin placed inside a BABY BOBBIN.

minor laces (general) Laces not entirely made using BOBBINS, or needle lace based on BUTTONHOLE STITCHES. They include needle laces based on techniques other than buttonhole stitches, those made using a needle to decorate fabric, and those made using implements other than bobbins or needles, such as tatting. Also called craft laces.

minor trail (bobbin) *See* SECONDARY TRAIL.

mistake made when pricking (bobbin) An unwanted hole ringed with a waterproof pen. It should not be confused with the INDICATOR for a RAISED or ROLLED TALLY, which looks the same but is found well within an area, whereas a mistake will usually be close to other pinholes. *See* Appendix.

mittens (bobbin) A Honiton WORKED VEIN produced by creating a division in WHOLE STITCH. Level with the first INDICATOR pinhole, with the RUNNERS at one EDGE, the DOWNRIGHTS are divided into two sections with the odd pair, if present, on the side away from the runners. The inner pairs from the sections work a HALF STITCH and the resulting pair furthest from the runners become runners and work towards the other edge. * The two pairs of runners work

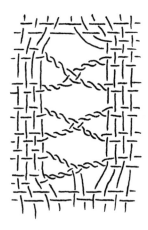

to the centre, TWIST twice, work whole stitch and twist twice. Repeat from * until level with the last indicator hole. Close the division when the runners are at the edges, by working a REVERSED HALF STITCH. Check which pair is to continue as runners and bring the other pair of runners through the first downright pair (figure). If the pattern widens the pairs can be twisted three times at the centre to open the division, reducing to two twists before it closes, and work to the other edge. Also called buckle stitch. *See* Appendix for worked vein indicator.

mixed lace (general) Lace made using more than one technique, usually a combination of bobbin and needle lace.

mock footside (bobbin) *See* FALSE FOOT.

mock ring (tatting) A CHAIN that bends round into a circle, imitating a RING.

mode (general) *See* FILLING.

mother and/in/'n babe (bobbin) A wooden or bone BABY BOBBIN having a hollowed SHANK with slots through which a MINIATURE BOBBIN, the babe, can be seen. *See also* COW AND CALF, GRANDMOTHER BOBBIN.

mottled bobbin (bobbin) A bobbin treated with AQUA FORTIS (also called AGNES FORTY), usually applied only to patches to give a tortoiseshell appearance (figure). Aqua fortis is very dangerous and should not be used without training.

mottled bobbin (bobbin) *See* INSCRIBED BOBBIN.

mouche (bobbin) A mistranslation from French. *See* BEE.

moulded pillow (bobbin) A pillow made, in a mould, from POLYSTYRENE or STYROFOAM. *See also* CARVED PILLOW.

mounting fabric in a frame (general) *See* STRETCHING FABRIC IN A FRAME.

mounting lace (general) A process of attaching lace to fabric or other material for the purpose of future use or display.

mourning bobbin (bobbin) Traditionally, when a loved one died the BOTTOM BEAD of a bobbin would be exchanged for a black one. After a family bereavement all the beads on a bobbin could be exchanged for black.

mousehole ring (tatting) *See* SPLIT RING.

moving up (bobbin) Relocating the PRICKING on the PILLOW, while lace is being made. (1) Secure the bobbins in a bundle within a COVER CLOTH and slide them up slightly to remove any tension on the threads, pin the bundle securely

to the pillow, remove all the pins. Holding the bundle of bobbins remove the pin securing it and relocate the pricking and re-pin the bundle of bobbins securely to the pillow, replace the lace on the pattern, replace sufficient pins, release bobbins and untangle them. (2) Place a BRIDGE beneath the pricking and work up onto it, the pins only passing into the bridge and not the pillow, secure the bobbins in a bundle within a cover cloth, slide them up to remove any tension on the threads and pin the bundle securely to the pillow, remove any pins still in the pillow, holding the bundle of bobbins remove the pin securing it, relocate the bridge and pricking and re-pin the bundle of bobbins securely to the pillow, release bobbins and untangle them. Also called lifting lace, PUTTING BACK and setting up.

multi-needle (needle) A gadget similar to the DAISY WINDER, differing by having the knob extended to form a handle

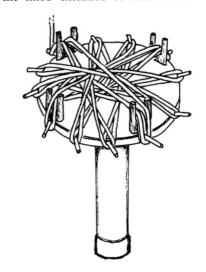

mottled bobbin

and a removable fitting, over which the threads are wound, that increases the length of some loops, resulting in square motifs (figure).

multi-sewing (bobbin) Where a single SEWING is made through loops from several pairs, more easily made using a LAZY LOOP or LAZY SUSAN than the conventional crochet hook.

multiple loop join (crochet) A method for joining strips of hairpin crochet, made as SINGLE LOOP JOIN but picking up more than two loops at a time instead of one, passing the hook through from front to back for each, and pulling all through the previous set of loops. *See also* LOOP JOIN.

multiple-pair plait (bobbin) (1) Work a plait with more than two pairs of bobbins in rows of half stitch, starting with the two right hand pairs and working towards the left. No pins are used, and there are no 'return rows' working towards the right. The best places for FIRMING UP are after the 'two over three' of the first stitch and the 'two over three' of the last stitch of the row. When two picots are at the same level, one on

either side of the plait, make both after completing a row (figure).
(2) Make a THREE- or FOUR-THREAD PLAIT using multiple threads instead of single threads. *See also* DOUBLE PLAIT. (3) THREE PAIR PLAIT. *See* Appendix for indicator.

mushroom pillow (bobbin) A slightly domed, circular, FLAT PILLOW (figure). Also called COOKIE PILLOW. *See also* U-SHAPED PILLOW.

N

named bobbin (bobbin) A BOBBIN inscribed with a person's name, usually that of the lacemaker, a member of his or her family or a loved one.

natural yarn (yarn) Yarn that is produced from natural fibres, such as cotton, linen, silk and wool.

Nazareth stitch (needle) *See* RODI STITCH.

neat (tambour) Zigzagging closely from one mesh to the next, working either along a row or diagonally, gives a more solid line. It can be used for overcasting (figure).

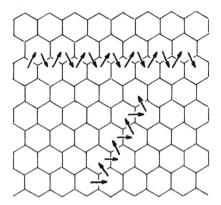

neck (bobbin) The narrow part of a BOBBIN, between the HEAD and the SHANK, on which the thread is wound. Also occasionally called shank.

needle (netting) *See* NETTING NEEDLE.

needle lace pillow (needle) A small PILLOW, of the BOLSTER variety, to which needle lace can be attached while it is being made. An average size is a diameter of about 14cm (5½in) and a length of about 30cm (12in). *See also* LIFTER.

needle(made) lace (needle) Lace made using a needle and thread.

needlepin (bobbin) A sewing needle, usually no. 8 or finer, set in a handle and used for taking NEEDLEPIN SEWINGS in Honiton lace. A good needlepin handle will taper towards the needle (figure).

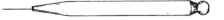

needlepin sewing (bobbin) Traditionally Honiton SEWINGS are made with a needlepin. One method is to insert the needlepin under the BAR, or EDGE PAIR, holding it as shown, arranging the pillow so that its tip points directly towards you (figure). Take the thread under the tip of the needle holding both hands level. (Ideally the thread should come from behind the point at which the sewing is to be made, if not and if the sewing is difficult, pin the thread behind but do not forget to release immediately the sewing has been made.) Holding a slight tension on the bobbin thread bring both hands towards you, the tip of the needlepin may enter the pinhole for a moment, then continue the movement until both hands face palm down. The thread should now lie on the top of the point of the needlepin to be lifted up while the bobbin thread tension is released – i.e., lift both hands upwards while continuing the turning movement slightly, allowing the bobbin to go closer to the lace. If the thread approaches from the left the head of the bobbin is held behind the needlepin with its head to the right. *See also* EDGE SEWING, SELF-SEWING, TOP SEWING.

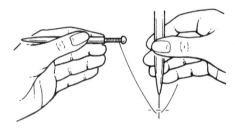

needlepoint lace (needle) Needle lace that is made using BUTTONHOLE STITCH and its variants. Not to be confused with counted thread embroidery called needlepoint.

needlerun (needle) A lace effect produced by embroidering machine net. When the stitches result in enlarging some of the MESHES it can be called openwork on net.

net/net filling (bobbin) *See* TROLLY NET.

net (general) The name for fine, simple GROUNDS of both hand- and machine-made lace. *See also* BOBBIN NET and BOBBINET.

net embroidery (needle) *See* NEEDLERUN LACE.

net (groundwork) stitch (netting) *See* FILET STITCH.

net stitch (bobbin) (1) *See* POINT GROUND STITCH. (2) *See* HALF STITCH.

net stitch (needle) *See* BRUSSELS STITCH.

netting (netting) A fabric consisting of a simple openwork mesh, particularly that made in the same way as fishing and trapping nets. Also called filet net and net work. *See also* FISHERMAN'S KNOT, PLAIN NETTING, SIMPLE KNOT, SQUARE NETTING, WORKING IN THE ROUND.

netting frame (netting) A square or rectangular frame, usually of stout wire,

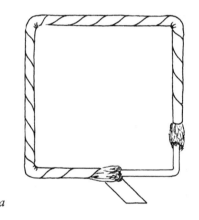

a

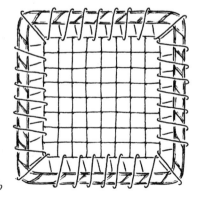

b

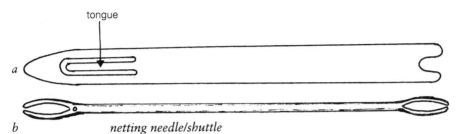

tongue

a

b   *netting needle/shuttle*

in which NETTING is stretched while it is being decorated. The frame needs to be prepared by being tightly bound with tape approximately 1.25cm (½in) wide with or without wadding. Sew the end to secure (figure a). The netting to be decorated is secured into the frame by lacing it in place (figure b).

netting gauge/stick (netting) *See* MESH BOARD/GAUGE/STICK.

netting knot (netting) *See* FISHERMAN'S KNOT, SIMPLE KNOT.

netted lace (netting) *See* NETTING.

netting needle/shuttle (netting) An implement for holding the thread while NETTING. There are several styles. The most popular for general use is flat, pointed at one end with a shallow fork at the other and a TONGUE in the centre (figure a). A long, narrow rod with flattened, split eyes at both ends is commonly used for fine work (figure b). *See also* LOADING A NEEDLE.

netting onto a handle/ring (netting) Tie the thread to the handle/ring and use the SIMPLE KNOT, allowing the knot to settle just below the ring (figure).

network (netting) *See* NETTING.

new middled (general) (1) The process of removing the lace edging from a worn

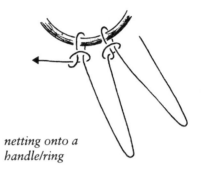

netting onto a handle/ring

out article and remounting it around new fabric. (2) Re-stuffing a pillow that has become soft in the centre.

nib (needle) A decoration on Branscombe lace BARS. The FOUNDATION THREADS of the bar are laid and the bar BUTTONHOLED as far as the centre. Lay a thread, making the next stitch further along the bar and work about eight buttonhole stitches back over this thread only (figure a). Slide the first stitch of this group (made over the foundation threads), to meet the first half of the buttonholed bar to make the nib, and

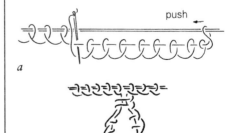

push

a

b

work two stitches around its neck to 'strangle' it (figure b).

nine-pin edging (bobbin) A HEADSIDE of PLAITS and PICOTS, where one or more plaits of two pairs loop out from the pattern and are held in place by one or more plaits crossing the loops with WINDMILLS. Where there are two or more sets of loops, they may cross with windmills. The number of picots may vary from pattern to pattern and there may, or may not, be a pin between the exit and re-entry points of each loop to the braid. The 'nine' refers to the number of pins often found on each loop – i.e., the exit and re-entry points, the windmills and the picots (numbered on the figure). This edging is typically found in Bedfordshire lace. The illustration shows a basic form but there are many variants (figure).

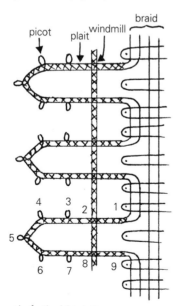

picot plait windmill braid
4 3 2 1
5
6 7 8 9

no stitch (bobbin) *See* HALF STITCH.

no-pin filling (bobbin) A Honiton filling consisting totally of LEADWORKS that are unsupported by pins. Always use the DOWNRIGHT pair, either to make the next leadwork or to sew out, before using the WORKING BOBBIN, and make sure that the working bobbin from one leadwork continues as the working bobbin for the next leadwork. Downrights should be FIRMED UP before sewing out (figure). Also called swing filling/leadworks.

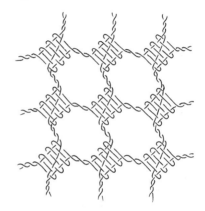

node stitch (tatting) The repeated alternation of two similar stitches – i.e. two PLAIN stitches followed by two PURL, repeated (figure).

non-continuous lace (general) *See* PART LACE.

nook pin (bobbin) The pin supporting a GIMP indented into the CLOTHWORK, with the pin also supporting the WORKERS (usually TWISTED twice). Workers or PASSIVES may change roles. If the gimp passes through one or more pairs of passives before meeting the workers, these pairs are not twisted before the gimp returns through them. There is no stitch worked at this pin. (1) When the gimp indents into the side of the clothwork, the worker crosses the gimp, passes round the nook pin and returns as the worker. There may be one or more passive pairs bridging the gimp (figure a). (2) When two cloth stitch sections join the workers from one section, cross the gimp and pass round the nook pin and back across the gimp, they remain there as a passive pair. The workers from the other section continue across the combined sections (figure b). (3) When clothwork divides, the workers continue to make one section and either the gimp is taken round and up to the point of division or a new gimp is introduced. The next passive pair is taken across the gimp and makes two twists as

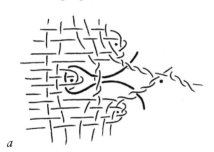

a

b

c

it passes round the nook pin, it recrosses the gimp and becomes the working pair for the other section (figure c).

noose (bobbin) (1) *See* HITCH. (2) *See* SLIP KNOT.

noose (general) A loop secured by a knot that tightens when one thread is pulled.

noquette (bobbin) A collar of thin horn, parchment, celluloid or acetate, sometimes secured round the neck of a bobbin with stitches, and used to keep the thread clean (figure).

stitches

nozzle (bobbin) (1) The socket in a CANDLE BLOCK/STOOL that holds the candle. It is adjustable so that the height of the candle can be altered as it burns lower. (2) The socket of a BOBBIN WINDER that holds the bobbin.

numbering bobbins (bobbin) Bobbins are always numbered from the left, unless otherwise instructed, and they are renumbered immediately after any action.

nuns' work (bobbin) An old term for BOBBIN LACE.

nutting day (tradition) 3 September, the first day of the season when candles were used in the Honiton lace schools.

O

occhiwork (tatting) Another name for tatting.

oeil de perdrix (bobbin) *See* PARTRIDGE EYE FILLING.

off-loom weaving (bobbin) Another name for BOBBIN LACE.

off-set footside (bobbin) The FOOTSIDE and CATCH PIN rows of Bucks point lace are not pricked in line with the adjacent GROUND, because to do so would result in distortion of the ground. To make the distance between the catch pin pair and the next ground pair (A) the same as the

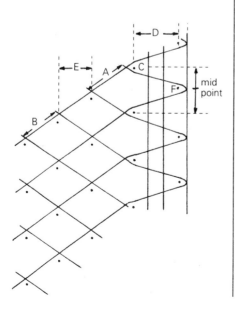

distance between two ground pairs (B), the catch pin (C) must be pricked at a wider vertical spacing (D) than the ground while remaining in line with the diagonal rows of the ground. The footside pins (E) must also lie with a wider vertical spacing (F), usually about the same as the space between the ground and catch pins to allow for the two PASSIVE pairs, and be placed midway between the catch pins. The actual amount of extra space allowed depends on the relative thickness of the thread, a finer thread requiring less extra space than a coarser one (figure). In practice these distances are not measured but are estimated by eye.

oil cloth (general) *See* ARCHITECTS' LINEN.

old maid (bobbin) A plain, slender EAST MIDLANDS BOBBIN.

one-piece lace (general) *See* CONTINUOUS (THREAD) LACE.

one-two-three stitch (bobbin) *See* CLOTH STITCH.

one-two-three stitch (needle) A filling composed of single rows of BRUSSELS STITCH, POINT DE SORRENTO and GREEK NET STITCH, worked in that order.

opaque lace (bobbin) *See* TISSUE LACE.

open (needle) When applied to a stitch, the term indicates that it is spaced from the previous one.

open buttonhole filling (needle) *See* POINT DE VENISE.

open-centred braid (bobbin) A braid with a patterned section through the centre, such as DIVIDED BRAID/TRAIL, MITTENS and twisted vein.

open-centred spider (bobbin) A motif started as a SPIDER, but the last 'legs' entering return, or pass through the centre, and make a stitch outside before returning. The spider is completed as usual (figure). *See also* GERMAN SPIDER.

open edge (bobbin) An edge made when the WORKERS are TWISTED before and after working the EDGE STITCH.

open stitches (needle) A series of enlarged stitches used to form divisions, such as veins, usually in CORDED BUTTON-HOLE STITCH, or to surround a section. After a row of corded buttonhole stitch, WHIP back to the start, working once only into alternate stitches (figure a). Work a row of stitches, making only one onto each space that was not whipped,

and whip back once through each stitch (figure b). Return to the original number of stitches by working two stitches into each space and making this the next row of corded buttonhole stitch (figure c).

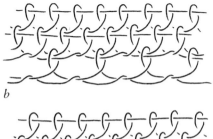

a

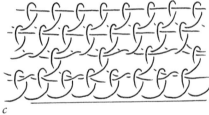

b

c

open torchon fan (bobbin) *See* SPANISH FAN.

opening (needle) *See* BUD (needle).

openwork on net (needle) Hand embroidered machine net. *See* NEEDLERUN.

ordinary cobweb (needle) *See* SORRENTO WHEEL.

ordinary sewing (bobbin) *See* EDGE SEWING.

ornamental turning (bobbin) A BOBBIN with a decorative shape produced while being turned on a lathe. *See also* BALUSTER-TURNED BOBBIN.

ornamented bobbin (bobbin) A BOBBIN decorated so that is looks attractive. The ornamentation has no significance in terms of the lace made. Some decorations can, in fact, be annoying when the bobbin is in use.

outlining pair (bobbin) *See* RING PAIR.

oval (tatting) *See* RING.

over and under joins (tatting) *See* UNDER AND OVER JOINS.

over-stitching (needle) The term used when a completed needle-made GROUND is decorated with further stitching.

over turning (tatting) Reversing the direction of the stitches at a set point, usually at a JOIN or PICOT.

overcast bar (needle) *See* TWISTED BAR.

overhand knot (netting) A knot made by looping the FREE END around the STANDING END (figure).

overlaid leaf/plait/tally (bobbin) A leaf, usually pointed, made using two pairs lifted from CLOTH or HALF STITCH. The cloth or half stitch is continued for a few rows, this being the length of the leaf, before the pairs of the leaf are absorbed back into the stitching by replacing them into the next row. Also called raised leaf/plait/tally, shell and surface tally. *See* Appendix for indicator.

oya(h) (needle) *See* BEBILLA.

P

packet (bobbin) *See* FLANDERS GROUND.

packet (yarn) A group of four PARCELS of SLIP THREAD, usually weighing 2oz (approximately 57g).

padding cord (crochet) Thick thread over which stitches are worked in Irish crochet. Its purpose is to thicken the work, and it results in the three-dimensional effect that is typical of the lace. Traditionally, it was a smooth, thick linen thread the same colour as the working thread although of heavier grade.

padding threads (needle) Threads, laid with the FOUNDATION THREAD, over which TOP STITCHING is worked. Their purpose is to thicken the work, resulting in the three-dimensional effect, called RAISED EDGE/WORK, frequently used in needle lace.

pair (bobbin) With a few exceptions, bobbins are always used in pairs. Also called couple. *See* Appendix for Bedfordshire indicator.

paired gimps (bobbin) *See* CABLE GIMP, CHAIN GIMP, RAISED GIMP.

palm (bobbin) *See* FEATHER, SPANISH FAN.

parcel (yarn) A continuous skein of SLIP THREAD, weighing ¼oz or ½oz (7–14g), which was divided into individual slips by a thick, coloured thread. *See also* PACKET (yarn).

parchment (bobbin) (1) The skin, usually of calf, sheep or goat, specially prepared for writing on and used for making PRICKINGS. Its special qualities are its resistance to tearing and general wear, and its translucence. MANILLA CARD is a suitable substitute. (2) Pricking made on any material.

parchment lace (bobbin) *See* CARTISAN(E).

parfilage (yarn) *See* DRIZZLING.

Paris fan (bobbin) *See* FRENCH FAN.

Paris/Parisian ground (bobbin) *See* KAT STITCH.

part lace (bobbin) Lace that is worked in small sections, joined together by SEWINGS and with any BARS or GROUND added later. Also called à pièces rapportées, free lace, non-continuous lace, piece(d) lace, sectional lace and sprig lace. *See also* CONTINUOUS LACE.

partridge eye filling (bobbin) A hole produced in the CLOTHWORK of Flemish laces where pairs are united around four pins with CLOTH AND TWIST (figure a) or

a

b

HALF STITCH (figure b). Two pairs, one either side of the top pin, are TWISTED and worked together. The two pairs of WORKERS (the second usually being the PASSIVE PAIR adjacent to the pairs that worked the top pin) work until they reach the centre pairs, twist, work with the nearest of the centre pairs and return to their original sides after pins have been set. The centre pairs work together and a pin is set between them. If the second pair of workers were passives adjacent to the centre pairs, they are returned, usually to the other side. Sometimes used in the centre of a SNOWFLAKE, the term can also apply to snowflake grounds containing this hole. Also called oeil de perdrix.

pass (bobbin) (1) A HALF STITCH that COVERS A PIN. (2) The movement of the working thread from one side to the other and back when making a tally.

passement (bobbin) Elaborate braids, often made from metallic yarns, from which bobbin lace developed, usually applied to clothing.

passive (bobbin) A pair of bobbins (or a single bobbin) that is replaced in its former position, or approximately so, after making a stitch with the WORKERS. Called downrights by Honiton workers; also called tracers, tracer/tracing threads and warps.

passive chain (tatting) A CHAIN with PICOTS to which the current ACTIVE CHAIN joins.

pattern draft (bobbin) A prepared pattern at the end of the drawing stage, usually still bearing the marks of its construction and often with some indication of how it is to be worked. The figure, for example, shows the pattern draft for a SIMPLE FAN. Not to be confused with INDICATOR, THREAD DIAGRAM or SCHEMATIC DIAGRAM.

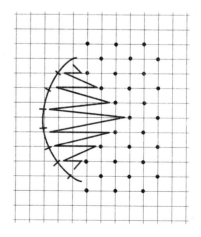

pattern foundation (crochet) The BACKING for Irish crochet consisting of glazed linen, brown paper or other backing onto which the pattern is drawn. The completed motifs are securely tacked to the backing and GROUND worked between them, holding them together. *See also* EMERALD FOUNDATION.

pea (bobbin) A small round or oval CLOTH STITCH motif, of which there are many variants, surrounded by a RING PAIR, sometimes with a small hole, PARTRIDGE EYE or other decoration (but never a pin) in the centre, sometimes with a GIMP surrounding the cloth stitch. Found in Flanders lace (figure).

pea stitch (needle) A FILLING, of which there are many variants, worked in BRUSSELS STITCH, with spaces producing a regular pattern of holes. Start with a row of fairly close buttonhole stitches.

  row 1: *work one stitch into each of the first two loops, miss two loops, repeat from * to end

  row 2: **work one stitch between the pair of stitches and a set of three into the long loop, repeat from ** to end

  row 3: *work one stitch into each of the two loops of the sets of three stitches of the previous row

Repeat rows 2 and 3 as required (figure). Also called perforated net.

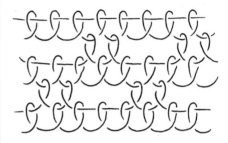

pearl (general) *See* PICOT.

pearl bar/tie (bobbin) *See* PURL-PIN BAR.

pearl chain (tatting) *See* DOUBLE PEARL CHAIN, SINGLE PEARL CHAIN.

pearl edge (bobbin) An edge decorated with PEARLS. *See also* PURL EDGE.

pea bobbin

pearl-pin bar (bobbin) *See* PURL-PIN BAR.

pearling (needle) *See* PURLING.

peel (bobbin) A local name for a PILLOW in Malmesbury.

penknife bobbin (bobbin) As the name implies, a BOBBIN made by whittling with a knife. Also called chip-carved bobbin and pocketknife bobbin.

pepper pot (bobbin) A wooden or bone BOBBIN that has a hollowed SHANK with slots through which peppercorns can be seen (figure). *See also* TWISTED CHAMBER BOBBIN.

perforated net (needle) *See* PEA STITCH.

perl(e) (general) *See* PICOT.

perlin(g) (needle) *See* PURLING.

petit point de Venise (needle) *See* POINT DE VENISE.

petit réseau (needle) *See* ALENÇON GROUND/MESH.

pewter inlay (bobbin) BUTTERFLY, LEOPARD and TIGER bobbins with pewter inlay. When the bobbins are wooden, the pewter tends to corrode in time, a chemical reaction between pewter and wood. Poor quality pewter resists corrosion better than the better qualities.

pick up the thread (crochet) *See* YARN OVER HOOK.

picking up (bobbin) A term used when a pair left out when working one section of the lace is brought into use when working another section.

picot (bobbin) Also called pearl(e), perl(e), purl(e), spine, thorn and turn pin. *See* CAUGHT PICOT, DOUBLE CAUGHT PICOT, DOUBLE PICOT, HEAD PIN, INNER PURL, LEFT-HAND PURL, RIGHT-HAND PURL, SINGLE LOOP PICOT and Appendix for indicator.

picot (general) A small loop used to decorate the edge, BARS and so on. Also called pearl(e), perl(e), purl and thorn. In many laces made by working two stitches next to each other – for example, Armenian, netting and tatting – the picot is the loop of intervening thread.

picot (needle) (1) In Armenian lace, make a loop into a row of loops and another into the same place (figure). (2) *See* BULLION (STITCH) PICOT, BUTTON-HOLED LOOPS, LOOPED PICOT, VENETIAN PICOT.

picot (tatting) Make a PLAIN stitch and hold it about the width of two stitches from the previous stitch, make a PURL stitch against the first half and push the completed DOUBLE STITCH against the previous one (figure). *See* LONG PICOT, SHORT PICOT.

pepper pot

Picot edge (general) An edge decorated with a row of PICOTS. *See also* PURL EDGE.

picot edge (needle) An edging for Tenerife lace in which both threads supported by a single pin are KNOTTED together with short sections of thread left between (figure).

piece(d) lace (bobbin) *See* PART LACE.

pillow (general) A piece of equipment to which the pattern and/or lace is pinned while lace is made. Also called cushion and fat hen. *See also* BOLSTER, FLAT PILLOW, FRENCH PILLOW, HONITON PILLOW, MUSHROOM PILLOW, NEEDLE LACE PILLOW, PEEL, ROUND PILLOW, SPANISH PILLOW, SQUARE PILLOW, SWEDISH PILLOW, TRAVELLING PILLOW.

pillow cloth (bobbin) The COVER CLOTH that protects the PILLOW from becoming soiled or damaged.

pillow horse/stand (bobbin) *See* HORSE.

pillow weight (bobbin) A weight with a sharp hook or tab, by which it is attached to the back of a ROUND PILLOW, or a ROLLER set in a pillow, that prevents the pillow from rotating while lace is being made.

pin (bobbin) *See* BRASS PINS.

pin (tatting) *See* TATTING PIN.

pin after two (bobbin) *See* FOOTSIDE.

pin by/on pin sewing (bobbin) The process of SEWING where two Honiton EDGES meet, each having its own pinhole. As the RUNNERS of the second braid reach their pinhole, TWIST three times and WHOLE STITCH with the EDGE PAIR, make an EDGE SEWING into the pinhole of the first braid and return through the edge pair. Twist both pairs three times and continue (figure).

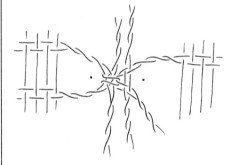

pin down (bobbin) Pushing pins down, particularly when making Honiton lace, so that the bobbins may use the space above them. To prevent the heads jamming or forming STAIRS, either remove alternate pins and push the remaining ones flush with the pillow (this may result in a wavy finish to the edge) or push down alternate pins, then the remainder. Even if these BRIDGE, the slight increase in height is negligible. Cover the pinheads with a COVER CLOTH or SLIDER before working over them.

pin (hole) side (bobbin) The side of a RIB supported by pins. Also called hole side. *See also* PLAIN SIDE.

pin lifter (bobbin) A small implement (figure) for lifting pinheads of pins that have been pushed down hard into a

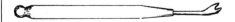

pillow. Care must be taken to avoid cutting threads when using. Also called lifter, push-me-pull-you.

pin out (general) *See* BLOCKING OUT.

pin spot inlay (bobbin) *See* PINNED BOBBIN.

pin stitch (mounting) The lace is tacked to the fabric, the thread fastened on at A, just below the lace, and a small stitch taken from B to the same point A (figure a). The needle is reinserted at B to come out at C, just within the lace (figure b), with the result that two threads lie

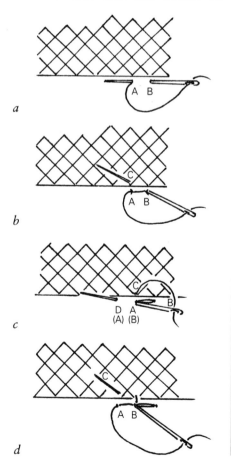

a

b

c

d

between points A and B. The needle is reinserted at A and a stitch taken to D. Rename D as A and A as B (figure c) and complete the next pin stitch (figure d). Continue as required, remove the tacking and trim away all the excess fabric. Pin stitch should be worked with a strong tension, bunching the threads of the fabric tightly together and leaving holes between the stitches. It is the tight stitches that prevent the fabric fraying. This method of mounting is more suitable for use with very fine fabrics such as lingerie silk, and it can be used around curves.

pin under four (bobbin) The term used when the pin is placed inside the STITCH ABOUT THE PIN when working a FOOT-SIDE.

pin under two (bobbin) *See* TWO TWIST EDGE.

pin-vice (bobbin) A pencil-shaped implement having a chuck or screw to hold a needle firmly in the end. The needle can be replaced when necessary. *See also* PRICKER.

pin work (bobbin) *See* BOBBIN LACE.

pincushion (bobbin) An item of equipment for holding pins not currently in use, usually firmly stuffed with sawdust or raw wool, the lanolin of which oils pins slightly and helps to reduce rusting. *See also* EMERY PINCUSHION, STRAWBERRY PINCUSHION.

pinhole (bobbin) (1) A hole in a PRICK-ING into which a pin is inserted when lace is made. If an extra pinhole has been made by mistake, a ring should be drawn around it indicating that it should not be used. (2) A space left when a pin is removed (figure). *See also* HOLE IN CLOTH STITCH, HOLE IN HALF STITCH, PLAIN HOLE.

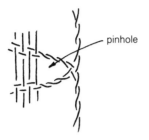

pinhole

pinhole (needle) *See* BUD (needle).

pinhole edge/side (bobbin) The side of a RIB where EDGE STITCHES are made along the single row of pins.

pinhole ground (bobbin) *See* SPANISH GROUND.

pinned bobbin (bobbin) A decoration of pins forced into the shank of a bobbin and cut off flush with its surface, sometimes used to form inscriptions. Also called brass pinned bobbin and pin spot inlay.

pinwork (needle) *See* FLY (STITCH).

piquéd bobbin (bobbin) *See* COLOURED DOTS ON BOBBINS.

pita thread (yarn) Thread that is made from leaf fibres of the century plant (Agave americana). It is washable but should not be exposed to sunlight while it is wet.

pivot (bobbin) When a sharp turn is required in Bruges lace several rows may all travel to one pin, the PIVOT PIN (P) on the inside of the turn (figure a). Each time the WORKERS approach the pivot pin, they do not make a stitch with the

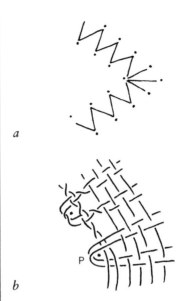

a

b

last pair of PASSIVES but pass over them, TWIST three times and return, passing under the same passives (figure b), the twisted workers of successive rows stacking up on the pivot pin. The next pin on the inside of the turn is worked as usual. At this point, remove the pivot pin and take up the slack on the passives. The pivot pin is not replaced. This is only one of several similar methods.

pivot loop (needle) In Tenerife lace the loop through which the thread passes after making each spoke of the web of a SHELL.

pivot pin (bobbin) A pin at the inside of a sharp turn, used several times. *See also* PIVOT.

plain (tatting) Hold the thread as for making a CHAIN or RING and pass the

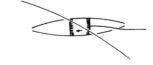

a

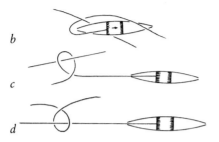

SHUTTLE under the thread across the fingers (figure a), pass the shuttle back over the thread (figure b). The shuttle thread makes a loop around the thread (figure c), and when you pull the shuttle thread and CAPSIZE the knot, the thread makes a loop around the shuttle thread (figure d). This is the first half of a DOUBLE STITCH.

plain crochet (crochet) *See* DOUBLE CROCHET.

plain edge/side (bobbin) The unpinned edge of Honiton RIBS and PURL-PIN BARS. Also called free edge. (1) Twist the RUNNERS once when they reach this

edge, leave them and return with the adjacent pair of DOWNRIGHTS as runners (figure a). (2) Return from this edge, with the same pair of runners (figure b). (3) The runners and last pair of downrights, at this edge, make a TURNING STITCH and the second pair from the edge returns as runners (figure c).

plain filet (netting) *See* SQUARE NETTING.

plain hole ground (bobbin) *See* TORCHON GROUND.

plain hole (bobbin) With the RUNNERS at the edge, divide DOWNRIGHTS into two equal sections, half stitch the two centre pairs, bring runners through to make a TURNING STITCH with the nearest of the centre pairs, return and MAKE UP THE EDGE. Take the other centre pair, as runners, out to the other edge, make up the edge, return to the centre and make a REVERSE HALF STITCH with the centre pairs. Use the original runners to continue (figure). This is useful when turning a corner. Also called pinhole. *See also* HOLE IN CLOTH STITCH, HOLE IN HALF STITCH *and* Appendix for indicator.

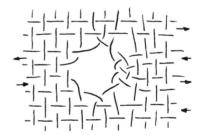

plain netting (netting) Filet net made by working one stitch into each mesh for each row without increasing or decreasing (figure). Also called diamond filet/net. Not to be confused with SQUARE NETTING.

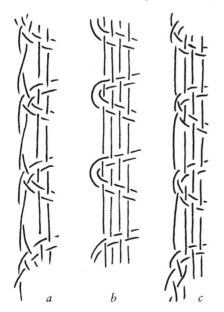

a b c

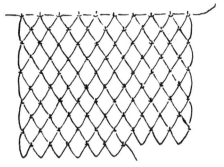

plain shank (bobbin) An undecorated BOBBIN with a plain turned SHANK.

plain work (general) *See* CLOTH WORK.

plait (bobbin) (1) A narrow connection made by working a series of HALF STITCHES with the same two pairs. It can be made with more pairs (figure). Also called bar, braid, half stitch bar. *See also* DOUBLE PLAIT, LEG, MULTIPLE-PAIR PLAIT, THREE PAIR PLAIT and Appendix for indicator. (2) In Bedfordshire lace a SQUARE-ENDED TALLY. *See also* BARLEY-CORN, GATE, LADDER.

plaited filling/ground (bobbin) The name that can be applied to any FILLING in Bedfordshire lace, mainly composed of PLAITS (TALLIES), particularly DIAMOND FILLING/GROUND.

plaited lace (bobbin) Lace consisting almost exclusively of PLAITS and LEAVES.

plat (needle) Flat (Fr.).

play pillow (bobbin) A pillow on which a child makes what he or she likes, as opposed to the one used for learning lacemaking.

plume (bobbin) *See* FEATHER.

ply (yarn) A yarn produced by twisting two, or more, SINGLES together. *See also* CORD, FOLD.

pocketknife bobbin (bobbin) *See* PENKNIFE BOBBIN.

point (general) Stitch (Fr.).

point à la vierge (bobbin) *See* POINT DE (LA) VIERGE.

point d'Alençon (needle) *See* ALENÇON GROUND/MESH.

point d'Angleterre bar (needle) A line of BAR ROSETTES divided by interlaced threads (figure).

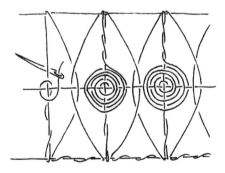

point d'Angleterre edging (needle)

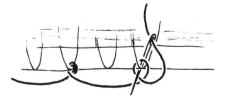

An edging of loops anchored by two BUTTONHOLE STITCHES, the thread of the second passing through the first (figure). Usually used for edging TAPE LACE. *See also* POINT DE SORRENTO.

point d'Angleterre filling/ground (needle) Lay a SQUARE FOUNDATION of threads across a space. The working thread is fastened on and whipped along one of the threads until it reaches a cross thread. A small rosette is worked with the working thread passing over, under and over the first three threads of the cross, *then under the next two, thus reversing the threads being passed over and under then over, under, over the next three threads, repeating from * as required, and with fine thread as many as ten times. The rosettes may touch or there may be spaces between them, in which case the working thread is whipped along the thread connecting the two rosettes (figure). *See also* BAR ROSETTE.

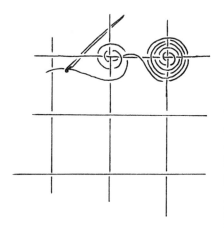

point d'Angleterre ground/net (bobbin) *See* DROSCHEL GROUND.

point d'Angleterre wheels (needle) Lay a grid of double threads with the spacing between the pairs about half that of the

space between adjacent pairs, and the pairs 'weaving' where they cross. Lay thread along one of the grid threads and darn the thread around the crossing four or five times. (Do not pull tightly as the centre should be open.) Then work a ring of BUTTONHOLE STITCHES over the darning (figure). Fasten the thread off into the back of the buttonhole stitches. Start the next ring with a new thread.

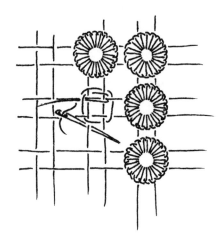

point d'Anvers (needle) (1) Rows of BUTTONHOLE STITCHES, each whipped on the return row with the needle passing upwards through each loop of the previous row. Subsequent rows of buttonhole stitches are worked through the mesh (figure a). (2) As (1) but with subsequent rows of buttonhole stitches worked between the buttonhole loops and the whipping. Also called ALENÇON GROUND/MESH, corded buttonhole stitch, point de Malines and wavily stitch (figure b). This form can also be made with the whipping thread passing down through the mesh (figure c). *See also* WHIPPED MESH/STITCH. (3) As a filling for tape lace groups, three or four buttonhole stitches are worked with spaces of the same width between them. These groups are repeated in subsequent rows, each time working slightly to one side. After a set number of rows the groups are worked to the other side. The final appearance is of zigzag bands (figure d). Also called wavily stitch (Branscombe lace). It can also be worked as a corded version using a RETURNING THREAD.

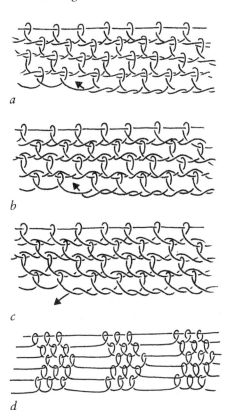

a

b

c

d

point de Brabançon (needle) A needle lace FILLING.

    row 1: seven close buttonhole stitches, space, one stitch, space repeated as required

    row 2: long space under the seven stitches, one stitch into each space in previous row

Repeat the two rows as required (figure). It can be made working two close stitches

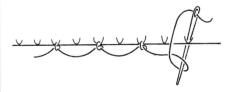

in place of the single stitches. Also called Brabançon stitch.

point de Brussels/Bruxelles (needle)
See BRUSSELS STITCH.

point de Brussels/Bruxelles edging (needle) A simple edging of loops attached by a KNOTTED BUTTONHOLE STITCH. The needle is passed through the edge, behind the thread and forwards through the loop (figure). It is usually used for edging TAPE LACE.

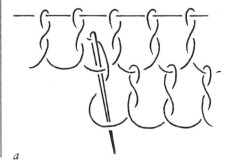

point de Dieppe (bobbin) *See* DIEPPE GROUND.

point d'entoillage (needle) *See* CORDED BUTTONHOLE STITCH.

point d'Espagne (needle) TWISTED BUTTONHOLE STITCH worked the opposite way for alternate rows, resulting in the threads crossing in different directions

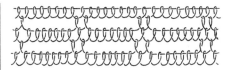

a

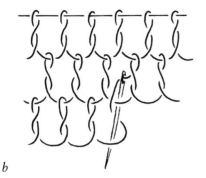

b

on alternate rows (figures a and b). Also called Spanish point. Not to be confused with POINT DE GAZE GROUND or TWISTED NET STITCH. *See also* HOLLIE STITCH.

point d'Espagne edging (needle) An edging consisting of a series of equally spaced BULLION PICOTS, each made with about 20 windings around the needle. Usually used for edging TAPE LACE.

point d'esprit (bobbin) (1) *See* SPOTTED GROUND. (2) TALLY.

point d'esprit (general) Net patterned with regularly spaced spots. Also called spotted ground/net.

point d'esprit (needle) *See* GHOST STITCH.

point de feston (needle) After making a BUTTONHOLE STITCH, the thread is left in a loop and the needle taken behind the stitch and forwards through the loop (figure).

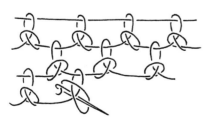

point de feston (netting) Starting at the corner of a mesh, make two BUTTON-HOLE STITCHES along one side, then one on an adjacent thread. Continue making stitches on these two threads, always two on one thread and one on the other. When finished the work fills one side of the mesh but only reaches halfway along the other (figure).

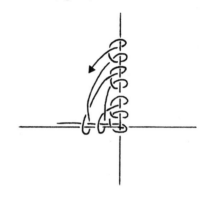

point de filet (needle) *See* FILET STITCH (needle).

point de gaze ground (needle) An open TWISTED BUTTONHOLE STITCH, used for the ground of point de gaze lace, having alternating rows in which the thread crosses three times for each stitch along one row and then twice for each stitch along the other, all threads crossing right over left regardless of the direction in which the row has been made (figure). Not to be confused with POINT D'ES-PAGNE or TWISTED NET STITCH.

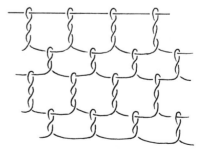

point de Grecque (needle) *See* GRECIAN POINT.

point de Grecque bar (needle) Lay a thread down through the centre of the space and out under the edge. Take the thread out under the left edge, leaving a loop, and pass the needle behind all three threads and forwards through the loop (figure a). Do not pull too tightly. Pass the needle out under the right edge and through the knot from right to left (figure b). Tighten and position the knot carefully.

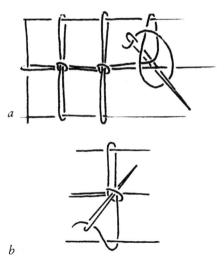

a

b

point de (la) vierge (bobbin) The

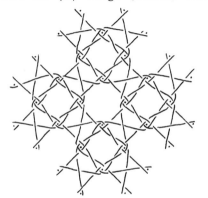

simplest of the ROSE GROUNDS, of which the others are variants. The pairs are linked with half stitches and each pin worked half stitch, pin, half stitch (figure). Also called cane bottom chair ground, cross stitch, fond à la vierge, maiden's net and virgin ground.

point de mariage (bobbin) One of the ROSE GROUNDS. The pairs are linked with cloth stitch and twist and each pin worked half stitch, pin, half stitch (figure). Also called double rose ground, fond de mariage and rose point de mariage.

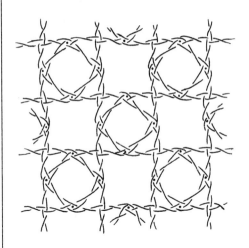

point de Malines (needle) *See* POINT D'ANVERS.

point de Paris (bobbin) *See* KAT STITCH.

point de rac(c)roc/raccroche (bobbin) A method of invisibly joining bobbin-made grounds thus producing large areas from narrow strips. The strips are pinned side by side, leaving a space of one mesh between them. (1) When joining POINT GROUND, the two strips are laced together using two needles, the lacing stitches forming an extra mesh between the strips (figure a). (2) When joining DROSCHEL and MECHLIN GROUNDS, two pairs are used to make a PLAIT, each pair is then TWISTED twice and SEWN into the upper part of the loop of the adjacent strip, then twisted twice and sewn into the lower part of the same loop. The pairs are twisted twice and are ready to make the next plait (figure b). Also called fine joining.

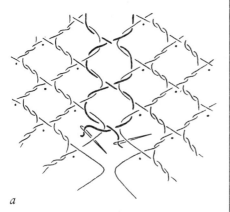

a

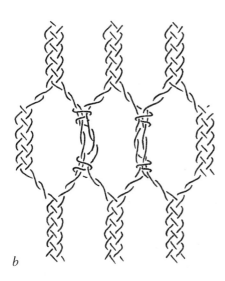

b

point de reprise (netting) Passing a needle under and over threads to imitate

weaving, working in one direction only across one or more meshes (figure). Not to be confused with POINT DE TOILE.

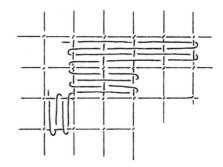

point de six (bobbin) *See* KAT STITCH.

point de Sorrento (needle) (1) Pairs of BUTTONHOLE STITCHES separated by spaces of the same size, with subsequent rows consisting of pairs of buttonhole stitches worked in the spaces (figure a). Also called double Brussels/buttonhole/ loop stitch. (2) Alternating rows of two and four buttonhole stitches with the groups of stitches worked in the spaces between the groups of the previous row (figure b).

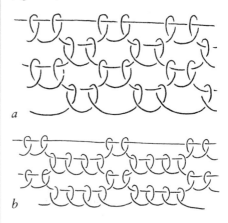

a

b

point de Sorrento stitch (needle) After working a BUTTONHOLE STITCH, take the needle over the same supporting thread and through the previous stitch (figure). *See also* SPANISH GROUND.

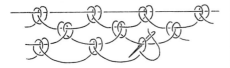

point de toile (bobbin) *See* CLOTH STITCH.

point de toile (netting) Stitch in which the thread is darned across one or more meshes so that it passes across and back and forth twice across each mesh (figure). Also called cloth stitch and linen stitch. Not to be confused with POINT DE REPRISE.

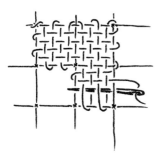

point de Tulle (needle) *See* BRUSSELS STITCH.

point de Turc/Turque (needle) *See* TURKISH STITCH.

point de Valenciennes (needle) A

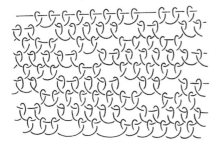

FILLING of diamonds of BRUSSELS STITCH.
row 1: groups of eight stitches with spaces for two stitches between them
row 2: five stitches worked centrally across the group of eight, two stitches worked in the spaces
row 3: two stitches worked in the spaces and four worked across the group of five, making groups of eight with spaces between them (figure)
Also called Valenciennes stitch.

point de Venise (needle) Make one BUTTONHOLE STITCH, then a second into the loop formed by the first stitch (figure). Also called open buttonhole filling, petit point de Venise, single point de Venise, Venetian point, Venetian point stitch and Venice point. There are many variants. *See also* DOUBLE POINT DE VENISE, CINQ POINT DE VENISE, PURLING.

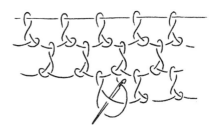

point de Venise bar (needle) After making a BUTTONHOLE(D) BAR, work POINT DE VENISE STITCH into every third stitch along each side (figure).

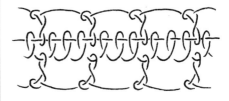

point de Venise edging (needle) *See* PURLING.

point double (bobbin) *See* KAT STITCH.

point feston doublé (needle) *See* ALENÇON GROUND/MESH.

point ground (bobbin) The characteristic GROUND of Bucks point lace made on a grid having an angle between 52 and 70 degrees. (1) Made by working a HALF STITCH, TWIST twice and SETTING A PIN between the pairs; the pin is UNCOVERED. The resulting ground has three sets of threads, two travelling diagonally, one towards the right, one towards the left and a third set travelling downwards (figure a). Also known as Bucks point ground. This ground is also used in other laces where it is known as fond claire, fond simple, hexagonal mesh and Lille ground/mesh. (2) A ground occasionally found in antique Bucks point lace that is made in strips joined together with POINT RACROC, the change in the number of twists being made to accommodate the number produced by the joining stitch. It is made by working a half stitch and twist and pinning between the two pairs, this resulting in all the threads snaking from side to side down the vertical rows of pins (figure b).

point ground stitch (bobbin) A characteristic stitch of POINT GROUND. With two pairs work half stitch twist twice, pin between the pairs (figure). Also called net stitch.

point noné *See* CLOSE STITCH.

point noué (needle) (1) A KNOTTED BUTTONHOLE STITCH. (2) *See* CORDED BUTTONHOLE STITCH.

point plat (needle) *See* FLATWORK.

point raccroc *See* POINT DE RAC(C)ROC.

point tape (needle) Machine-made tape with cords running through to gather it as required.

pointed tally (bobbin) *See* LEAF.

pokerwork (bobbin) A BOBBIN decoration produced by pyrography – i.e., scorching the surface of the wood with a very hot implement.

polar co-ordinate paper (general) GRAPH PAPER having a series of equally spaced concentric circles crossed by equally spaced radial lines, used for drafting circular patterns (figure).

a

L – lead(ing) bobbin/thread

b

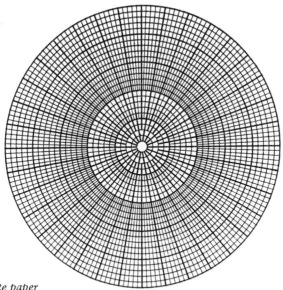

polar co-ordinate paper

polish (bobbin) Wooden bobbins may be polished with a mixture of beeswax and turpentine, but this should never be used on the head or neck, where it might stain the thread.

Polo Mint circle/ring (bobbin) *See* BEDFORDSHIRE CIRCLE.

polychrome lace (general) Lace of more than one colour.

polystyrene pillow (bobbin) A pillow made from carved or moulded polystyrene. *See also* STYROFOAM.

Pompadour bead (bobbin) *See* VENETIAN BEAD.

pony beads (bobbin) Plain glass WOUND

BEADS, usually made in blue, that were originally produced for trade in Africa and North America where they are said to have been used for decorating ponies (figure).

pop (needle) A tiny motif used to decorate CARRICKMACROSS APPLIQUÉ, formed by working two BUTTONHOLE STITCHES across each of six MESHES surrounding a single mesh (figure).

porte (needle) *See* BUD (needle).

porthole church window bobbin (bobbin) A CHURCH WINDOW BOBBIN with a series of holes, often with shallow incisions around them, drilled through the SHANK instead of slits. This 'porthole' decoration was characteristic of early twentieth-century Indian craftsmen (figure).

pouncing (needle) An early method of transferring a pattern to fabric. The pattern was evenly pricked along all the lines and placed in position on the fabric. TRACING POWDER was shaken over the pattern and the pattern tapped or rubbed with a pad, so that the powder passed through the holes. The pattern of chalk spots was often replaced by tacking stitches or painted with watercolour paint, because the powder would soon rub away.

powdered (general) Machine- or handmade net decorated with TALLIES or small motifs.

powderings (crochet) Irish crochet motifs, sprigs or sprays arranged haphazardly within the area of the lace, leaving large areas between for fillings.

pricker (bobbin) A needle, having the same diameter as the pins to be used in the pattern, held in a PIN-VICE. Used for making a PRICKING (figure). *See also* BEESWAX, CHUBBY PRICKER.

pricker

pricking (bobbin) A card or PARCHMENT pattern having a series of pinholes into which pins are inserted to support threads while lace is being made. GUIDELINES and/or INDICATORS may be added. Also called card. *See also* DOWN, ECHE, MANILLA CARD.

pricking (needle) A parchment pattern with holes pricked for the couching of the FOUNDATION THREAD. Used by Alençon lacemakers among others.

pricking (out) (general) A technique used for many forms of lacemaking. The pattern draft is secured on the PRICKING CARD or other material and pinholes made, where marked, with a PRICKER. Care should be taken to ensure that the pricker is kept vertical at all times. Also called making a pricking and stabbing. *See also* PRICKING BOARD.

pricking board (bobbin) A board on which a PRICKING is made. It should be sufficiently firm to support the card, sufficiently soft to allow the PRICKER to pass freely through and sufficiently deep to protect the underlying table. Suitable materials include cork (beware of varieties with hard pieces that may deflect the pricker), tentest board and several layers of corrugated cardboard, held together with sticky tape.

pricking card (bobbin) Card from which a PRICKING is made. *See also* MANILLA CARD, PARCHMENT.

princess ganse (bobbin) *See* VENETIAN BAR (BOBBIN).

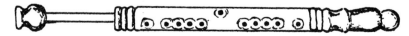

porthole church window bobbin

progressive darned centre (needle) The term used when the CENTRE of a Tenerife medallion is darned by dividing the threads into an even number of groups and advancing the darning by one thread, or pair of threads, at each round, which results in a spiral effect (figure).

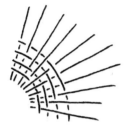

prong (crochet) *See* HAIRPIN.

prop (bobbin) *See* SUPPORT PIN.

psocid (general) A small insect belonging to the order Psocoptera that sometimes infests straw and bran lace pillows. It is harmless and does not transmit diseases. *See also* STERILIZING PILLOW FILLINGS.

pulled fabric/thread work (needle) Where the threads of a fabric are pulled together to form a decoration of holes.

pulled over picot (tatting) PICOT, on a slack CHAIN, that has been pulled over to the wrong side, dampened and allowed to dry.

pulling up (bobbin) *See* FIRMING UP.

puncetto work (needle) *See* PUNTO AVORIO.

punto (general) Stitch (Italian).

punto alpino/avorio (needle) Strong needle-knotted lace made using VALSESIAN STITCH and BAR STITCH. Also

called alpine point, ivory point/stitch and Saracen point.

purl (bobbin) *See* PICOT.

purl (tatting) Hold the thread as for making a CHAIN or RING. Pass the SHUTTLE over the thread across the fingers (figure a), pass the shuttle back under the thread (figure b), the shuttle thread makes a loop around the thread (figure c) and when you pull the shuttle thread and CAPSIZE the knot the thread makes a loop around the shuttle thread (figure d). This is the second HALF STITCH of a DOUBLE STITCH.

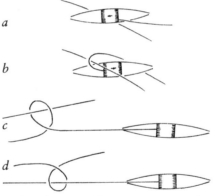

purl edge (bobbin) Honiton edge

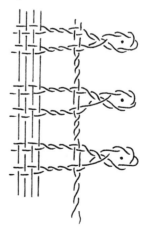

worked with a PURL at every pinhole and three TWISTS between the edge two pairs of DOWNRIGHTS; the edge downright is twisted three times between pinholes (figure). *See also* FORGOTTEN PURLS and Appendix for indicator.

purl filling *See* CINQ POINT DE VENISE.

purl locking stitch (tatting) A PURL stitch that has not been CAPSIZED and locks the chain. *See also* LOCKING STITCH.

purl pin (bobbin) *See* PICOT.

purl-pin bar (bobbin) In Honiton lace, a narrow strip made with PURLS along a single row of pinholes, and the RUNNERS returning from the other edge without pinning. It can be made with as few as four pairs (figure). Also called pearl bar/tie. *See* PLAIN EDGE/SIDE for alternative plain edges.

purling (general) An early term for narrow ornamental braids made by twisting threads.

purling (needle) This is used to edge Branscombe lace. A buttonhole stitch is taken into the edge and the thread taken back to cross the loop it has made. A stitch is made over the loop (figure a) and tensioned carefully; this is the stitch that determines the size and position of the cluster. The next buttonhole stitch is worked over the double thread (figure b), then the remaining three stitches of the cluster of five (figure c). Also called perlin(g).

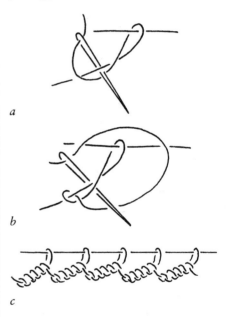

a

b

c

push-me-pull-you (bobbin) *See* PIN LIFTER.

put up a pin (bobbin) *See* SET UP A PIN.

putting back (bobbin) Bedford and Buckinghamshire term for MOVING UP.

pyramid stitch (needle) *See* BUTTERFLY STITCH.

Q

quartern bead (bobbin) A WOUND BEAD, usually transparent and often coloured, longer than its width and pressed into a somewhat rectangular shape with a ridge implement. Said to represent a quartern of butter (figure).

queen of lace (bobbin) A term applied to Bucks point lace or to Honiton lace, according to the preference of the speaker.

quick windmill (bobbin) *See* WINDMILL.

quill (bobbin) A wooden BOBBIN with a very long NECK on which could be stored a complete skein of GIMP and from which yarn would be transferred to the working bobbins. Quills were not used for making lace.

quille/quilling (general) Lace designed to be used gathered along one edge, having a fine, soft, fairly plain ground that would gather easily. It was sometimes powdered with small spots or tiny motifs, usually regularly spaced and only a few so that they did not interfere with the effect of the gathered ground. The FREE EDGE of the lace would be decorated with larger, stiffer motifs, which would cause it to stand out and, because it was away from the close gathering, more attractive designs would be used along this edge.

quint(a)in (general) A BURATO-like fabric, produced in Brittany, that had double weft threads.

R

rac(c)roc stitch (bobbin) *See* POINT DE RAC(C)ROC.

radially pinned wheel (needle) A Tenerife wheel worked with the pins inserted into its edge with the points towards the centre, often made by gathering a piece of fabric over two circles of cardboard, the pins being inserted between the two cards, sometimes with a thin layer of batting or wadding between the cards and under the upper layer of fabric (figure).

rag lace (bobbin) (1) Poor quality Honiton lace made in the latter half of the nineteenth century. (2) Torchon lace, particularly poor quality. Also called dishcloth lace.

raised cordonnet/top stitching (needle) *See* RAISED EDGE (needle).

raised crumb bead (bobbin) A CRUMB BEAD, used to weight BOBBINS, on which the tiny chips stand proud from the surface.

raised edge (bobbin) *See* LEAF WITH RAISED VEIN.

raised edge (needle) TOP STITCHING worked over a number of PADDING THREADS to make it thicker and stand out. Also called raised cordonnet/top stitching.

raised edge sewing (bobbin) (1) *See* DOUBLE SEWING. (2) *See* TOP SEWING.

raised eye (bobbin) An EYE or spot decoration standing proud from the surface. Also called horned eye/spot and raised spot. *See also* EVIL EYE BEAD, KITTY FISHER'S EYES.

raised gimp (bobbin) A method of using a pair of gimps that results in the appearance of a raised cord or chain. When used through the GROUND, each thread is usually finer than if a single gimp were used. It is useful when coloured gimp is used because it does

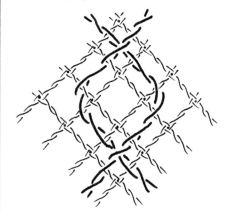

not obscure the threads passing through (figure). Also called corded gimp, cording, doubled gimp, Irish gimp and surface gimp. *See also* CABLE GIMP, CHAIN GIMP.

raised Honiton (bobbin) An effect produced when whole stitch, half stitch or a filling is worked over a previous piece of work, RIB or ROLL, and to which it is attached by SEWINGS, the former piece standing proud when the lace is turned over. *See also* LEAF WITH RAISED VEIN *and* Appendix for indicator.

raised leaf/plait/tally (bobbin) *See* RAISED TALLY.

raised needlelace/needlepoint (needle) (1) Having a RAISED EDGE. (2) *See* APPLIED PIECE.

raised rib (bobbin) RAISED HONITON where the raised part is a RIB. *See also* LEAF WITH RAISED VEIN.

raised rib cobweb (needle) *See* SPIDER WEB WHEEL.

raised rib leaf/tally (bobbin) (1) *See* LEAF WITH RAISED VEIN. (2) A LEAF-shaped TALLY where the WORKING THREAD is taken right round the central thread instead of passing over or under it, and made so that the central 'ridge' is

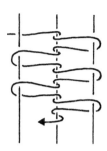

b

on the right side when finished. For lace made 'right side' uppermost, * pass the working bobbin under the left and central threads, back over then under the central thread, over the right thread, under the right and central threads, back over and under the central thread and over the left thread. Repeat from * as required (figure a). For lace made wrong side uppermost, *pass the working bobbin under the left thread and over the central thread, back under the central thread, over the central and right threads, back under the right thread, over the central thread, back under the thread and over the central and left threads. repeat from * as required (figure b). Also called ribbed leaf.

raised sewing (bobbin) (1) *See* DOUBLE SEWING. (2) *See* TOP SEWING.

raised spot (needle) Take the thread

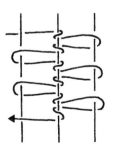

a

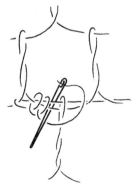

a

under the mesh from right to left and bring it through a mesh. Make three BUTTONHOLE STITCHES into the mesh on the right (figure a), over the three stitches make a buttonhole stitch in the other direction (figure b), and before pulling it tight, slide the needle through the three buttonhole stitches from right to left (figure c). Tighten by pulling both ends and trim.

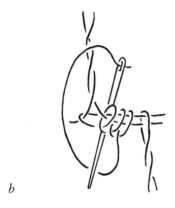

b

c

raised tally (bobbin) (1) *See* OVERLAID LEAF/PLAIT/TALLY. (2) A TALLY that stands up, usually from cloth or half stitch in Bedfordshire lace. Using adjacent pairs, or two pairs having left one pair between them, make a square ended tally twice as long as it is wide. Return the pairs to their original positions and continue working, lifting the tally so that the cloth, or half stitch, closes up. Sometimes the shape is kept by inserting a cocktail stick through the fold of the tally. If the underside of the lace is to be the right side, the loop of tally will have to be pushed through when the lace is taken off the

pillow (figure). Also called bobble, Florentine knot, raised leaf, raised plait and tuft. (3) *See* ROLLED PLAIT/TALLY *and* Appendix for indicator.

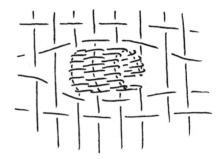

raised vein *See* LEAF WITH RAISED VEIN.

raised work (bobbin) Any technique that makes the lace three-dimensional. *See also* OVERLAID LEAF/TALLY, RAISED HONITON, RAISED TALLY, ROLLED TALLY.

raised work (needle) Any technique that makes the lace three-dimensional. *See also* APPLIED PIECES, PADDING THREADS, TOP STITCHING.

raising (general) Using a small implement under RAISED WORK to make it stand up. *See also* AFFICOT.

Raleigh bar (**ground**) (needle) A regular or irregular ground of BULLION BARS.

raw silk (yarn) Between seven and ten filaments of silk, loosely spun together as they are taken from the cocoons; it is still coated with a gum from the cocoon which makes up about 25 per cent of the weight. Also known as 20/22 silk from the DENIER.

reef knot and a half (bobbin) A reef knot followed by the first half of a reef knot, used in Honiton lace when tying off pairs (figure).

*reef knot
and a half*

regenerated fibre (yarn) A fibre produced by chemically changing natural fibres. The new fibre has very different properties – rayon, for example.

regrounding (general) Replacing some or all of the GROUND, either to repair damage or to make the lace fashionable. The ground removed is replaced with a similar hand-made ground, a different hand-made ground or machine-made net. Net behind motifs is removed. Not to be confused with APPLIQUÉ LACE.

reinforced foot (bobbin) *See* FOOTSIDE.

removing bobbins from work (bobbin) *See* RESERVE PAIRS, THROWING BACK.

removing a pair from half stitch (bobbin) In Honiton lace work a WHOLE STITCH with the DOWNRIGHT pair adjacent to the COARSE PAIR, or edge downrights, as well as the coarse pair. After MAKING UP THE EDGE, lift the two central threads from the two whole stitches and make a REEF KNOT AND A HALF (figure).

removing completed lace from foundation (needle) The two layers of the

BACKING are separated. (1) By cutting the couching stitches between them with scissors or a razor blade. (2) By ripping the couching stitches by pulling the two backing layers apart so that the lace falls free. Use tweezers to remove any remaining pieces of couching thread.

removing knots (bobbin) Knots are not used to join threads that are running out. (1) In close CLOTH STITCH the offending thread can simply be lifted back and a new thread laid in. (2) DOUBLING UP. (3) In Honiton HALF STITCH, when the offending thread reaches an appropriate place it is removed as in REMOVING A PAIR FROM HALF STITCH, a replacement pair being added at the other end of the same row. (4) Where the offending thread reaches a footside that is to be sewn to fabric, it is THROWN BACK and another used to replace it, neither thread being cut. When the work is mounted on the fabric the loose threads are used for mounting or sewn off.

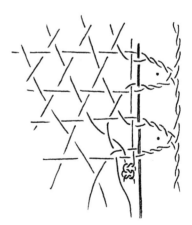

repairing net (general) Trim away damaged portions of net, following the lines of holes, and tack to a BACKING of strong fabric or stiff paper or mount in

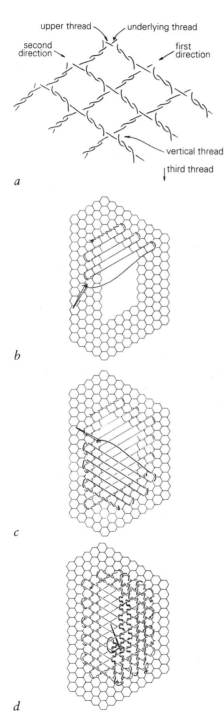

a

b

c

d

a frame. Check the threads of the net to determine in which direction to start – i.e., net is formed from three sets of threads, two intersecting diagonally, with the third connecting them vertically. This is easily seen by looking for the singly crossed threads; the underlying thread shows the first direction for working (figure a). Lay the first set of threads, starting from the third hole from the cut edge and laying it across the space to the third mesh from the opposite cut edge of the same line. Continue to take it back and forth until the area has been covered (figure b). Lay a second layer of threads over the first, in the direction of the upper thread of the singly crossed threads (figure c). Lay the last set of threads in the third direction, whipping along the meshes of the net, then, when the loose threads are reached, whipping the underlying thread twice in each space between the over-lying threads (figure d). Careful tensioning is required to shape the meshes. The work may be turned so that each row may be worked in the easiest direction.

repeating pattern/pricking (bobbin) A single pattern repeat plus one row of holes made using ACETATE FILM or other transparent material. A straight line is scratched on the PRICKING CARD for the FOOTSIDE, and the pattern is transferred by pricking. * The repeating pattern is moved down until its top line of pinholes lines up with the last through the pricking card and its footside is along the scratch, then the remainder of the pattern is copied. Repeat from * as required.

reprise bar (needle) *See* WOVEN BAR.

réseau (general) *See* GROUND (general).

réseau ordinaire (needle) *See* ALENÇON GROUND/MESH.

reserve pairs (bobbin) In Bucks point those pairs that are no longer required in the work and are laid along the gimp. They may be brought back into the lace later or THROWN OUT.

resting bobbins/workers (bobbin) *See* EDGE PAIR.

returning cord/thread (needle) (1) The thread that is thrown back along a row and then subsequently worked over. Also called fil de retour, lay(ing) a cord/thread, returning cord/thread, straight stitch return and throw(ing) a thread. *See also* CORDED BUTTONHOLE STITCH. (2) The thread returning from across a space so that subsequent stitches can be worked in the required direction. *See* BUTTONHOLE(D) LOOP where the FOUNDATION THREAD, forming the core of the loop, is laid across a third time so that the BUTTONHOLE STITCHES will be worked towards the point at which the loop started – i.e., bringing the working thread to the position required for continuing. Also called fil de retour.

returning row (general) (1) A plain row when there are alternating patterned and plain rows. (2) The returning thread being whipped along the previous row.

reverse (tatting) After completing a section, turn over the work and continue with it in this position.

reverse catch-pin (bobbin) A CATCH-PIN lying by the side of HEADSIDE PASSIVES (figure) or to the right of a VERTICAL GIMP.

reverse(d) half stitch (bobbin) Using

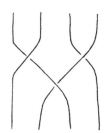

a

two pairs of bobbins, TWIST each pair, 2 over 1 and 4 over 3, then CROSS the centre bobbins, 2 over 3 (figure). Also called half passing.

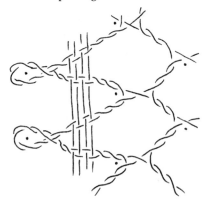

reverse twist (bobbin) Pass the left-hand bobbin of a pair over the right-hand one (figure).

reversing chain (tatting) A chain in which the knots lie on the other side can be made either by REVERSING the chain at a given point or by using two shuttles and exchanging them at a given point, the knots subsequently lying on the other side.

rib (bobbin) In Honiton lace a narrow strip made with EDGE STITCHES, along a single row of pinholes, the PINHOLE SIDE, and the RUNNERS returning from the PLAIN EDGE without pinning (figure).

Also called stem, stem stitch and TEN STICK. *See* PLAIN EDGE/SIDE for alternative plain edges.

rib and leadwork vein (bobbin) A Honiton vein made by working two RIBS joined at regular intervals by LEAD-WORKS (figure). The rest of the leaf is SEWN to the ribs.

ribbed cutwork (needle) A Branscombe term for RAISED RIB COBWEB.

ribbed leaf (bobbin) *See* RAISED RIB LEAF.

ribbed spider (netting) Lay two diagonals across a square of four meshes (figure) and work a RAISED RIB COBWEB around the centre point.

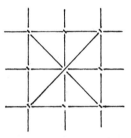

ribbon (bobbin) *See* BRAID.

ribbon bead (bobbin) A round bead, used to weight bobbins, having a strip of decoration around the centre. The decoration can be striped and straight or wavy (figure). Also called rope bead. *See also* SERPENT'S EYE.

right-handed purl (bobbin) A Honiton PURL worked on the right-hand side of a BRAID OR RIB. When the RUNNERS reach the right side, TWIST them seven times, place the point of a pin under the thread farthest from the work, point towards you, pass the point over the bobbin HEAD and into the pinhole in the pricking (figure a). Do not allow the thread to pull tight round the pin at this stage. Take the second thread around the pin in the same direction (figure b). Take up the slack, gently at first with a see-sawing motion, then more firmly. Twist the pair once (figure c).

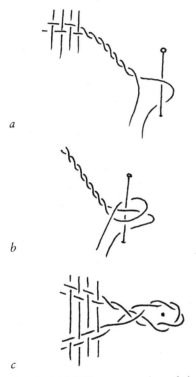

a

b

c

rim (bobbin) The outer edge of the top of the HEAD. *See also* BOBBIN.

ring (tatting) With the last part of the previous work held between the left index finger and thumb, the SHUTTLE THREAD is taken across the backs of the fingers of the left hand, and under the fingers to be held between the first finger and thumb to control the tension. The fingers of the left hand are spread out and DOUBLE STITCHES are worked over the section of thread between the first and second fingers. When the ring has the required number of stitches

it is CLOSED (figure). Also called circle and oval (according to shape). *See also* SCALLOP, SPLIT RING.

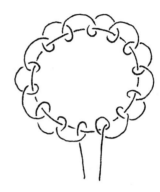

ring and pin (tatting) A TATTING PIN linked to a ring by a fine chain. The ring is placed over the left thumb to keep it available (figure).

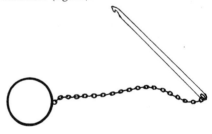

ring pair (bobbin) In Flanders laces the pair worked around the outside of the

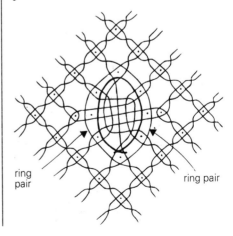

ring pair

ring pair

181

pins surrounding CLOTH STITCH areas and from which it is separated by TWISTS (figure). Also called outlining pair.

ring picot (needle) *See* BUTTONHOLED LOOP.

ring stick (needle) A narrow, cylindrical implement with the diameter reducing at regular intervals. Used for making BUTTONHOLE(D) RINGS (figure). Also called couronne stick.

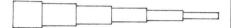

ringed bobbin (bobbin) A BOBBIN with narrow, incised rings that have been coloured (figure).

Rodi stitch (needle) The stitch used for Rodi lace, which is similar to Armenian lace (figure). Also called Nazareth stitch and Smyrna stitch.

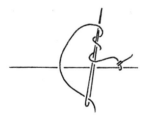

roll (bobbin) (1) In Honiton and similar laces, the bunch of threads, sometimes bound with one of the pairs, THROWN UP and STITCHED to an existing EDGE that is part of the boundary of the next section. The new section is then BACKED. When completed and turned over, the roll stands up as RAISED WORK. Also called

rope. *See also* ROLL AND TIE. (2) When DARNING AWAY in difficult situations – e.g., along HALF STITCH or GROUND – the threads may be laid in a roll along the finishing line, and one thread, from the first knot, whips around the roll attaching it to the starting edge of the lace (figure). Each thread is laid out after it has been whipped three times and the stitching thread is secured at the end. The ends are trimmed off closely.

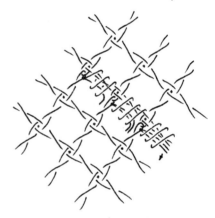

roll (tatting) Pass the shuttle repeatedly in the same direction through the ring currently being made, then pull the SHUTTLE THREAD tightly to CAPSIZE the twists.

roll and tie (bobbin) A method of attaching a ROLL. The pairs of the roll, usually between five and seven, are laid along the EDGE to which it is to be SEWN. A pair binds them twice into a roll, then makes an EDGE SEWING to the edge and is tied. This pair continues binding the roll and making sewings, usually to every second or third pinhole, as far as it needs to be attached. Alternatively,

ringed bobbin

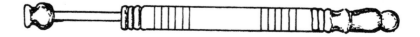

the roll is bound with one pair, the separate threads of which may pass in opposite directions, and the sewings taken by another pair, which is tied after each sewing. Finally the roll becomes a RIB or the pairs are used to BACK the area (figure). *See also* GARTER STITCH.

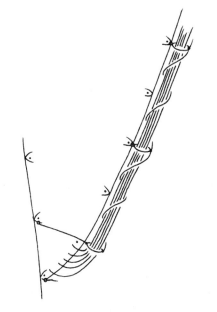

roll stitch (crochet) Yarn over hook between eight and twelve times, insert hook through the work or chain loop, yarn over hook and draw through a loop, yarn over hook and draw loop through all loops on the hook, keeping a firm tension on the thread and easing the loops off the hook with the right middle finger. To finish, make one CHAIN and draw up the thread (figure). Also called bullion stitch and coil stitch.

rolled tally/leaf/plait (bobbin) Mainly in Bedfordshire lace, a TALLY that stands

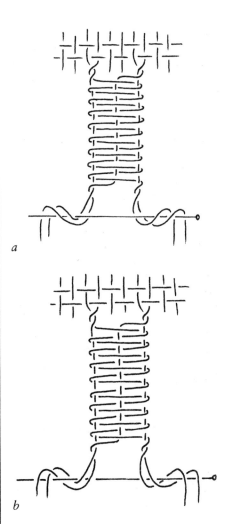

a

b

up, usually from CLOTH STITCH, HALF STITCH or CROSSINGS. Using adjacent pairs, or two pairs having left one pair between them, make a SQUARE-ENDED TALLY twice as long as it is wide. Hold a pin horizontally on the tally, lift the right-hand pair over the right-hand end of the pin and lift the left-hand pair over the left hand end of the pin (figure a). The tally will roll up over the pin. Return the pairs to their original positions and continue working. If the underside of the lace is to be the right side, the pairs must be taken down and up behind the pins (figure b), and the roll will have to be pushed through when the lace is taken off the pillow. Also called Florentine knot. *See also* RAISED TALLY and Appendix for indicator.

roller (bobbin) (1) A cylindrical section of FRENCH and SWEDISH PILLOWS to which the PRICKING is pinned, with the pattern meeting accurately. As the lace progresses, the roller is rotated, presenting an apparently continuous pricking. *See also* PILLOW WEIGHT. (2) A cylindrical implement, like a child's rolling pin, on which lace can be wound and stored as it is made (figure).

roller pillow (bobbin) A pillow with a ROLLER. *See also* FRENCH PILLOW, SWEDISH PILLOW.

rope (bobbin) (1) *See* ROLL. (2) In Cantù lace the group of threads attached to the edge of the CLOTHWORK by WRAPPING.

rope bead (bobbin) *See* RIBBON BEAD.

rose ground/stitch (bobbin) A variant of TORCHON GROUND in which the pairs are linked, two at a time, with CLOTH AND TWIST or HALF STITCH (indicated by crosses L), before working a set of two, or more usually four, pinholes (figure). The sets of pinholes may be worked as any variety of torchon ground (T) and there are additional variations. *See also* CLOSED CHECK, FOURS, LINK (STITCH), POINT DE MARIAGE, POINT A/DE (LA)

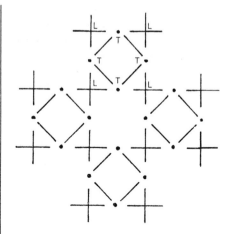

VIERGE, SLAVIC/SLAVE GROUND *and* Appendix for indicator.

rose net ground/rose point (bobbin) *See* HONEYCOMB FILLING/GROUND.

rose point de mariage (bobbin) *See* POINT DE MARIAGE.

rose point edge (needle) Make a series of large BUTTONHOLE STITCHES for the foundations of the loops and buttonhole the first loop (A), start the next (B), stopping when the buttonholing reaches the centre, throw the thread back to the centre of the previous loop and buttonhole over this one (C) (figure). Complete the buttonholing of the previous loop (B). Repeat as required. Also called trefoil edge.

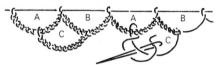

rose point loop (needle) *See* BUTTON-HOLED LOOP.

rosebud knot (needle) Whip the junction of four threads and continue to the

far side (figure a). Make three BUTTON-HOLE STITCHES across the other diagonal of the junction A–C (figure b), make two stitches across these, B–D (figure c), then one in the opposite direction, D–B (figure d). Make sure that this last loop tightens underneath the edges of all the stitches.

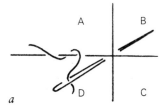

a

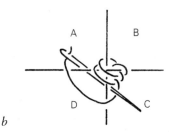

b

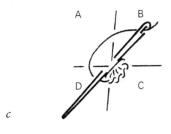

c

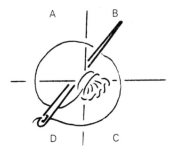

d

rosette (needle) (1) A decoration on BRUSSELS GROUND in which a thread has been run around a single MESH over which buttonhole stitches have been worked (figure). (2) *See* MEDALLION.

round ground/round Flemish mesh (bobbin) The early Valenciennes GROUND. When two PLAITS meet, each pair TWISTS twice, those from the left plait having REVERSE TWISTS, the centre pairs CLOTH STITCH and twist twice, the right pair having reverse twists. Plait each pair working cloth stitch, twist twice for the length required, usually twice, ending with the twists in the required directions (figure). *See also* DIAMOND FILLING/GROUND.

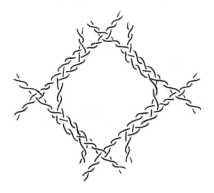

round pillow (bobbin) A pillow that rotates as it is used, enabling lengths of lace to be made without MOVING UP, as opposed to a FLAT PILLOW that remains flat in use. Also called cylindrical pillow. *See also* BOLSTER, FLAT PILLOW, FRENCH PILLOW, ROLLER, SWEDISH PILLOW.

round spool (netting) A cylindrical MESH BOARD/GAUGE/STICK (figure). *See also* FLAT SPOOL.

rubbing (bobbin) A copy of a pricking produced by TAKING A RUBBING.

rubbing wax (bobbin) Wax that is specially produced for taking brass rubbings. It makes a better copy when TAKING A RUBBING than HEELBALL.

rueda (needle) A circular MEDALLION produced in Ñanduti and Tenerife lace.

run out line (tatting) When the stitches of a CHAIN of rather tight stitches are stretched apart so that usual curve disappears or even curves the other way.

running end (netting) When a SLIP KNOT is made, this is the end that moves through the knot as opposed to the STANDING END.

runner/runner pair/runners (bobbin) The Honiton term for WORKER.

runner end (bobbin) An edging that has the HEADSIDE continuing across both ends. It is started along a FALSE FOOTSIDE

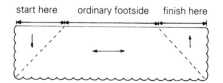

and worked towards the headside until the diagonal to the corner is reached. It is then worked in the usual manner until the diagonal meeting the other corner is reached, when it is worked towards the 'footside', where it is finished. This has the advantage that both ends are neat, as required for a runner (figure).

running line/thread (tatting) Derived from knotting, this is the thread over which a knot is made and along which it can slide. *See also* AUXILIARY THREAD.

run through (bobbin) Workers working through the available pairs.

Russian bars (needle) A narrow filling with a herring bone appearance (figure). The number of twists may vary but should be the same on both sides. Also called twisted filling stitch.

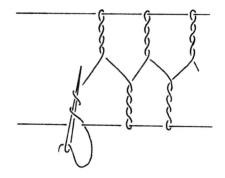

S

S twist (yarn) A yarn spun so that the twist travels in a clockwise direction. This can be checked by looking at the yarn side-on (figure a) or by looking at the end of the yarn (figure b).

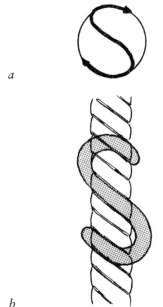

a

b

Saint Catherine (general) The patron saint of lacemakers.

Saracen point (needle) *See* PUNTO AVORIO.

sawdust (bobbin) A filling for pillows and pincushions. It is inclined to pack down and loosen, and it is heavy.

scallop (tatting) A RING that has not been completely CLOSED (figure). Also called HALF-RING.

scallop fan (bobbin) *See* CORONET FAN.

scalloped cordonnette (needle) *See* LOOPED CORDONNETTE.

schematic diagram/drawing (bobbin) A diagram that shows the path of each pair of threads. The illustration, for example, is the schematic diagram for a SIMPLE FAN. Such a diagram is sometimes drawn using a variety of colours, each indicating a different stitch or technique. Also called schematic drawing, technical

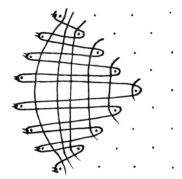

drawing and working diagram. Not to be confused with INDICATOR, PATTERN DRAFT or THREAD DIAGRAM. *See also* BELGIAN COLOUR CODE.

Scotch gauze (needle) A very fine, loosely woven fabric intended for PULLED THREAD WORK in which the threads can be pulled together to produce lace-like grounds.

screwthread bobbin (bobbin) A BOBBIN with a close spiral running the length of the SHANK (figure).

scroll (bobbin) The term used when a braid turns tightly at its end (figure).

scroop (yarn) The feel and sound of new silk caused by treatment with acetic acid. It is removed by washing but not by dry cleaning.

sealing wax (bobbin) Used to decorate HEADPINS and STRIVERS, and occasionally used in depressions in bobbins.

seaming lace (general) A lace INSERTION used between two pieces of lace.

secondary trail (bobbin). This, in Bedfordshire lace, is a TRAIL that joins a DOMINANT TRAIL. Also called minor trail.

sectional lace (bobbin) *See* PART LACE.

sectional paper (general) *See* GRAPH PAPER.

sectioned bobbin (bobbin) A BOBBIN that consists of two different woods or of wood and bone joined together, sometimes joined with rivets. *See also* SPLICED BOBBIN.

seed stitch (needle) *See* CINQ POINT DE VENISE.

self-sewing (bobbin) SEWING in which only one bobbin is involved – i.e., the thread making the loop is from the bobbin passing through it. It is used for SEWING IN A PAIR and attaching the BACKING to a piece of work underlying it (figure). It may take the form of an EDGE or TOP SEWING.

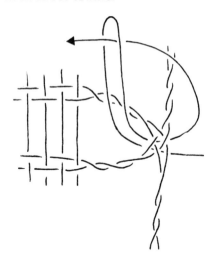

semi-circle (needle) *See* DARNED SEMI-CIRCLE.

serpent's eye (bobbin) A RIBBON BEAD, used to weight bobbins, with the 'ribbon' (the serpent) undulating around the widest part and a spot (an eye) in each indulation (figure, p.189).

screwthread bobbin

serpent's eye

set (bobbin) Lace is left pinned to the pillow for a period, usually for two weeks, so that the appearance is improved by the threads setting in position.

set(ting) in (bobbin) Starting work on a fresh piece of lace. Also called setting up.

set(ting) up (bobbin) (1) *See* SETTING IN. (2) *See* MOVING UP.

set(ting) up a pillow (bobbin) DRESSING A PILLOW and getting the bobbins ready for working.

set(ting) (up) a pin (bobbin) Placing a pin in position in a pinhole when making lace. Also called put up a pin and setting up a pin.

set(ting) up at a point (bobbin) In Honiton lace place six or eight pairs (depending on whether the point is sharp or widens quickly), HALF STRADDLED over a pin and twist each resulting pair twice. Separate off the RUNNERS and EDGE PAIRS and slide the COARSE THREAD, if there is one, under the remaining DOWNRIGHTS* laying the bobbins to the back. The illustration shows the layout when commencing work from the right (figure a). Work an EDGE STITCH, continue across one row in WHOLE STITCH and make up the other edge. Lay the coarse thread bobbins, if present, in working position (figure b) and continue. (*The coarse pair may be

threaded over and under the downrights.) Also called starting at a point.

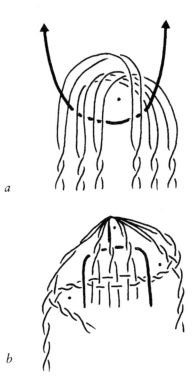

a

b

set(ting) up at a point with a purl (bobbin) In Honiton lace at the pinhole to one side of the point (in this case the left) set up as for SETTING UP AT A POINT using six pairs plus a COARSE THREAD and work from the left-hand side towards the right until the right EDGE PAIR is reached. WHOLE STITCH the edge pair and make a RIGHT-HAND PURL setting up the pin at the point. Make the TOP HOLE PURL and TWIST both pairs three times. Bring down the coarse threads, return through the coarse pair and tie the RUNNERS (figure a). Work across the DOWNRIGHTS and through the coarse pair, twist the runners three times and make a LEFT HAND PURL setting the pin at the first pinhole used – i.e., remove the pin to the left of the point and use it to make the purl and setting it up in the same hole, having carefully moved the starting point out of the way. Work through the edge pair, twist both pairs three times, whole stitch the runners with the coarse pair and tie the runners (figure b). Work across and make a PURL EDGE at the right-hand side. Continue making purl edges on both sides. Also called starting at a point with a purl.

seven-pin honeycomb ring (bobbin) In Bucks point a group of seven HONEY- COMB STITCHES around a space, all surrounded by a gimp (figure).

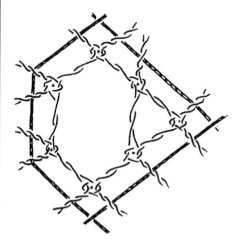

sewing (bobbin) The process of joining work to an existing piece of lace, using a crochet hook or NEEDLEPIN to bring a loop of thread from one bobbin through the existing lace and passing the other bobbin through the loop. Also called accrochetage, connecting stitch, crochet hook join, crochetage, hooking and join. *See also* DOUBLE SEWING, EDGE SEWING, HELP THREAD, LAZY LOOP, NEEDLEPIN SEWING, PIN-BY-PIN SEWING, SELF-SEWING, TAKING A SEWING, TOP SEWING *and* Appendix for indicator.

sewing and sewing across the pair on the return/way back (bobbin) *See* CONTINENTAL BAR.

sewing in (bobbin) Joining to an exist- ing EDGE using SEWINGS, particularly when joining new pairs to an edge by sewings. Several pairs may be added by laying some along the edge and making one sewing across them (figure). Also called hooking in. *See also* SELF-SEWING.

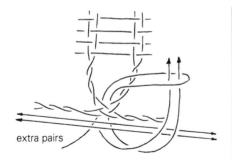

extra pairs

sewing on forgotten purls (bobbin) *See* FORGOTTEN PURLS.

sewing out (bobbin) Having completed a section by meeting an existing section, the pairs are SEWN into the existing section and tied off with a REEF KNOT AND A HALF. Also called tying out. In Honiton lace this is usually followed by BUNCH AND TIE.

shackle (bobbin) A loop of wire that is used to link a SPANGLE to the bobbin TAIL (figure).

shading (needle) *See* HORIZONTAL SHADING, VERTICAL SHADING.

shadow-holes (bobbin) Unwanted holes that sometimes appear in lace, especially next to twists.

shadow stitch (needle) Spaced BRUSSELS STITCHES that, when used with more closely worked stitches, give the appearance of shading.

shank (bobbin) Usually applied to the part of the bobbin that is used as a handle. Also called handle and stem. *See* BOBBIN.

sheathed bobbin (bobbin) *See* HOODED BOBBIN.

shell (bobbin) *See* OVERLAID LEAF/TALLY.

shell (needle) A decorative edge used around Tenerife medallions (figure a). The web is STRETCHED between a loop of the medallion, the PIVOT LOOP, and each pin in turn (figure b). Darning is worked across the threads and into loops on either side of the one supporting the web. As darning continues threads are left out. Finally a round of KNOT STITCH is worked around the edge, starting and finishing at one of the medallion loops. The webs of adjacent shells are INTERLOCKED.

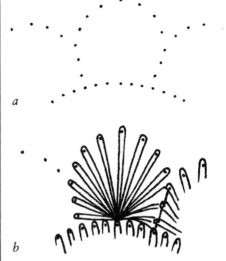

a

b

shell, shell edge/fan (bobbin) (1) *See* FRENCH FAN. (2) *See* SIMPLE FAN.

shell stitch (needle) *See* CINQ POINT DE VENISE.

shield (bobbin) *See* GUARD.

shiny thread (yarn) A Honiton term for a soft, lustrous linen yarn used as the COARSE THREAD.

short neck (bobbin) A groove around the head of a bobbin with a DOUBLE HEAD in which the HITCH lies. *See* BOBBIN.

short picot (tatting) A PICOT that is smaller than usual, often made for joining a chain or ring onto later. A picot of the usual size may look unsightly after a join has been made. Also called small picot.

short row (bobbin) *See* GAP ROW.

shortening bobbin thread (bobbin) While holding the bobbin horizontally, pull out the HITCH with a pin and gently rotate the bobbin to wind up the required amount of thread, then tighten the hitch by twisting sharply (figure). *See also* LENGTHENING BOBBIN THREAD.

shrinkage allowance (bobbin) Usually estimated as one-fifteenth of the finished length, but tightly made BRAID LACE made with a thickish yarn can shrink by one-tenth and fine lace with open grounds by very little.

shuttle (netting) *See* NETTING SHUTTLE.

shuttle (tatting) The implement used to make tatting (figure).

shuttle thread (tatting) When making a RING, the thread from the shuttle that is wound around the left hand and over which the stitches are made. *See also* AUXILIARY THREAD.

side loop (needle) In Armenian lace a loop projecting from the side of a stitch. *See also* DOUBLE SIDE LOOP, SINGLE SIDE LOOP.

side sewing (bobbin) *See* EDGE SEWING.

side vein (bobbin) *See* BRANCHED VEIN.

silk (yarn) Filaments produced by the silk moth (Bombyx mori) to make its cocoons. These are unravelled and spun into yarn. *See also* CONTINUOUS FILAMENT, DENIER, RAW SILK, SCROOP, SPUN SILK, YARN, YARN COUNT.

silk system (yarn) Yarn thickness expressed as the weight in drams of 1000 yards of yarn, if the yarn is 50 1000 yards of it will weigh 50 drams. *See also* DIRECT COUNT SYSTEM, CONVERSION FACTOR, YARN COUNT.

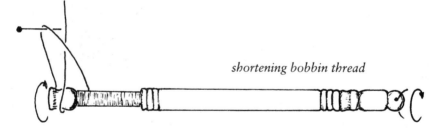

shortening bobbin thread

silver bobbin (bobbin) A BOBBIN made of silver for presentation, not for use. Some 'silver' bobbins are, in fact, made of pewter.

silver lace (bobbin) *See* BULLION LACE.

simple fan (bobbin) A torchon fan with a curve at the HEADSIDE supported by a V of pinholes and made by the WORKERS working alternately to the headside and the supporting V of pinholes. The appearance can be altered by using CLOTH (figure a) or HALF STITCH and including TWISTS in selected places. Half stitch fans should be protected with a CLOTH AND TWIST EDGE (figure b) unless the article is to be completely protected after it is made – in a paperweight, for example. Also called shell, shell edge/fan and torchon fan. *See also* SOLID FAN *and* Appendix for indicator.

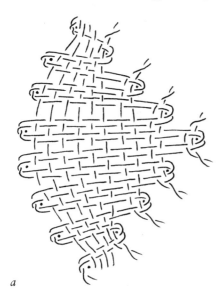

a

simple knot (stitch) (netting) This knot, which is easier than the FISHERMAN'S KNOT, has a tendency to slip below the loop while being made, making it useful when WORKING IN THE ROUND and NETTING ONTO A HANDLE/RING. Holding the MESH STICK horizontally below the FOUNDATION THREAD or loop, pass the thread down in front of the stick, up the back and through the loop from back to front. Lay the thread over to the left and hold with the left thumb (figure a), take the SHUTTLE to the right, pass behind the foundation loop and over the SHUTTLE THREAD (figure b). Pull up until the thread lies snugly round the mesh stick with the knot at the top. Usually the knot is worked around the base of the previous loop (figure c), but when it is used to start circular netting or when starting with a ring or handle, it must lie below the item (figure d).

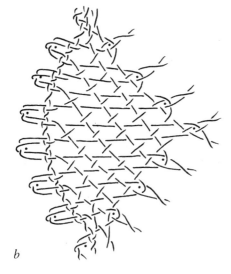

b

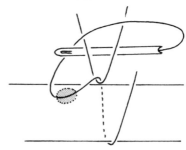

a

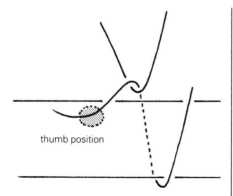

b

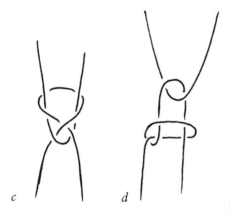

c   *d*

simple picot (bobbin) *See* SINGLE LOOP PICOT.

simple picot (needle) (1) *See* FRENCH KNOT PICOT. (2) *See* LOOP(ED) PICOT.

simple round stitch (bobbin) *See* EVERLASTING STITCH.

simple spider (bobbin) *See* SPIDER.

simple twisted vein (bobbin) *See* TWISTED VEIN.

simulated footside (bobbin) *See* FALSE FOOT.

simulated picot (tatting) *See* CLIMBING OUT OF A RING.

single Brussels/buttonhole stitch (needle) *See* BRUSSELS STITCH.

single corded Brussels/Bruxelles/ buttonhole stitch (needle) *See* CORDED BUTTONHOLE STITCH.

single cording (bobbin) *See* CABLE GIMP, RAISED GIMP.

single crochet (crochet) *See* SLIP STITCH.

single darned centre (needle) A Tenerife medallion CENTRE darned with the needle passing under and over single threads (figure).

single head (bobbin) A simply shaped bulbous top to a BOBBIN without a groove (figure). *See also* DOUBLE HEAD.

single horse (bobbin) A bar, often slightly bowed, on three legs, used to prevent the PILLOW from slipping off the lap (figure).

single knot stitch (needle) *See* VALSESIAN STITCH.

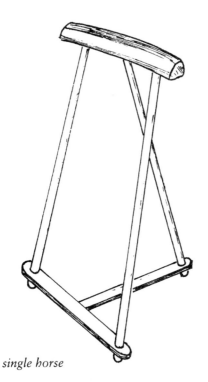

single horse

single loop join (crochet) A method of joining strips of hairpin crochet. Holding two strips side by side, start at the lower edges by passing the hook

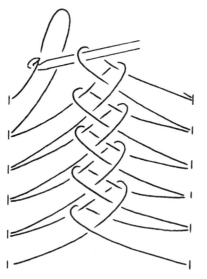

from front to back through the first loop of the right strip, then front to back through the first loop of the other strip. Pull the first loop through the second. Continue picking up loops from each strip alternately, each time drawing it through the loop already on the hook (figure). *See also* LOOP JOIN.

single loop picot (bobbin) A weak SINGLE THREAD PICOT that usually disappears when the lace is used and washed. When made on the right-hand side of a PLAIT, place the point of a pin behind the thread pointing to the left, lift the point forwards over the bobbin head and place in the pinhole. When made on the left-hand side of a plait, place the point of a pin behind the thread pointing to the right, lift the point forwards over the thread above the pin and place in the pinhole (figure). Also called simple picot, single picot and twisted picot. *See also* CAUGHT PICOT, SINGLE THREAD PICOT.

single loop stitch (bobbin) *See* BRUSSELS STITCH. This term is usually used by embroiderers.

single neck (bobbin) A BOBBIN with a SINGLE HEAD. There is, therefore, only one narrow section – i.e., where thread is wound. There is no separate groove in which the HITCH can rest (figure).

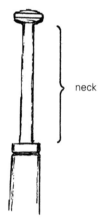

neck

single pearl chain (tatting) Using two SHUTTLES and an AUXILIARY THREAD, work DOUBLE STITCHES with each shuttle in turn, arranging the stitches so that those from one shuttle face one way and those from the other shuttle face the other way (figure). *See also* DOUBLE PEARL CHAIN.

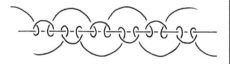

single picot (bobbin) *See* LOOP(ED) PICOT.

single picot (needle) *See* FRENCH KNOT PICOT.

single ply (yarn) A singly twisted unit of thread with all fibres twisting together. *See also* YARN.

single point de Venise (needle) *See* POINT DE VENISE.

single running stitch foundation (needle) In Tenerife lace the circle of running stitches that supports the WEB. The web is STRETCHED by passing the needle out through one stitch and back through the next (figure).

single side loop (needle) In Armenian lace a loop projecting from the side of a stitch into a row of loops. Make a loop (figure a), make a loop to its top (this forms the side loop (figure b). *See also* DOUBLE SIDE LOOP.

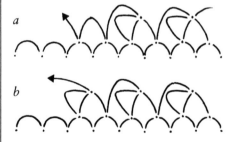

a

b

single stitch (tatting) One half of a DOUBLE STITCH.

single thread picot (bobbin) A PICOT made using a single thread. *See also* CAUGHT PICOT, SINGLE LOOP PICOT.

single twist(ed) bar (bobbin) After TWISTING the pair on the right-hand side by placing the point of a pin behind the thread pointing to the left and lifting the point forwards over the bobbin head as many times as required, SET UP A PIN and return across the row (figure a). When making twists on the left-hand side, place the point of a pin behind the thread pointing to the right, lift the point forwards over the thread above the pin, repeating as required (figure b). Make a sewing when the other end of the bar is reached.

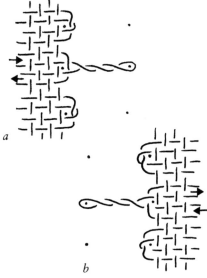

a

b

singles (yarn) A singly twisted unit of yarn with all fibres twisting together in one direction, its thickness being gauged by the number of hanks of a given length of yarn that can be spun from a set weight. The 's' included when a number is quoted as 2/120s refers to each unit being a 120 singles. *See also* FOLD, YARN.

siunashar (needle) In Armenian lace make a long loop (figure a), make a stitch at the top of the loop above the previous knot so that both threads lie parallel (figure b). Also called column.

a

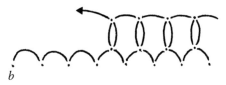

b

six pair/plait crossing (bobbin) Using pairs, work (figure):

pair 2 over 3, 4 over 5
twist centre pairs (3 over 2)
pair 2 over 3, 4 over 5
twist outer pairs (2 over 1 and 6 over 5)
pin between pairs 3 & 4
pair 2 over 3, 4 over 5
twist centre pairs (3 over 2)
pair 2 over 3, 4 over 5

Also called three-plait crossing. *See* Appendix for indicator.

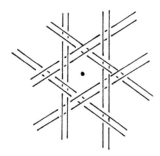

six-pin honeycomb ring (bobbin) A HONEYCOMB RING having six stitches surrounded by a gimp (figure).

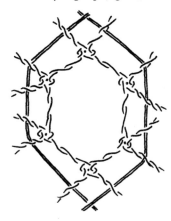

six-pointed star ground (bobbin) *See* KAT STITCH.

six thread plait (bobbin) *See* THREE-PAIR PLAIT.

skip thread (yarn) *See* SLIP THREAD.

slack (tambour) A filling of CHAIN STITCHES made using a large hook with fine thread, which results in loose loops that fill areas better than tighter crisp ones.

slanting (bobbin) *See* BIAS GROUND.

slash mark (bobbin) A mark used in SCHEMATIC DIAGRAMS to indicate twists. *See* Appendix.

Slavic/slave ground (bobbin) One of the ROSE GROUNDS. LINK pairs together with HALF STITCHES, centre pairs half stitch, pin, half stitch, half stitch left two pairs, half stitch right two pairs, centre pairs half stitch, pin half stitch (figure).

slider (bobbin) A thin layer of horn, sheet of talc, perspex or acetate film used between COVER CLOTHS that makes it possible for pricking and lace to be seen while protecting them from wear and dirt, and also prevents threads from catching on pins.

slip knot (bobbin) A loop secured with a knot so that the loop, or noose, can be made larger or smaller by sliding the knot along the thread. Make a circle of thread (figure a) and pass a loop from the upper thread (A) through the circle from back to front, ease up gently, (figure b). Usually (B) is the STANDING END leading to the ball or shuttle, and (C) the TAIL or FREE END.

slip stitch (crochet) Insert hook under top two threads of previous row, yarn

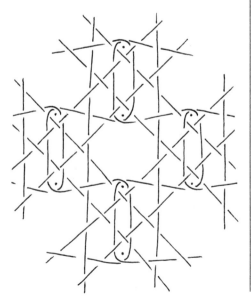

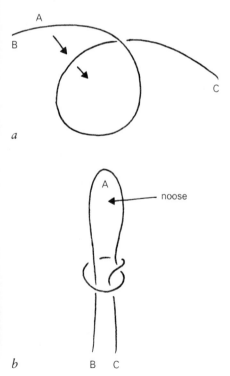

over hook and draw loop through all loops on hook (figure). Also called single crochet.

slip thread (yarn) A continuous skein divided into sections or slips of 96 yards (about 105 metres), by a thick coloured thread, usually red or dark pink. The size was determined by the number of slips per skein – i.e., 12 × 96 yard sections per skein for 12 slip thread. *See also* PACKET, PARCEL.

slipping a mesh (netting) Make a knot but remove the MESH STICK before pulling the knot tight. Sometimes used when DECREASING.

small circle (needle) In Tenerife lace a circle of 20 pins (figure a), with the WEB STRETCHED by bringing the thread between pins 1 and 20 and around the remaining pins in the following order: 9, 18, 7, 16, 5, 14, 3, 12, 1, 10, 19, 8, 17, 6, 15, 4, 13, 2, 11 and 20 (figure b). This results in a hole forming in the centre of the web, the edge of which is bound by oversewing with the thread passing around the group of threads encircling the centre and passing up through the space made by a pin, taking

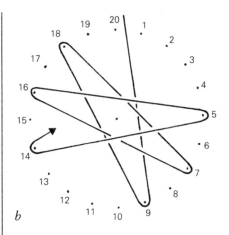

b

each pin in turn. The outer edge is secured by a round of KNOT STITCH.

small snowflake (bobbin) A group of Flanders FILLINGS with pairs travelling across each other, based on a square grid

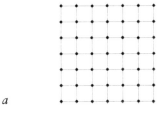

a

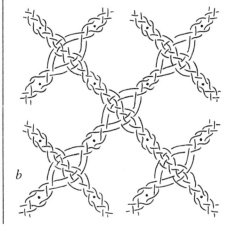

b

a

(figure a). There are several variants, one of which is illustrated (figure b). Also called little snowflake. *See also* FLIES, LARGE SNOWFLAKE, SNOWBALL.

Smyrna stitch (needle) *See* RODI STITCH.

snake bead (bobbin) A hand-made bead, used to weight bobbins, having a spiral decoration that starts at the hole on one side and ends at the hole on the other (figure). Also called evil eye bead.

snarling (needle) The word used when the yarn kinks and twists close to the eye of the needle or when it passes through the work, thus preventing the smooth passage of the yarn. Remove by allowing the yarn to hang freely and untwist. It is particularly troublesome when using highly twisted yarn.

snatch (bobbin) A WHOLE STITCH block of six pins with SNATCH PINS worked down each side, found in some Honiton fillings including TOAD-IN-THE-HOLE (figures a and b).

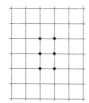

a   plot on 1mm graph paper

b

snatch pin (bobbin) A Honiton term for RUNNERS passing around a pin with seven TWISTS instead of working an EDGE STITCH, as used for a SNATCH (figure). Also called WINKIE PIN.

snowball (bobbin) A Flanders filling in which some pairs change direction within the units. There are several variants, one of which is illustrated (figure). There is no standard grid pattern. *See also* LARGE SNOWFLAKE, SMALL SNOWFLAKE.

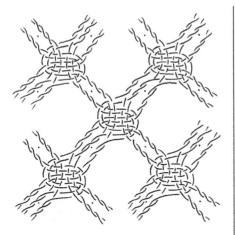

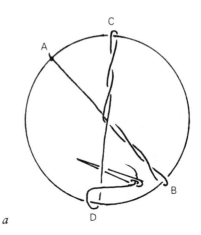

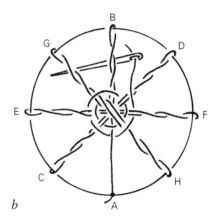

a

b

snowflake filling/ground (bobbin) A Flanders filling with pairs travelling across each other. *See also* LARGE SNOWFLAKE, SMALL SNOWFLAKE, SPIDER GROUND.

solid fan (bobbin) A SIMPLE FAN made completely in CLOTH STITCH with TWISTS as the WORKERS pass around the pins.

Sorrento bar (needle) *See* TWISTED BAR.

Sorrento edging (needle) An edging made as ANTWERP EDGING but with alternating long and short spaces between stitches (figure).

Sorrento stitch (needle) *See* SPANISH GROUND.

Sorrento wheel (needle) A decoration for a small space. Lay the thread from A to B and whip back along it to the centre. Take it across to C and whip back to the centre, across to D, whip back to the centre (figure a) and continue until the thread has reached the centre after point H. Darn around the centre, going under bars G, C, H and D, then over bars G and E, and continue going round over, or under, G and E together, otherwise the needle will always be working over and under the same threads (figure b). When the centre has reached the required size, whip along the bar to H. Also called cobweb, darning stitch web, ordinary cobweb, spider, stitched ring and web in darning stitch. *See also* BAR ROSETTE, FLAT CUTWORK, RAISED RIB COBWEB.

South Bucks bobbin (bobbin) A thick,

*South
Bucks
bobbin*

*Spanish
bobbin*

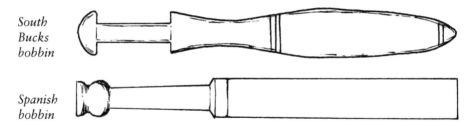

unspangled BOBBIN with a SINGLE HEAD (figure). Also called bobtailed bobbin, dump and thumper. *See also* EAST MIDLANDS BOBBIN.

spaced (needle) A term applied to needle lace stitches that are not closely worked so that two or more stitches may be worked through the gaps between them.

spangle (bobbin) A circle of beads attached with wire to the TAIL of an EAST MIDLANDS BOBBIN, to add weight and aid tension (figure). Sometimes called gingle. *See also* BOTTOM BEAD, SHACKLE, STAPLE, TOP BEAD.

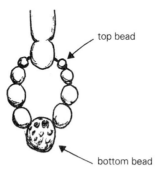

top bead

bottom bead

spangling (bobbin) The process of stringing appropriate beads on a wire and attaching them to a BOBBIN to form a SPANGLE.

spangling (tambour) Working with sequins.

Spanish bobbin (bobbin) An unspangled BOBBIN with a DOUBLE HEAD and thick, straight shank (figure).

Spanish fan (bobbin) A torchon fan having a curve at the HEADSIDE supported by a V of pinholes and having a double line of pinholes from the point of the V to the centre of the curve. The WORKERS alternate between headside and the central division. The appearance can be altered by including TWISTS in various places or varying the thickness of the workers by using a double or thicker thread or by substituting a GIMP (figure). Also called cloth and twist fan, open torchon fan, palm and twisted torchon fan. *See also* FEATHER *and* Appendix for indicator.

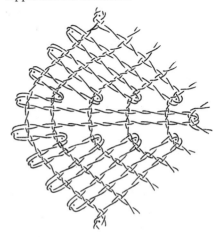

Spanish ground/mesh (bobbin) The most frequently used TWISTED HALF

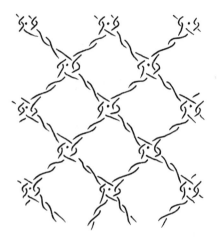

STITCH GROUND of torchon lace (figure), made by working:
  half stitch and twist
  pin
  half stitch and twist
Also called double twisted ground and pinhole ground.

Spanish ground (needle) Worked as follows:
  row 1: make groups of three
  POINT DE SORRENTO STITCHES
  with spaces between them
  row 2: make two stitches between the groups of three
  row 3: make three stitches in the gaps between the pairs of stitches
Repeat rows 2 and 3 as required (figure).

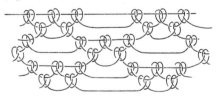

Spanish pillow (bobbin) A long, cylindrical PILLOW, tapering slightly at one end, made from a bundle of straw tightly rolled in brown paper with other layers pasted over. It is used with the upper end supported, often against a wall, and the lower, tapering end between the knees (figure). The same style is used in Malta.

Spanish point (needle) *See* POINT D'ES-PAGNE.

spider (bobbin) TWIST the pairs making the spider (there is no set number of twists but make approximately the same number as pairs entering per side). CLOTH STITCH the pairs from one

side across those of the other, set a pin in the centre and cloth stitch the pairs back. TWIST each pair as before (figure). Also called simple spider. *See also* BEDFORDSHIRE SPIDER, COBWEB (bobbin), CUT SPIDER, GERMAN SPIDER, HALOED SPIDER, SIMPLE SPIDER, SPIDER GROUND *and* Appendix for indicator.

spider (web) (needle) *See* SORRENTO WHEEL.

spider ground (bobbin) An area of spiders running one into another, without intervening lines of torchon ground, usually having only two 'legs' entering from each side (figure). Also called compound spider and snowflake ground. *See* Appendix for guidelines.

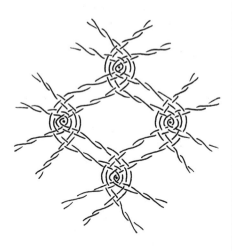

spider in/with a ring (bobbin) *See* HALOED SPIDER.

spider lace/work (netting) *See* FILET LACE. Also known as decorated netting.

spider web wheel (needle) A needle-made wheel with a back-stitched centre (figure). Also called English wheel, raised rib cobweb and web in rib stitch.

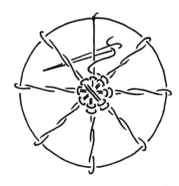

See also RIBBED CUTWORK, SORRENTO WHEEL.

spider with eye (bobbin) *See* GERMAN SPIDER.

spine (bobbin) *See* PICOT (bobbin).

spine (crochet) *See* SURFACE SPINE.

spiral bead (bobbin) A hand-made bead, used to weight bobbins, made by winding hot glass around a piece of wire (figure). *See also* WOUND BEAD.

spiral inscription (bobbin) A BOBBIN bearing an inscription, such as a saying, name or date, as a decoration. The letters, which are formed by a series of dots, either coloured or burnt or painted in a spiral round the SHANK, are read by rotating the bobbin, usually starting from the bottom. *See also* COMMEMORATIVE BOBBIN.

spiral line (tatting) *See* TWISTED CHAIN.

spiral pewter (bobbin) An INLAID BOBBIN with a spiral of PEWTER inlay around the SHANK.

spiral ring (tatting) *See* TWISTED RING.

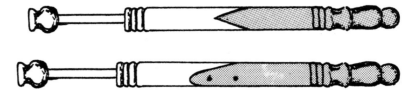

spliced bobbin

spliced bobbin (bobbin) A BOBBIN made of more than one type of wood, or of wood and bone, joined together with a V (figure a) or with a diagonal joint (figure b), often secured with rivets. *See also* SECTIONED BOBBIN.

split ring (tatting) Using two shuttles to make a CHAIN and REVERSE WORK. Using shuttle 1, start making the RING with the second half of a DOUBLE STITCH and work as usual as far as required. Then work the other side with shuttle 2 without CAPSIZING the knots. Use shuttle 1 to draw up the ring. The following chain or ring will continue from a point other than that at which the ring was started (figure). Also called mousehole ring.

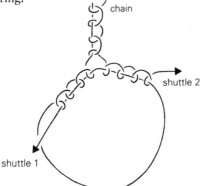

chain

shuttle 2

shuttle 1

split threads (needle) These can be unsightly and are less likely to happen when a ballpoint or tapestry needle rather than one with a sharp point is used.

spool (netting) *See* MESH STICK.

spool holder (general) A spike supported by a base for holding spools of yarn while yarn is being unwound (figure).

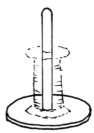

spot flower (tambour) Enlarge a single mesh with a stiletto and work CHAIN STITCH into each of the six holes surrounding it (figure). Spot flowers can be worked in a regular pattern to form a filling.

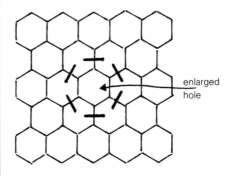

enlarged hole

spot (stitch) (bobbin) *See* TALLY.

spotted ground (general) Net or simple ground scattered with regularly or irregularly spaced spots. In bobbin lace the spots are generally TALLIES. Also called point d'esprit.

sprang (general) A possible precursor of bobbin lace. A fabric produced by winding a thread round two threads supported by a frame and threading a cord through the centre (figure a). Starting from one side, the threads are manipulated by the fingers twisting one or more across one or more, and a rod is passed through them to maintain their new positions. The cord is then removed. When the row is complete the rod is pushed up (figure b) and down, moving the twists to the ends. The cord is replaced and another row started. When the two sections approach the centre they are secured by a row of stitches or the work is folded across the

centre, the sides sewn together and the loops that are produced along the fold are knotted to form a bag.

sprig lace (bobbin) *See* PART LACE.

spun silk (yarn) Short filaments from cocoons that have been damaged by grubs eating their way out are spun into SINGLES and plied. The resulting thread is numbered using the COTTON COUNT SYSTEM (Ne). *See also* YARN.

square cushion (bobbin) *See* SQUARE PILLOW.

square cut (bobbin) A glass bead used in SPANGLES to weight bobbins. It is made by pressing hot glass into a cube between files, so that a pattern of dimples is created on the sides (figure). Also called cut bead.

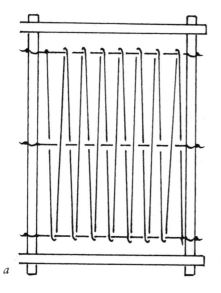

a

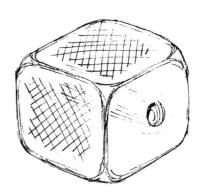

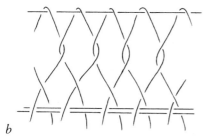

b

square-ended tally/plait, square dot (bobbin) A TALLY that is the same width throughout. In Bedfordshire lace also called plait; Honiton workers call it cutwork, leadwork and ludwork. *See also* GATE, LADDER.

square foundation (needle) A series of parallel threads with a similar set lying at right angles over it (figure).

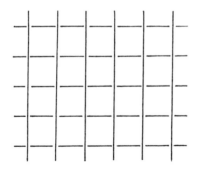

square ground/mesh (bobbin) (1) *See* FLANDERS GROUND. (2) A form of torchon ground that is worked horizontally (figure). *See also* BOBBIN FILET.

square netting (netting) NETTING in

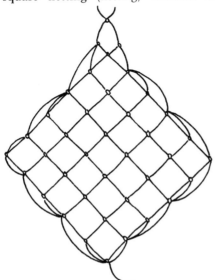

which the sides of the meshes are parallel with the sides of the piece. This is produced by starting with two meshes and INCREASING each row by one mesh worked at the end of the row until it is the required size, then DECREASING by one mesh at the end of each row (figure). Also called plain filet. Not to be confused with PLAIN NETTING.

square pillow (bobbin) Take a 90cm (36in) square of strong fabric, bring the corners together and sew three of the seams, leaving part of the fourth open for stuffing. Stuff very firmly with straw and close the opening (figure). Traditionally a Midlands pillow. Also called square cushion.

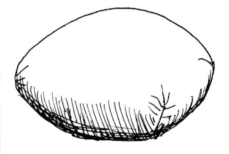

square plait (bobbin) A Bedfordshire term. *See* SQUARE-ENDED TALLY.

square tally (bobbin) *See* SQUARE-ENDED TALLY.

stabbing (bobbin/tambour) *See* PRICKING (OUT).

stacking pins (bobbin) Long pins, approximately 17cm (6¾in) in length, used to store CONTINENTAL BOBBINS while working. Place the first pin towards the back of the PILLOW at about the centre of the SHANK (figure a), slide the point of another pin under between

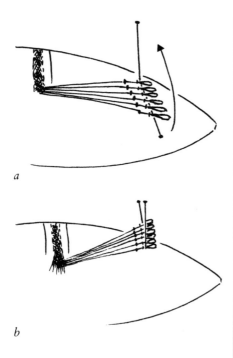

a

b

six and eight bobbins, insert the point a little way into the pillow about 1cm (⅖in) from the first and lift until almost vertical, then push firmly into the pillow. The bobbins slide down between the two pins (figure b). To bring the bobbins back into use, let the second pin down slowly and the bobbins should return to their former positions. Also called support pins. *See also* DIVIDER.

stained bobbin (bobbin) A BOBBIN that has been coloured by being immersed in stain. The bobbin is sometimes partially turned after staining to reveal contrasting natural wood or bone.

stairs (bobbin) Pinheads sitting one on

top of another so that they gradually rise up (figure). *See also* BRIDGE, PIN DOWN.

stand (bobbin) *See* HORSE.

standing end/part (netting) The end of the string that is attached, as opposed to the FREE END.

staple (bobbin) A U-shaped piece of stiff wire driven into the TAIL end of a bobbin and through which the wire of the SPANGLE passes (figure).

star centre (needle) A Tenerife lace medallion with curved indentations into which circular medallions can be sewn (figure).

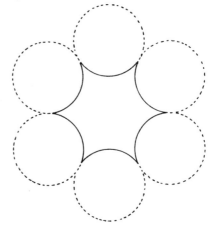

star mesh (bobbin) *See* KAT STITCH.

starting at a point (bobbin) *See* SETTING UP AT A POINT.

starting with a picot (tatting) *See* FALSE PICOT (tatting).

starting with a purl (bobbin) *See* SETTING UP AT A POINT WITH A PURL.

stem (bobbin) *See* SHANK.

stem (stitch) (bobbin) *See* RIB.

stem stitched centre (needle) The centre of a Tenerife lace medallion made by passing the needle over two threads or pairs and bringing it back under one (figure).

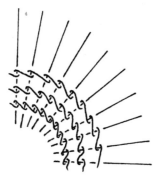

sterilizing pillow fillings (general) PILLOWS filled with natural materials, such as straw and bran, can become infested with small insects, particularly PSOCIDS. These can be destroyed: (1) By baking the pillow in an oven (not a gas oven or microwave oven) at 45°C (115°F) for three hours. (2) By placing the pillow in a polythene bag with dichloros-impregnated strips for three days, removing it for ten days and replacing it for another three (air well outdoors to remove fumes before using). (3) By placing it in a deep freeze for

three days, removing it for ten days and replacing it for another three.

stick (bobbin) *See* LACE STICK.

stick (netting) *See* MESH STICK.

stiletto (general) A pointed implement for making holes in fabric and enlarging meshes of machine-made net (figure).

stirrup (netting) A loop of thick thread, string, tape and so on, 150cm (60in) long, which is tied in a loop and passed under a foot and to which the working thread is attached when netting (figure). *See also* FOUNDATION LOOP.

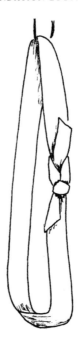

stitch about a/the pin (bobbin) A stitch made outside the EDGE PIN when making a FOOTSIDE (figure). Also called edge stitch.

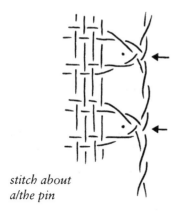

*stitch about
a/the pin*

stitched foundation (needle) In Tenerife lace a circle of running stitches that supports the web. *See also* DOUBLE RUNNING STITCH FOUNDATION, SINGLE RUNNING STITCH FOUNDATION.

stitched ring (needle) *See* SORRENTO WHEEL.

stitches without pins (bobbin) In floral Bucks and similar laces, unpinned ground stitches may be made where a pin would deflect the GIMP line but failure to make a stitch would result in an unsightly hole. Careful FIRMING UP will hold the stitches in place without

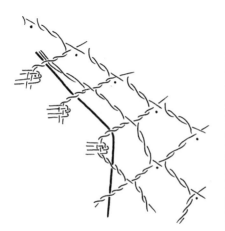

the usual pin. If an extra pair is required, it should be introduced previously and run along the gimp through one pair (figure).

stitching (bobbin) TAKING SEWINGS, particularly used when attaching a ROLL.

storing lace and yarn (general) Store lace and yarn made from natural fibres, preferably unfolded, between layers of ACID FREE TISSUE PAPER in cardboard boxes or drawers. Roll large pieces around a cardboard tube covered with acid free tissue paper and with a final layer of tissue paper round the lace. Such rolls can be conveniently stored by placing in one leg of an old pair of tights, tying the top and suspending from a hook or hanger. Keep yarn in cardboard boxes, lined with acid free tissue paper. Lace and yarn should never be stored in polythene bags or boxes, because both need to be in freely circulating air, and linen lace and yarn must never be allowed to become too dry or the fibres will crack. For information on storing man-made materials, contact the manufacturer.

straddling a pin (bobbin) *See* HANGING ON STRADDLE WISE.

straight edge (bobbin) *See* FOOTSIDE.

straight lace (bobbin) *See* CONTINUOUS (THREAD) LACE.

straight start (bobbin) Starting horizontally across the top of the work.

straight stitch return (needle) *See* RETURNING THREAD.

strap (general) *See* BAR (general).

strip lace (bobbin) *See* CONTINUOUS
LACE.

straw (bobbin) Used to stuff PILLOWS.
BARLEY is the best kind, but wheat straw
can be used, although the nodes are
somewhat harder.

strawberry pincushion (bobbin) A traditional PINCUSHION used by lacemakers.
Fold a 20cm (8in) square of fabric, right
sides facing, along a diagonal, and stitch
a seam along one and a half sides (figure
a). Turn to the right side. Stuff firmly,
turn in the edges of the opening and slip

stitch together. Pull the points together,
then stitch securely and add a bow to
cover the stitches. A narrow lace edging
is usually gathered and stitched along
the seam line (figure b). Also called
heart-shaped pincushion, lacemaker's
pincushion and sweetheart pincushion.
See also EMERY PINCUSHION.

stretching fabric in a frame (general)
Turn in the edges of the fabric to
strengthen and reduce fraying and
stitch. Working from the centre first pin,
both edges are pinned, then they are
stitched. Stitch opposite edges to the
tapes of the frame and lace the sides
(figure a). Including string or cord in the
turnings reduces the tendency for
stitches to tear the fabric (figure b). For

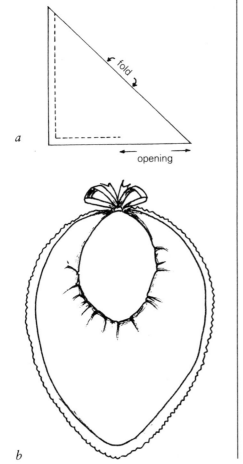

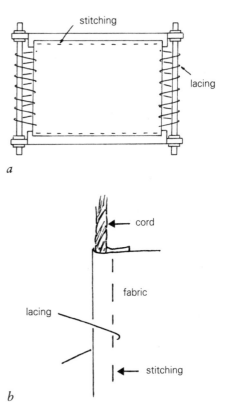

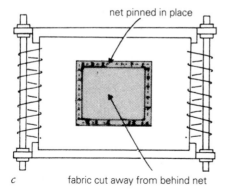

net pinned in place

c fabric cut away from behind net

small pieces and net mount a strong piece of fabric as described. Place the piece of net to be mounted in position and, starting from the centres of opposite sides and stretching, pin in place. Lifting the foundation fabric with a pin, cut out a portion behind the pinned-on piece, (figure c). It is not necessary to stitch the net in place, pinning has the advantage that the piece can be easily tensioned by repinning one pin a time, particularly for tambour work. *See also* NETTING FRAME.

stretching the web (needle) In Tenerife lace the process of winding the thread around the pins or threading through a STITCHED FOUNDATION before stitching. Also called warping.

strip grouping (crochet) A method for linking strips of hairpin crochet. *See also* BUD GROUP, FAN GROUP.

strip lace (bobbin) *See* CONTINUOUS (THREAD) LACE.

striver (bobbin) A DECORATED PIN, its name reflecting its function – i.e., to mark a position at which to aim in order to work quickly, such as when working a pattern repeat or a length to be made in a certain time. Often workers would compete against each other. Today, the name can be used for any decorated pin. *See also* BUGLE, BUR(R) HEAD, SEALING WAX.

striver bar (bobbin) *See* THREAD CLAMP.

styrofoam pillow (bobbin) A PILLOW made from styrofoam, either CARVED or MOULDED.

support pin (bobbin) (1) In freestyle and floral laces the pin placed between pairs to hold them in place but not supporting WORKERS or stitches (figure). Also called prop. (2) *See* STACKING PIN. (3) A pin over which pair(s) are hung when starting a piece. It is usually removed soon afterwards to allow the pair to settle into the work without leaving a loop.

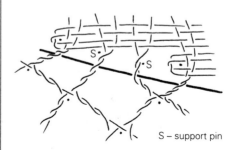

S – support pin

support pin (needle) A pin used to hold a loop of thread to the required size or position while stitches are made around it. *See also* LOOP(ED) PICOT.

support thread (needle) A temporary thread used to hold a loop of thread to the required size or position, while stitches are made around it. Often, both ends of the thread are supported by being wound around pins. *See also* LOOSE LEAF.

surface gimp (bobbin) *See* RAISED GIMP.

surface spine (stitch) (crochet) Tie the thread to the PRONG of a HAIRPIN and wind the thread round the prongs, ensuring that there are the same number of loops on each, and tie the end to a prong. Start working the spine by fastening on at the lower end with a DOUBLE CROCHET around the first loop. Keeping the working thread to the back, * insert the hook over the next double loop across the prongs, yarn over hook and draw through the one on the hook. Repeat from * for the length of the strip and fasten off. Remove carefully from the hairpin (figure). *See also* HAIRPIN CROCHET.

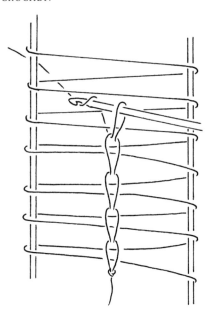

surface stitch (needle) Embroidery worked over a framework of threads as in FILET LACE.

surface tally *See* OVERLAID TALLY.

suspended leadwork (bobbin) In Honiton lace a single LEADWORK worked in the centre of a space, either between two sections of work or in a hole left within a braid.

Swedish bobbin (bobbin) An un-spangled BOBBIN with a SINGLE HEAD and bulbous SHANK for weight (figure).

Swedish pillow (bobbin) An oval FLAT PILLOW with a ROLLER set towards the back, which is convenient for making lengths of lace because the pattern can be joined in a continuous loop, the sloping FRONT being comfortable for spreading bobbins while working (figure).

sweetheart (bobbin) *See* BUR(R) HEAD.

sweetheart bead (bobbin) *See* VALENTINE BEAD.

sweetheart pincushion (bobbin) *See* STRAWBERRY PINCUSHION.

swing filling/leadworks (bobbin) *See* NO-PIN FILLING.

swing leadwork (bobbin) Single LEAD-WORK used to fill a small space.

Swedish bobbin

sympathetic knot (bobbin) A knot used to restrain the worker when it exchanges with a passive within the work (figure). A Bedfordshire term. *See also* TYING THE RUNNERS.

synthetic yarn (yarn) Yarn that has been chemically produced.

sympathetic knot

T

tail (**bobbin**) The end portion of an EAST MIDLANDS BOBBIN through which the hole is drilled for the SPANGLE wire; often divided from the shank by a groove. *See also* BOBBIN.

tail (general) A loose end of thread, often the starting end that floats loose when the thread is knotted to the FOUNDATION THREAD.

taking a rubbing (bobbin) An early method of copying a pricking. A piece of thin paper is fixed over the wrong side of a PRICKING and the surface rubbed with HEELBALL or RUBBING WAX, as for taking a brass rubbing. Lace can be copied in a similar way.

taking out pairs (bobbin) *See* THROW(ING) OUT PAIRS.

taking (up/a) sewing (bobbin) Making a SEWING.

taking up the slack (bobbin) *See* FIRMING UP.

taking up the thread (crochet) *See* YARN OVER HOOK.

talc (bobbin) *See* SLIDER.

tally (bobbin) A square, rectangular or leaf-shaped motif produced by weaving a single thread across three others. Also called fat hen, grain, jewel, matting stitch, paddle, point d'esprit, seed, spot stitch, square dot and woven plait. *See also* BARLEYCORN, BEEHIVE TALLY, DIVIDED TALLY, GATE, LEAF, PASS, PLAIT, RAISED RIB LEAF, POINT D'ESPRIT, SQUARE-ENDED TALLY, WHEATEAR, WORKER *and* Appendix for indicator.

tambour frame (tamboured lace) Originally a circular frame used for embroidery, but square or rectangular frames are preferable when tambouring net. *See also* EMBROIDERY FRAME, STRETCHING FABRIC IN A FRAME.

tambour hook (tambour) A fine-pointed hook inserted into a handle. The opening of the hook should be aligned with the retaining screw. When the hook is permanently fixed into the handle there may be a dot or inlay design indicating the alignment of the hook. When it is in use, the screw or dot, and hence the hook, faces the line of work (figure).

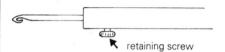

retaining screw

Tanders day (tradition) 30 November, a lacemakers' holiday and feast day when special home-brewed drinks and cakes were made. The name is a corruption of Saint Andrew's day.

tape (bobbin) *See* TRAIL.

tape lace (needle) Lace made using a machine-made tape that is tacked over a design drawn on ARCHITECTS' LINEN or paper covered with plastic film, and tacked to a stiff fabric BACKING. The tape is sewn together where it touches, and needle-made FILLINGS are used in some or all the spaces between the different parts of the braid. Also called braid lace and ladies' work. *See also* BOBBIN TAPE LACE, HONITON BRAID, LACET (BRAID), MEZZO PUNTO.

taps (bobbin) A Honiton technique for raising the edge between several areas that abut one after the other. It usually starts with a section having a RAISED RIB. As the BACKING is completed, the pairs are reduced to those required for a ROLL and secured with a BUNCH AND TIE. * A roll is STITCHED along part of this section, turning into a RIB as it breaks away, and the abutting section is backed. Repeat from * as required. To work the pricking (figure a), start the rib from A to the tip of section B and back this section, make first a roll, then a rib to the tip of section C and back the section. Repeat this for section D. Roll up the central rib, rib to the tip of section E and back the section, roll, rib and back section F then G. Alternatively make a bunch and tie after completing section D and cut off pairs. SEW IN for the rib to the tip of E, continue as above (figure b).

tatting Lace consisting almost entirely of DOUBLE STITCHES made using a SHUTTLE or needle, taking the form of rings and/or CHAINS, usually decorated with PICOTS.

tatting pin (tatting) A short, fine crochet-type hook, used for JOINING. *See also* RING AND PIN.

Tawdry lace (tradition) A cheap, poor quality lace that was often sold at fairs. The name is a corruption of Saint Audry whose day, 17 October, was celebrated in some villages.

technical drawing (bobbin) *See* SCHEMATIC DIAGRAM.

tell (tradition) *See* LACE TELL.

template (general) Tracing or pricking on ACETATE that can be used to transfer the design. *See also* GRID.

temporary pin (bobbin) *See* AUXILIARY PIN.

ten stick (bobbin) Originally used for a RIB made using ten bobbins (sticks), now applied to any rib.

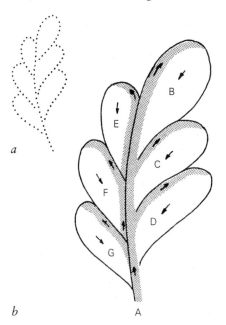

a

b

Tenerife wheel (needle) An implement with prongs or pins around the edge on which Tenerife lace can be made. *See also* RADIALLY PINNED WHEEL.

tex system (yarn) A yarn thickness expressed as the weight in grams of 1 kilometre of yarn, if the yarn is 50 tex, 1 kilometre will weigh 50 grams. *See also* CONVERSION FACTOR, DECITEX, YARN COUNT.

thistle head (bobbin) *See* DOUBLE HEAD.

thorn (general) *See* PICOT.

thorn bobbin (bobbin) A BOBBIN with a design or inscription of spots made by driving thorns into the shank.

thread clamp (bobbin) A wooden bar with two holes, which is placed over bobbin threads and pinned down to secure the bobbin threads in position during transportation (figure). Also called striver bar.

thread (general) *See* YARN.

thread count (general) *See* YARN COUNT.

thread diagram (bobbin) A diagram that indicates the path of every thread individually. See, for example, the illustration for a SIMPLE FAN. Not to be confused with GUIDELINE, PATTERN DRAFT or WORKING DIAGRAM.

thread lace (general) Lace made using

thread of vegetable origin – e.g., cotton or linen as opposed to metal thread.

thread over hook (crochet) *See* YARN OVER HOOK.

threaded couronne (needle) A couronne that appears to pass through the work, made by laying the RING STICK against the work and passing the thread winding around it through the work on each turn. The portion of threads above the work is buttonholed in the usual way. Also called disappearing couronne.

three-fold darning (needle) Darning across three threads or groups of threads. *See also* LEAF IN THREE-FOLD DARNING.

three-in-one bobbin (bobbin) *See* GRANDMOTHER BOBBIN.

three-pair plait (bobbin) (1) *Pairs 2 & 3 cloth stitch, pairs 1 & 2 cloth stitch, repeat from * as required. Also called six-thread plait (figure). (2) *See* MULTIPLE-PAIR PLAIT.

three part/thread plait (bobbin) A plait made using three threads or groups of threads, and made when plaiting hair

– i.e., 1 over 2, 3 over 2, repeated as required (figure).

thread part/thread plait

three-plait crossing (bobbin) *See* SIX PAIR/PLAIT CROSSING.

three stitch join (bobbin) *See* JOINING-ON-A-LEG.

three-twist bobbinet (machine) A machine-made net having four twists on each pair of threads, resulting in a light, diamond-shaped mesh used for APPLICATION and NEEDLERUN LACE (figure). The name comes from hand-bobbin workers' terminology, the stitch being a HALF STITCH and three TWISTS. Also called Brussels net.

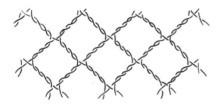

throw(ing) a thread (needle) *See* RETURNING CORD/THREAD.

throw(ing) back/off (bobbin) Bobbins are lifted and laid back over the work. Later, and before the pins are removed, the bobbins are cut off, sometimes trimmed off closely, sometimes after knotting (figure). Also called laying back pairs and throwing back pairs.

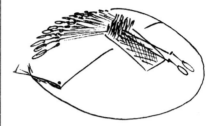

throw(ing) out (bobbin) Removing pairs of bobbins no longer required for making the lace; in some laces they are DOUBLED WITH THE GIMP through two or three pairs before being THROWN BACK (figure). Also called discarding pairs/threads and throwing out pairs.

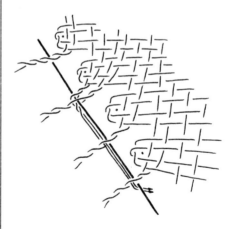

throwing up a roll (bobbin) Making a Honiton ROLL and STITCHING it on.

thumper (bobbin) *See* SOUTH BUCKS BOBBIN.

ticket number (yarn) The total yarn thickness expressed as the COTTON COUNT SYSTEM (Ne) three-fold equivalent – e.g., 3/60s Ne = ticket no. 60, while 2/40s = ticket no. 60. That is, the ticket number is the equivalent SINGLES (Ne)

tiger bobbin

number of the finished yarn multiplied by 3. *See also* CONVERSION FACTOR, TEX SYSTEM, YARN COUNT.

tie (general) *See* BAR (general).

tie out (bobbin) *See* BUNCH AND TIE.

tie pair (bobbin) A pair that has just been tied in a knot – e.g., having just made a BUNCH AND TIE.

tiger bobbin (bobbin) An INLAID BOBBIN with narrow bands of inlay around the shank (figure). *See also* COMPOUND INLAY BOBBIN, LEPTIG.

tinsel inlay (bobbin) *See* FAIRING.

tinting (general) Colouring lace using tea or coffee.

tissue lace (bobbin) A very fine Flanders lace, made at the end of the seventeenth century and during the eighteenth century. Also called opaque lace.

toad-in-the-hole (bobbin) A Honiton

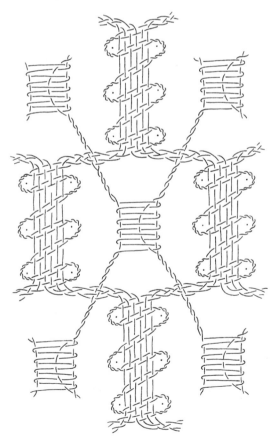

toad-in-the-hole

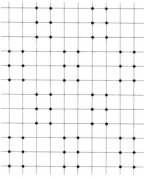

plot on 1mm graph paper

filling with LEADWORKS suspended between SNATCHES. After working a snatch, TWIST each pair and make a WHOLE stitch with the two right pairs. Whole stitch the leadwork pairs through the snatch pairs. Whole stitch and twist each two pairs the leadwork pairs have passed through. Twist the leadwork pairs five times, make the leadwork and again twist five times (figures a and b).

toad's foot (bobbin) *See* FRENCH FAN.

toggle (netting) A loop of fine cord suspending a shanked button (figure), used to support a GROMMET when starting netting from a circle.

toile (general) A French term. *See* CLOTH WORK.

tongue (netting) The narrow section of a NETTING NEEDLE/SHUTTLE attached by one end and used to retain thread (figure). *See also* LOADING A NEEDLE/SHUTTLE.

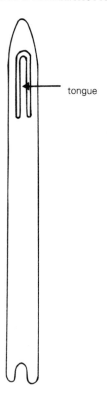

tongue

top bead (bobbin) A small bead adjacent to the BOBBIN or SHACKLE. Also called closing bead. *See also* SPANGLE.

top hole purl (bobbin) A purl at the point when SETTING UP AT A POINT WITH A PURL.

top sewing (bobbin) A SEWING, typical of Honiton lace, made over one BAR of the EDGE STITCH, usually the lower bar (figures a and b), although the upper bar may be used if it will produce a better

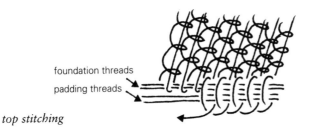

foundation threads

padding threads

top stitching

result. It is usually easier to make if the NEEDLEPIN is inserted through the PIN-HOLE and brought out between EDGE STITCHES than if it is worked the other way. Also called raised edge sewing. *See also* BOTTOM SEWING, NEEDLEPIN SEWING.

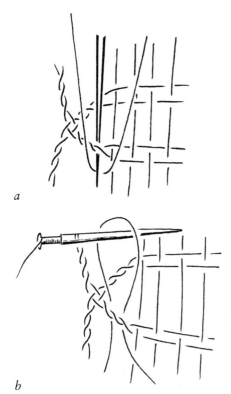

a

b

top stitching (needle) A final edging of BUTTONHOLE STITCH worked over the couched FOUNDATION THREAD in needle lace (figure), sometimes thickened with

PADDING THREADS, occasionally worked as an ARDENZA BAR, sometimes embellished with PICOTS and/or COURONNES. Also called le brodé, broiders, cordonnette and la feston. *See also* CRIN (LE), LOOPED CORDONNETTE, RAISED WORK (needle).

torchon double ground (bobbin) *See* WHOLE STITCH TORCHON GROUND.

torchon edge (bobbin) *See* FOOTSIDE and TORCHON FOOTSIDE.

torchon fan (bobbin) *See* SIMPLE FAN.

torchon foot(side) (bobbin) The FOOTSIDE characteristic of torchon lace, worked by taking the last of the GROUNDWORK PAIRS and working CLOTH AND TWIST with the FOOTSIDE PASSIVES. The WORKERS twist and a pin is SET UP under them. The workers make a cloth stitch and twist

with the EDGE PAIR and remain at the edge as the new edge pair, the former edge pair returning as workers making a cloth stitch and twist with the passives. The edge pair may be twisted two or three times according to taste (figure).

torchon ground/net (bobbin) A typical ground of torchon lace, with a diamond-shaped MESH having an ANGLE TO THE FOOTSIDE of 45 degrees, made by working HALF STITCH, pin, half stitch (figure). Also called plain hole ground. This basic ground can be modified by adding one or two twists between the pins and/or as the pins are set and substituting half stitch with CLOTH STITCH. See also CLOSED CHECK, DIEPPE GROUND, ROSE GROUND, SPANISH GROUND, TWISTED HALF STITCH GROUND, WHOLE STITCH TORCHON GROUND.

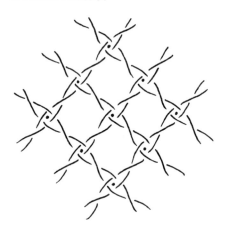

torchon honeycomb (bobbin) See BRABANT GROUND.

torchon pillow (bobbin) See FRENCH PILLOW.

tracers/tracer threads (bobbin) See PASSIVES.

tracing (needle) Outlining the design with the FOUNDATION THREAD.

tracing powder (needle) Fine powder used for POUNCING, powdered chalk, French chalk, light clay or charcoal, or any combination of these different colours to produce a suitable contrasting colour.

tractor (bobbin) See WIG HOOK.

trail (bobbin) A band of CLOTH or HALF STITCH zigzagging or undulating through the work, occasionally containing TWISTS. Also called tape. See also DOMINANT TRAIL, SECONDARY TRAIL and Appendix for indicator.

trail lace (bobbin) See BRAID LACE.

transferring (general) Removing lace motifs from net and remounting. See also APPLIQUÉ LACE, REGROUNDING.

traveller pair/travellers (bobbin) See WORKER.

travelling pillow (bobbin) A small, light PILLOW suitable for carrying and packing in a suitcase. See also HANDBAG PILLOW.

traversed net (general) A net in which some threads travel diagonally across the net.

treble Brussels stitch (needle) See GREEK NET STITCH.

treble crochet (crochet) YARN OVER HOOK, insert hook into next chain, yarn over hook and draw through a loop (three loops on the hook), yarn over hook and draw a loop through two loops (two loops on the hook), yarn over hook and draw a loop through both loops on hook (figure).

trefoil edge (needle) *See* ROSE POINT EDGE.

trellis stitch (bobbin) *See* TWISTED LINEN STITCH.

triangle (needle) *See* DARNED POINT, DARNED TRIANGLE.

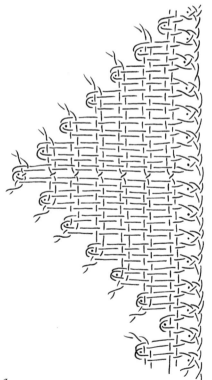

a

triangular area against the footside (bobbin) An area of CLOTH OR HALF STITCH. (1) The pairs reaching the vertical edge of the triangle alternately meet the pairs from the adjacent part of the work with the intervening row turning at that edge (figure a). (2) WORKERS reaching the vertical edge are used to make the FOOTSIDE and alternate with the EDGE PAIR (figure b). *See* Appendix for indicator.

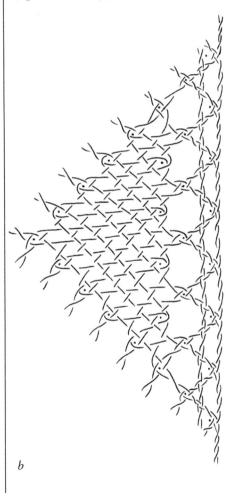

b

triangular graph paper (general) A triangle of GRAPH PAPER with an all-over pattern of triangles having ⅒in 2mm sides and every tenth line printed boldly. Used for pattern designing and drafting, it is particularly useful for Bucks point motifs because it has an angle of 60 degrees (figure). *See also* ISOMETRIC PAPER.

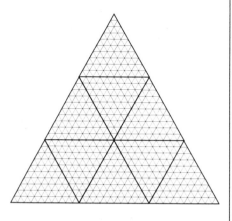

triangular ground (bobbin) A FILLING used in torchon lace (figures a and b).

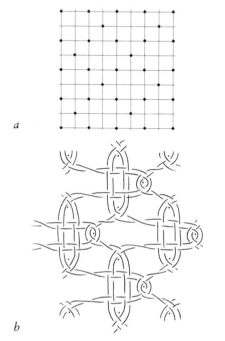

a

b

triangular loops (needle) *See* YERANG-YOUN.

triple Brussels stitch (needle) *See* GREEK NET STITCH.

trolly bobbin (bobbin) (1) A Honiton name for bobbins used to make CONTINUOUS (THREAD) LACE. (2) A bobbin slightly thicker than the rest of the bobbins being used, used for the GIMP. (3) *See* BEDFORDSHIRE TRAILER.

trolly lace (bobbin) A CONTINUOUS (THREAD) LACE made in Devon, similar to that made in the Midlands.

trolly net (bobbin) UNCOVERED GROUND or filling in Honiton lace having a grid at 45 degrees and worked HALF STITCH, TWIST twice (figure). Also called net filling.

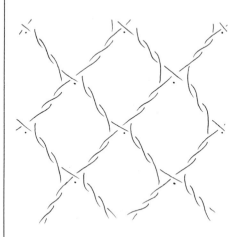

trou trou (bobbin) *See* EYELET LACE.

tuft (bobbin) *See* RAISED TALLY.

tulle du Puy filling (bobbin) A filling used in Milanese lace. At each pinhole the pairs already having one twist are worked cross, twist, cross, pin, cross, twist, cross, twist (figure).

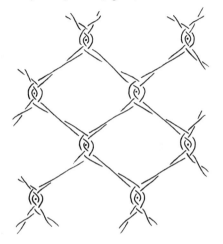

Tulle stitch (needle) (1) *See* BRUSSELS STITCH. (2) *See* BUTTERFLY STITCH, (3) *See* TWISTED NET STITCH.

Turkish stitch (needle) A KNOTTED BUTTONHOLE STITCH where the thread is taken over in a loop and the needle taken down behind the supporting thread and through the loop. At the end of the row a RETURNING THREAD is laid and included when working the following row (figure). Also called point de Turc/Turque.

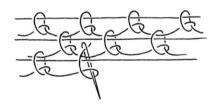

turn (bobbin) (1) *See* TWIST. (2) *See* BOBBIN WINDER.

turn pin (bobbin) (1) East Midlands term for a PICOT. (2) A pin at the end of a row where the direction of the work reverses.

turned shank (bobbin) A decoratively turned BOBBIN. There are many variations including BALUSTER BOBBIN.

turning/turning picot (tatting) When a CHAIN is turned over at a small PICOT, thus reversing its curve (figure).

turning a pillow (bobbin) Rotating the pillow through 180 degrees so that the work and bobbins are facing the opposite way.

turning stitch (bobbin) *See* CHANGING WORKERS.

turning stitch (bobbin) (1) Used at the PLAIN EDGE of a Honiton RIB. When the RUNNERS meet the edge DOWNRIGHTS at the plain edge they work WHOLE STITCH followed by a REVERSE HALF STITCH (figure). Can be used in other PART LACES. (2) *See* CHANGING WORKERS.

turnside/turn side (bobbin) *See* HEADSIDE.

twippering (bobbin) When CLOTHWORK, particularly in Bedfordshire lace, puckers due to being made from too thick a thread, containing too many PASSIVES or being inadequately FIRMED UP.

twirling (needle) The PICOT edge of CARRICKMACROSS APPLIQUÉ and GUIPURE, formed by twisting the FOUNDATION THREAD clockwise as it laid and securing with a single stitch. After drawing up the loop to the required size, a further two stitches are made across the overlap and two stitches made across the foundation thread before making the next loop (figure). The size of the loops may be regulated using a knitting needle or similar implement.

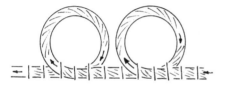

twist (bobbin) One of the basic moves. With a pair of bobbins pass the right-hand bobbin over the left-hand bobbin (figure). Also called turn.

twist (tatting) Make one half of the DOUBLE STITCH repeatedly and the work twists. When made with PLAIN stitches, the work twists in one direction, when made with PURLS it twists the other way.

twist net (bobbin) GROUND made by working HALF STITCHES followed by TWISTS and leaving pins UNCOVERED – e.g., POINT GROUND.

twist net (machine) A machine-made net, made by twisting threads, imitating POINT GROUND. *See* TWO-TWIST BOBBINET.

twist pair (bobbin) Twisted edge PASSIVES of a CLOTH AND TWIST EDGE.

twisted buttonhole stitch (needle) BUTTONHOLE STITCH with extra twists. *See also* GRECIAN POINT, POINT D'ESPAGNE, POINT DE GAZE GROUND, TWISTED NET STITCH.

twisted bar (needle) A single thread laid across a space and overcast back to the original side, resulting in a twisted appearance (figure). Also called bar in overcasting, Sorrento bar and whipped bar. Not to be confused with CORDED BAR.

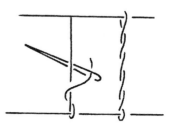

twisted chain (tatting) A CHAIN made by repeating the same half of a DOUBLE STITCH, which results in a spiral of stitches. Also called spiral line.

twisted chamber bobbin (bobbin) A BOBBIN of the CHURCH WINDOW type with the slots twisting around the shank. It may be used to contain a BABY BOBBIN, glass beads, lead shot or peppercorns (figure, p.227). *See also* LANTERN BOBBIN, PEPPER POT.

twisted chamber bobbin

twisted cloth stitch (bobbin) *See* CLOTH AND TWIST.

twisted edge stitch (needle) Over the FOUNDATION THREAD work a single row of spaced TWISTED BUTTONHOLE STITCHES with the thread crossing three times and the spaces equal to the width of three BUTTONHOLE STITCHES (figure a). Whip back across the row (figure b) and continue working making three stitches into every space (figure c). This and subsequent rows do not need to lie parallel with the edge. Also called twisted open edge stitch.

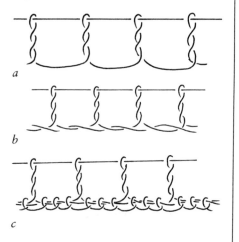

a

b

c

twisted footside (bobbin) A FOOTSIDE, in which the passives are worked in CLOTH AND TWIST (figure), used in Cluny lace. *See also* BEDFORDSHIRE FOOT(SIDE).

twisted half stitch ground (bobbin) A TORCHON GROUND worked with an extra TWIST either side of the pin, resulting in a larger hole around the pin. Also called closed pin stitch. *See* SPANISH GROUND for the most popular variety; other

varieties have more or fewer twists between the pins.

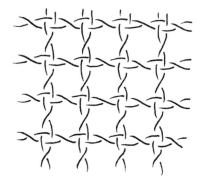

twisted footside

twisted filling stitch (needle) *See* RUSSIAN BARS.

twisted linen stitch (bobbin) Rows worked in CLOTH STITCH AND TWIST (figure). Also called trellis stitch.

twisted net stitch (needle) A TWISTED BUTTONHOLE STITCH in which the thread crosses twice. It is produced by passing the needle downwards through a space in the previous row, then over and under the working thread (figure). Also called double twisted net stitch, tulle stitch and twisted stitch. Not to be confused with POINT D'ESPAGNE or POINT DE GAZE GROUND. *See also* HOLLIE STITCH.

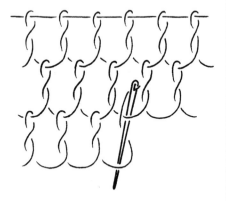

twisted open edge stitch (bobbin) *See* TWISTED EDGE STITCH.

twisted picot (bobbin) *See* SINGLE LOOP PICOT.

twisted picot (tatting) A very long PICOT made on a RING or CHAIN. Later, this is twisted tightly before a ring or chain is JOINED to it (figure).

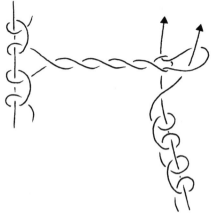

twisted ring (tatting) A RING made by repeating the same half of a DOUBLE

STITCH, which results in a spiral of stitches. Also called spiral ring.

twisted stitch (needle) *See* TWISTED NET STITCH.

twisted torchon fan (bobbin) *See* SPANISH FAN.

twisted vein (bobbin) A WORKED VEIN produced in CLOTHWORK by TWISTING the WORKERS one, two or three times between the same PASSIVES, starting with one twist, where the vein starts, and increasing by one twist each row until there are the required number of twists, then reducing by one twist each row before stopping the twists at the end of the vein (figure). Also called ladder braid/trail and simple twisted vein. *See* Appendix for indicator (worked vein).

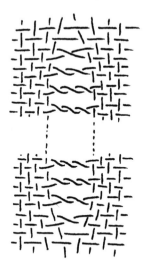

two-colour work (tatting) Using different coloured threads for BALL and SHUTTLE THREADS, or two shuttles wound with different colours. A RING takes the colour of the shuttle thread and a CHAIN the colour of the AUXILIARY THREAD.

two-fold darning (needle) Darning across two threads or groups of threads. *See also* LEAF IN TWO-FOLD DARNING.

two plait crossing (bobbin) *See* WINDMILL.

two-twist bobbinet (machine) Machine-made net that imitates POINT GROUND. The name comes from the bobbin laceworkers' terminology for the stitch – i.e., half stitch and two twists that results in the three twists found in this net (figure).

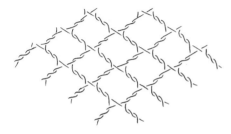

two twist edge (bobbin) When the WORKERS are TWISTED twice when passing round the EDGE PIN (figure). Also called pin under two.

tying tail to tail (bobbin) When tying a knot with two bobbins they are usually held TAIL pointing to tail (figure).

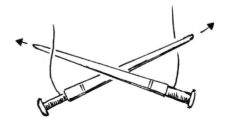

tying out (bobbin) *See* SEWING OUT.

tying the runners (bobbin) In Honiton lace, when the work turns a sharp corner or widens, a knot can be made with the RUNNERS immediately following the WHOLE STITCH with the COARSE PAIR or equivalent DOWNRIGHTS (figure), thus preventing the downrights from pulling away from the edge. *See also* SYMPATHETIC KNOT, TYING TAIL TO TAIL.

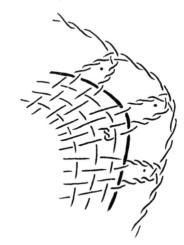

U

U-shaped pillow (bobbin) A pillow that combines the advantages of a MUSHROOM PILLOW and a BLOCK PILLOW (figure).

uncovered ground/pin (bobbin) A pin or pins without a following stitch made by the two pairs it separates – e.g., POINT GROUND.

under and over join (tatting) When a CHAIN or RING crosses over another chain or ring, with or without a JOIN. Also called crossing one line with another.

V-ground/stitch (needle) *See* BUTTER-
FLY STITCH.

Valenciennes ground (bobbin) (1)
Valenciennes square ground. *See* DIA-
MOND GROUND. (2) Valenciennes round
ground. *See* ROUND GROUND.

Valenciennes stitch (needle) *See* POINT
DE VALENCIENNES.

Valentine bead (bobbin) A flat, heart-
shaped bead with a ridged surface and
the hole passing down from the V to the
point (figure). Also called Pompadour
bead and sweetheart bead.

Valsesian stitch (needle) The basic knotted stitch of PUNTO AVORIO. Sometimes

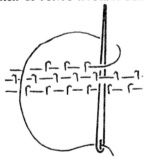

the first row is worked along the folded
edge of the fabric. Pass the needle, point
away from you, through the fabric or
under first part of the thread, and
through the loop of the WORKING THREAD
passing first behind then over it (figure).
Also called single knot stitch.

van dyked (bobbin) A deeply, and
usually sharply, indented edge.

vein (bobbin) *See* BRANCHED VEIN, LEAF
WITH RAISED VEIN, MIDRIB, MITTENS,
RAISED HONITON, RAISED RIB LEAF, RIB
AND LEADWORK VEIN, TWISTED VEIN,
WINDOWS, WORKED VEIN.

vein (needle) (1) By making a series of
holes – e.g., in CORDED BUTTONHOLE

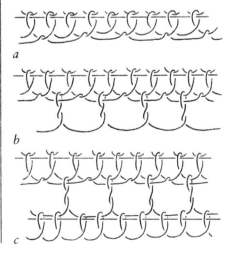

a

b

c

STITCH – whip the RETURNING THREAD through alternate stitches (figure a), work the returning row in TWISTED NET STITCH (figure b), followed by the returning thread and continuing with corded buttonhole stitch (figure c). (2) Laying the FOUNDATION THREAD along the vein and TOPSTITCHING with BUTTONHOLE STITCHES or ARDENZA BAR.

VELLUM (bobbin) A PARCHMENT made from calf skin. Also called vilain.

Venetian bar/cord/plait (bobbin) A bar formed by a single thread lacing from side to side, across a pair of threads, which are usually thicker than the working thread or may be a double thread. In the latter case the thread is usually wound double onto each bobbin. Mainly found in Cluny lace (figure). Also called bride de Venise and princess ganse.

Venetian bar (needle) *See* BUTTONHOLE(D) BAR.

Venetian bar ground (needle) Work a row of SPACED BUTTONHOLE STITCHES, * and return along the row closely buttonholing these loops. Work one buttonhole stitch into each loop. Repeat from * as required (figure).

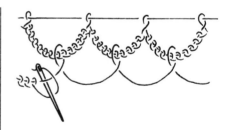

Venetian bead (bobbin) A highly decorated bead having raised lines and spots of several colours. Also called pompadour bead.

Venetian cloth stitch (needle) *See* CORDED BUTTONHOLE STITCH.

Venetian cobweb (needle) See BUTTONHOLED COBWEB/SPIDERS.

Venetian loop picot (needle) *See* LOOP(ED) PICOT.

Venetian picot (needle) Making the picot when progressing towards the left bring the thread down, round a SUPPORT PIN (or stitch in the BACKING), back over the foundation thread to the left of the last stitch, down under it and back round the pin from right to left. Pass the needle, from right to left, through the loop from front to back and over the working thread (figure). This makes the first stitch of the picot. Buttonhole stitch across the three threads until the previous work is reached. Also called knotted picot. Not to be confused with VENETIAN LOOP PICOT.

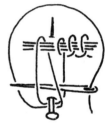

Venetian point (stitch) (needle) (1) *See* POINT DE VENISE. (2) *See* CINQ POINT DE VENISE.

Venetian stitch (needle) *See* BUTTERFLY STITCH.

Venice point (needle) *See* POINT DE VENISE.

vertical gimp (bobbin) A GIMP travelling straight down the lace, parallel to the FOOT(SIDE) (figure). *See also* REVERSE CATCH-PIN STITCH.

vertical shading (needle) Work across the space in CORDED BUTTONHOLE STITCH as far as required. Fasten on a thread of a different shade at the other side of work. Work a row in the original shade as far as required then, from the other end, work in the other shade, ensuring that the second thread passes through the first stitch of the first part of the row. Stagger the junctions in subsequent rows.

vilain (general) *See* VELLUM.

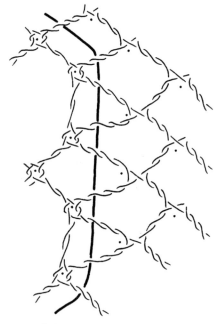

vertical gimp

virgin ground (bobbin) *See* POINT DE LA VIERGE.

vrai droschel/réseau (bobbin) *See* DROSCHEL GROUND.

W

waisted bobbin (bobbin) A BOBBIN with a SHANK that tapers towards the centre then widens to its original width (figure).

warp (bobbin and general) In weaving, the threads running the length of the fabric through which the WEFT thread is woven. *See also* PASSIVE.

warping (needle) *See* STRETCHING THE WEB.

washing lace (general) *See* CLEANING LACE.

wavily stitch (needle) *See* POINT D'ANVERS.

web in darning stitch (needle) *See* SORRENTO WHEEL.

weft (bobbin and general) (1) In weaving, the thread that weaves back and forth across the warp. (2) In bobbin lace see WORKER.

weaver (bobbin) *See* WORKER.

weavers' knot (general) Used by weavers to join threads. The ends can be trimmed off closely without the knot

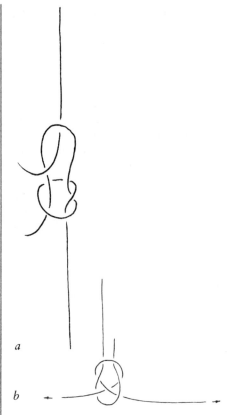

a

b

coming undone. Make a SLIP KNOT with the TAIL being the RUNNING END and pass the NOOSE over the end to which it is to be joined (figure a) and just close the knot, pull the running end until no

light can be seen through the knot, pull the two ends of the slip knot apart and the tail that passed through the slip knot should flip over as the knot locks (figure b). This method, only one of several, does not lock every time and several attempts may have to be made. However it is the best method when attempting to tie a bobbin to a short, broken thread.

weaver-legged spider (bobbin) A SPIDER where the last 'legs' entering become WEAVERS for part of the centre (figure). There are many variants.

weaving the coarse thread (bobbin) In Honiton lace when the COARSE THREAD passes across WHOLE or HALF STITCH it weaves through the DOWNRIGHTS, passing over the ones the previous thread passed under and vice versa. When there is a coarse thread on both sides of the work, one coarse thread can weave across, pass round the other and weave back; this allows one side to remain straight while the other indents (figure a). Alternatively, one thread weaves across and the other pair weaves back; this results in both sides indenting (figure b).

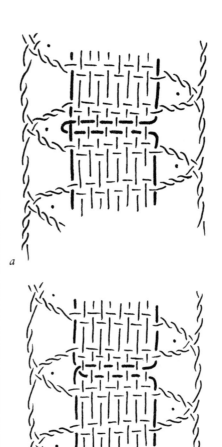

a

b

weaving stitch (bobbin) *See* CLOTH STITCH.

weaving thread (bobbin) *See* WORKER.

web (needle) (1) In Tenerife lace radial threads supported by the pins or teeth of the wheel. (2) In PUNTO AVORIO a motif worked in VALSESIAN STITCH within a framework of the same stitches. In the instructions the work on either side is represented by the groups of four stitches at the beginnings and ends of the rows.

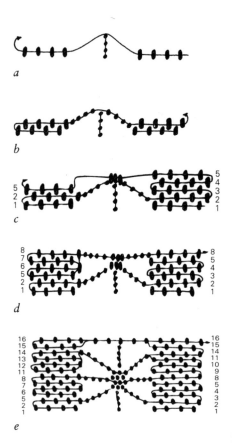

a

b

c

d

e

row 1: 4 stitches, miss space of 2, leave loose thread, 1 COLUMN, leave loose thread, complete the row (figure a)
row 2: 4 stitches, 4 stitches on each loose thread, 4 stitches (figure b)
rows 3 and 4: 4 stitches
row 5: 4 stitches, leave loose thread, 3 stitches in centre, leave loose thread, 4 stitches (figure c)
rows 6 and 7: 4 stitches (including the loose thread when appropriate)
row 8: 4 stitches, 4 stitches on loose thread, 3 stitches in centre, 4 stitches on loose thread, 4 stitches (figure d)
rows 9 and 10: 4 stitches
row 11: 4 stitches, leave loose thread, 3 stitches in centre, leave loose thread, 4 stitches

rows 12 and 13: 4 stitches (including the loose thread when appropriate)
row 14: 4 stitches, 4 stitches on loose thread, 3 stitches in centre, 4 stitches on loose thread, 4 stitches
row 15: 4 stitches, leave loose thread, 1 column stitch, leave loose thread, 4 stitches
row 16: 4 stitches, 2 stitches on loose thread, 1 stitch into column, 2 stitches on loose thread, 4 stitches (figure e)
Finish by working three rows the full width. *See also* COBWEB, RAISED RIB COBWEB, SORRENTO WHEEL.

web in darning stitch (needle) *See* SORRENTO WHEEL.

web in rib stitch (needle) *See* RAISED RIB COBWEB.

wedge (bobbin) *See* BRIDGE (bobbin).

weft (weaving) A thread wound on the shuttle that passes back and forth through the WARP threads.

weighted cushion (netting) A firmly padded cushion containing a heavy weight such as a brick, and with a non-slip base, that can be placed on a table to support netting without having to be attached to the table by a clamp or some other means.

wheatear (bobbin) *See* LEAF.

wheat straw (bobbin) A pillow filling that has tougher nodes than BARLEY STRAW.

wheatsheaf (needle) In Branscombe lace a decorative stitch used to fill narrow spaces by throwing a thread across a space and whipping back across it to the original side (as many times as required to give a close twisted appearance). This is repeated a little way further on then another started the same distance from the second and whipped back to the centre, when all three bars are joined by two buttonhole stitches worked around all bars, then the whipping of the last bar is completed (figure). *See also* BAR CLUSTER.

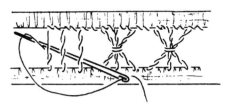

wheel (bobbin) In Bedfordshire lace an EIGHT-PAIR CROSSING encircled by PLAITS. Extra pairs are introduced at (A), the start of the circle of plaits, and removed, in a MULTIPLE PAIR PLAIT (B) (figure) where they can be thrown out or taken to the next section. *See also* CROSS STRANDS *and* Appendix for indicator.

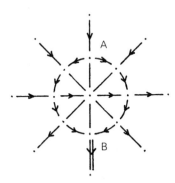

wheel (needle) (1) A small design worked over the crossing of several, usually four, threads. *See also* SORRENTO WHEEL, SPIDER WEB WHEEL and so on. (2) An implement used for making Tenerife lace, either in the form of a pincushion with a firm covering into which pins are inserted; or having pins, or prongs,

around the edge to support the WEB. *See also* RADIALLY PINNED WHEEL.

whipped bar (needle) *See* TWISTED BAR.

whipped mesh/stitch (needle) When the rows have a thread whipped one or more times along the lower edges of each MESH – e.g., POINT D'ANVERS.

whole stitch (bobbin) (1) A Honiton term, and also used elsewhere, meaning CLOTH STITCH. (2) Used by others to mean CLOTH AND TWIST.

whole stitch footside (bobbin) *See* CLOTH STITCH FOOTSIDE.

whole stitch honeycomb (bobbin) Bucks point filling, alternate CONTINUOUS and GAP ROWS worked CLOTH STITCH AND TWIST, pin cloth stitch and twist (figure), may contain TALLIES.

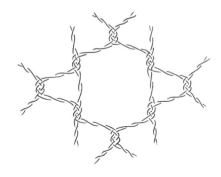

whole stitch (torchon) ground (bobbin) TORCHON GROUND WORKED CLOTH STITCH AND TWIST, pin, cloth stitch and twist (figure p.238). Also called torchon double ground.

whole stitch round a pin (bobbin) A method of starting with two pairs at a pin. Place each pair on a SUPPORT PIN and work HALF STITCH, SET UP A PIN, CROSS. Remove the support pins and the

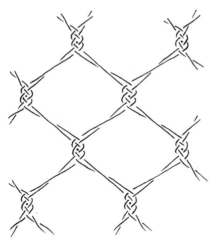

whole stitch (torchon) ground

'WHOLE STITCH' settles around the remaining pin (figure).

wig hook/wig makers' needle (bobbin) A very fine hook used by some for Honiton sewings. Use with care as it can cut threads and is dangerous because it is sharp and barbed. Also called tractor.

winder (bobbin) *See* BOBBIN WINDER.

winding (knots) back (bobbin) When making Honiton lace bobbins are not LINKED but wound separately and knotted in pairs. About 23cm (9in), or more, are taken off one bobbin and the thread wound onto the other, the knots being removed later if necessary.

winding bobbins (bobbin) The thread is placed against the LONG NECK (figure a), the end pointing towards the HEAD and the thread wound clockwise (looking down on the head). Make several turns round the bobbin until the thread stops slipping (figure b), then continue winding by rotating the bobbin rather than taking the thread round it, this avoids changing the twist of the thread. Wind several layers over the 5mm (¼in) closest to the head, then continue winding as evenly as possible, this reduces the tendency for the bobbins become unwound. Never allow the wound thread to become wider than any part of the head and secure the thread by making a HITCH, or HALF HITCH WITH EXTRA TURN around the SHORT NECK, if there is one; otherwise make the hitch on the thread. *See also* WINDING (KNOTS) BACK.

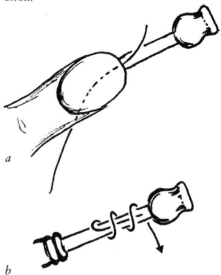

a

b

windmill (bobbin) The CROSSING of two PLAITS, or LEAVES; pairs should not be twisted either before or after the crossing is made. (1) Using pairs as single bobbins make a HALF STITCH, SET UP THE PIN and COVER by passing the second pair over the third – i.e. make a CLOTH STITCH with pairs, placing a pin in the centre (figure a). Also called big stitch, cloth stitch crossing, crossing, crossing plaits, four pair crossing, quick windmill and two plait crossing. (2) Work cloth stitches with the following pairs – centre pairs, left pairs, right pairs, pin, centre pairs (figure b). FIRM UP carefully around the pin. *See* Appendix for indicator.

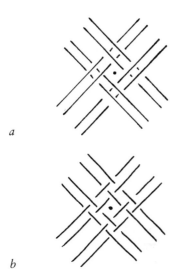

a

b

windows (bobbin) (1) In Honiton lace a series of holes formed by working a row of WHOLE STITCHES with each pair being TWISTED three times, followed by a row of whole stitches with the RUNNERS only twisted three times after every stitch. In practice it can be FIRMED UP more neatly by twisting the DOWNRIGHTS after the firming up (figure). (2) *See* BOXED PINHOLE.

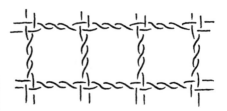

winkie pin (bobbin) A pair TWISTED twice or more times as it passes round a pin where pairs have been neither taken in from, or released into, the adjacent GROUND or FILLING – e.g., down either side of an EYELET or BRAID (figure). *See also* SNATCH PIN.

wire beaded (bobbin) *See* BEADED BOBBIN.

wire bound (bobbin) *See* BOUND BOBBIN.

wire ground (bobbin) *See* KAT STITCH.

wired bobbin (bobbin) *See* BOUND BOBBIN.

woollen lace (bobbin) *See* YAK LACE.

work around (needle) A Branscombe technique for filling small spaces. A row of SPACED, TWISTED BUTTONHOLE STITCHES is worked round the space (figure a), and

the thread whipped through each loop in turn. The thread is whipped out to the edge to complete the first stitch (figure b).

worked vein (bobbin) In Honiton lace a vein produced within an area by changing the stitches, no pins being used – e.g., MITTENS and TWISTED VEIN. *See* Appendix for indicator.

worker (bobbin) (1) The pair of bobbins that works across the row when making CLOTH and HALF STITCH, also called active pair, leaders, RUNNERS, travellers, weavers and working pair. *See* Appendix (most guidelines indicate the path of the worker). (2) The single bobbin that weaves backwards and forwards to form a TALLY, also called weaver. (3) A COVER CLOTH placed over the PILLOW and PRICK-

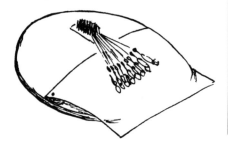

ING to keep them clean and placed just below the section of the pricking being used and reaching the FRONT of the pillow. It should extend the full width of the pillow and be firmly secured with strong pins (figure).

working diagram (bobbin) *See* SCHEMATIC DIAGRAM.

working in the round (netting) PLAIN NETTING worked from a circular foundation. Make a GROMMET with the required number of SIMPLE KNOT STITCHES and tie an OVERHAND KNOT, at the required distance, to simulate the last 'loop' (figure). (Subsequent knots are usually FISHERMAN'S KNOTS.) The first row usually consists of two stitches into each loop with one in the last followed by an overhand knot to simulate the second one, as before. Any netting stitches, and variations, can be used for the remainder of the piece, with the last 'stitch' of each circle involving a knot with the TAIL. Also called circular netting.

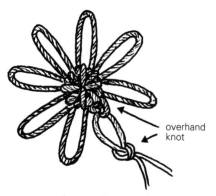

overhand knot

shown without toggle

working thread (general) Thread that has most recently been making, or is about to make the most movements.

worsted lace (bobbin) *See* YAK LACE.

wound bead (bobbin) A bead, used to weight bobbins, made by winding semi-molten glass round a metal wire.

woven bar (needle) Two threads, or pairs of threads, are thrown across a space and the area between them darned. The work is tensioned so that the bar remains the same width throughout (figure a). Also called bar in darning stitch, basket stitch, basketwork bar, darned bar, feuille bar and reprise bar. The work can be tensioned so that the bar narrows in the centre, with the thrown threads meeting each other, or the supporting threads can be crossed (figure b). Also called basket stitch.

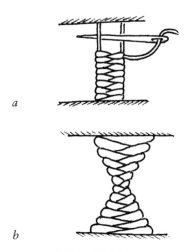

a

b

woven plait (bobbin) *See* TALLY.

woven wheel (needle) A circular motif made at the junction of two BUTTON-HOLE STITCHES. Sometimes made when a row of SPACED TWISTED BUTTONHOLE STITCHES is worked round the space, the thread whipped through each loop in turn and small wheel worked round each junction (figure).

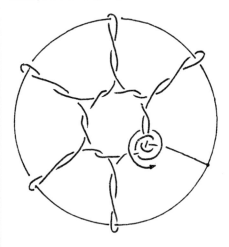

wrapping the rope (bobbin) In Cantù lace the WORKERS meet the ROPE immediately after a CLOTH STITCH, the right worker thread passes over the rope, the left under, the workers TWIST, the right worker thread passes over the rope, the left under and the pair continues across the braid (figure).

X

x-ray plate (bobbin) Sometimes used as a substitute for ACETATE FILM.

Y

yak bobbin (bobbin) A large bobbin for making YAK LACE.

yak lace (bobbin) Woollen lace, usually made from worsted yarn. The name may be a corruption of 'Yorkshire' a county closely associated with the wool trade, or it may have been taken from the hairy animal of the same name. Also called worsted lace.

yard lace/work (bobbin) *See* CONTINUOUS (THREAD) LACE.

yarn (yarn) Constructed by spinning fibres or filaments together to form SINGLES. These are usually spun in small

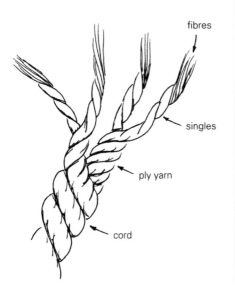

fibres

singles

ply yarn

cord

groups to form PLY yarn. Two or more ply yarns may be spun together to form CORDS (figure). *See also* CONTINUOUS FILAMENT, COTTON, LINEN, REGENERATED FIBRE, SILK, SYNTHETIC THREAD.

yarn count (yarn) Systems used to indicate the thickness of YARN, sometimes stated in two parts; a single digit, the FOLD number, and a larger number indicating the thickness of each SINGLES, see CONTINUOUS FILAMENT, DECITEX SYSTEM, DENIER, DIRECT COUNT SYSTEM, CONVERSION FACTOR, FOLD, INDIRECT COUNT SYSTEM, METRIC TICKET NUMBER, SINGLES, TEX SYSTEM, TICKET NUMBER AND APPENDIX FOR TABLE OF YARN COUNT SYSTEMS.

yarn over hook (crochet) When the hook is inserted under the yarn prior to pulling it through the loop(s) on the hook to make another loop (figure).

yarn winder (bobbin) *See* BOBBIN WINDER.

yarningle (general) The arm of a skein holder. When yarn was supplied in skeins, these were sometimes attached to bobbin winders (figure, p.244). Also called blade.

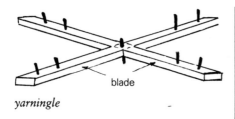

yarningle

blade

yellow pins (bobbin) *See* LONG TOMS.

yerangyoun (needle) In Armenian lace a triangle of loops. Lay a thread across a number of small loops *and knot to the top of the furthest one (figure a). Make a series of loops by knotting over this thread into each loop, ending with the one at the start of the laid thread. Lay the next thread back to the start of this row, and repeat from *, each row having one loop fewer, the last row having only one loop. Take the thread down the side of the triangle by making one knot into the end loop of each row. The thread is ready for making the next triangle (figure b). Also called triangular ground.

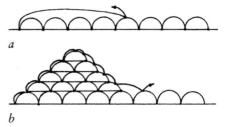

a

b

Z

Z **twist** (thread) Yarn spun so that the twist travels in a counterclockwise direction, which can be determined by looking at the direction of the twists of the thread (figure a) or by looking at the end of the thread (figure b).

a

b

Appendix

Indicators and Guidelines Found on Bobbin Lace Prickings

Most guidelines and indicators are drawn using a waterproof pen, but for Honiton lace the dots are pricked and the lines scratched. Indicators and guidelines are not always present on prickings, and many lacemakers have their own personal versions.

Balance marks (any lace).

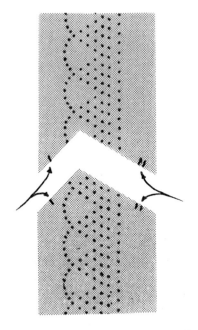

Bedfordshire spider (Bedfordshire), cloth or half stitch, that is surrounded by plaits (figure a); surrounded by leaves (figure b).

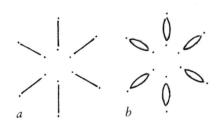

Brabant ground (torchon).

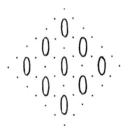

Catherine stitch, plaits with picots (Bedfordshire and braid).

Coarse threads crossing, single prick where the edge indents, not used as a pinhole (Honiton).

Coronet fan (torchon); twists may be added.

Cucumber tally (Bedfordshire and Bucks point).

Diamond (torchon) cloth or half stitch.

Eight pair crossing (Bedfordshire and braid) plaits crossing (figure a), leaves crossing (figure b) or any combination of the two.

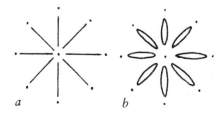

Feather (torchon) twists may be added.

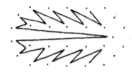

French fan (torchon) twists may be added.

Gimp (torchon and others) passing through ground.

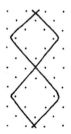

Half stitch (Honiton) indicated by the two close dots in the centre.

Kiss (Bedfordshire) drawn (figure a), with marker pin (figure b). (A pin may be inserted through the stitch into this hole.)

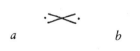

Leaf (various laces).

Mayflower (Bucks point); old mayflower (figure a), new mayflower (figure b). The dots and crosses are interchangeable.

Mistake made when pricking (any lace) usually close to other pinholes where it might be used.

Multiple pair plait (various laces) .

Overlaid tallies and plaits (Bedfordshire).

Pair or plait (Bedfordshire and braid); sometimes the line for the plait is thicker than for the pair.

Plain hole (Honiton) in whole or half stitch, single prick in the centre of an area, not used as a pinhole.

Plait (braid) to distinguish from pair.

Plait with picot (Bedfordshire and braid).

Plait which has picots both sides (Bedfordshire and braid).

Purl edge (Honiton), starts at a set of four pinholes, and follows the line to end at the other set of four pinholes.

Raised edge (Honiton).

Raised or rolled tally (Bedfordshire) found well inside the outline of pinholes (figures a and b).

Rose ground (torchon) (figures a and b), both have the same meaning.

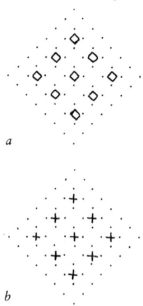

a

b

Sewing (braid) the small crescent between the two loops.

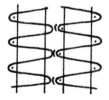

Simple fan (torchon) in cloth or half stitch, twists may be added.

Six pair crossing (Bedfordshire and braid) plaits crossing (figure a), leaves crossing (figure b) or any combination of the two.

a

b

Slash marks (schematic diagrams).

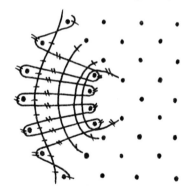

Spanish fan (torchon) twists may be added.

Spider (torchon).

Spider ground (torchon).

Tally in point ground (Bucks point).

Trail (Bedfordshire).

Trail (torchon) cloth or half stitch.

Triangle against the footside (torchon) cloth or half stitch (figures a and b).

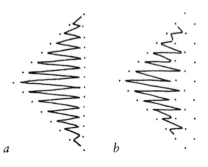

a   *b*

Wheel (Bedfordshire).

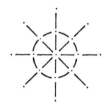

Windmill (Bedfordshire and braid), plaits crossing (figure a), leaves crossing (figure b) or any combination of the two.

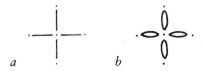

a   *b*

Worked vein (Honiton) opening at the first of the widely spaced pinholes and closing at the last, the pinholes are not used.

Appendix

Yarn Count Systems

Direct systems: count in Tex = conversion factor × count in direct system

System	Unit of mass	Unit of length	Conversion factor
Tex	gram	1,000 metres	1
Decitext	gram	10,000 metres	10
Denier	gram	9,000 metres	0.1111
Linen (dry spun)	pound	14,400 yards	34.45
Silk	dram	1,000 yards	1.938

Indirect systems: count in Tex = conversion factor ÷ count in indirect system

System	Unit of mass	Unit of length	Conversion factor
Cotton count (Ne)	1 pound	840 yards	590.5
Cotton (Continental)	500 pound	1 kilometre	500
Linen (wet spun)	1 pound	300 yards	1,654
Metric (Nm)	1 kilogram	1 kilometre	1,000
Spun silk system	1 pound	840 yards	590.5

See also METRIC TICKET NUMBER and TICKET NUMBER.